FILM GENRE:

Theory and Criticism

edited by

BARRY K. GRANT

The Scarecrow Press, Inc.
Metuchen, N.J. & London
1977

PN
1995
.F458

Library of Congress Cataloging in Publication Data
Main entry under title:

Film genre : theory and criticism.

    Bibliography: p.
    Includes index.
    1. Moving-pictures--Addresses, essays, lectures.
I. Grant, Barry K., 1947-
PN1995. F458   791. 43'015   77-8908
ISBN 0-8108-1059-X

To Robbie, all ways

ACKNOWLEDGMENTS

For their respective contributions to the development of this book, I wish to thank the following: Robbyn C. M. Grant; Professors Jim Leach and Maurice Yacowar, Dr. John McEwen, and Ms. Debbie Thorne (Brock University); Ms. Jenny Leach; Professor Art Efron and Dr. Gerald O'Grady (SUNY at Buffalo); Professor Stuart Kaminsky (Northwestern University); and Media Study/Buffalo.

McConnell, Frank D.: "Leopards and History: The Problem of Film Genre," from The Spoken Seen: Film and the Romantic Imagination (Baltimore: Johns Hopkins University Press, 1975), pp. 118-126. Copyright © 1975 by Johns Hopkins University Press. Reprinted by permission of the author and Johns Hopkins University Press.

Tudor, Andrew: "Genre," from Theories of Film (New York: Viking Press, 1973), pp. 131-150. Copyright © 1973 by Andrew Tudor. Reprinted by permission of the Viking Press and Martin Secker & Warburg Ltd.

Buscombe, Edward: "The Idea of Genre in the American Cinema," from Screen, Vol. 11, No. 2 (March-April 1970), pp. 33-45. Copyright © 1970 by Screen. Reprinted by permission.

Sobchack, Thomas: "Genre Film: A Classical Experience," from Literature/Film Quarterly, Vol. 3, No. 3 (Summer 1975), pp. 196-204. Copyright © 1975 by Literature/Film Quarterly. Reprinted by permission.

Hess, Judith: "Genre Films and the Status Quo," from Jump Cut, No. 1 (May-June 1974), pp. 1, 16, 18. Copyright © 1974 by Jump Cut. Reprinted by permission of Jump Cut and the author.

Bourget, Jean-Loup: "Social Implications in the Hollywood Genres," from Journal of Modern Literature, Vol. 3, No. 2 (April 1973), pp. 191-200. Copyright © 1973 by Journal

CONTENTS

INTRODUCTION

The work of defining film genres is surprisingly difficult and complex. This anthology was conceived both as a
basic sourcebook for film genre study and as an attempt to
confront some of these complexities. Part One is comprised
of theoretical essays concerned with the questions of what
film genres are and how we experience them, and Part Two
is a series of examinations of particular genres.

Recognition of the importance of genre in the cinema
is a relatively recent development, although chronologically it
narrowly predates the early work of auteur criticism. The
first significant essays of film genre criticism are those on
the Western written by Robert Warshow and Andre Bazin in
the late 1940s and early '50s, respectively. Earlier, films
were more loosely "typed" by reviewers and audiences alike:
a film was a "western" or a "war movie," and the phrase
was used merely as a convenient label to give one an idea of
what the story was like, what to expect generally from a
film.

Then film critics began to realize that, for example,
if those convenient descriptive labels actually evoked certain audience expectations--and apparently they did--then a
film's meaning might in part arise out of the relationship
between those expectations and a film's awareness and/or
treatment of them. But one first has to understand a genre
--the various relationships among a group of films--before
one can appreciate an individual expression responding to it.
"Genre" became a critical term, providing another conceptual
framework for understanding movies. It is invoked usually in
discussions of the American cinema, since Hollywood films
traditionally have been made in a large, profit-motivated
studio system, a situation which, as sound business practice,
has insisted upon the exploitation and repetition of successful
formulae in order to guarantee acceptance at the box office.

As genre criticism has evolved, it has begun to confront its essential critical problems. For instance, if a film

1

genre is an especially well-codified artistic tradition, then
what is and what should be the relation between that tradition
and the individual artist working within it? This question
has been particularly crucial for twentieth-century art, with
its characteristic self-consciousness, at least since T. S.
Eliot's famous essay, "Tradition and the Individual Talent"
(1919). Both the artist and the audience have become aware
that s/he exists as a part of a given tradition, his/her work
at once modifying it and modified by it; the degree to which
s/he is aware of this relationship can be either a boon or a
burden. With film, the question often is discussed in terms
of a tension between the genre and auteur approaches. Also,
the recent rise of Marxist film criticism (prompted largely
by the post-1968 film experiments of Jean-Luc Godard), with
its condemnation as bourgeois of both the traditional narrative and the idea of the individual artist as creative genius,
has further intensified the issue by adding to the historical
and aesthetic perspectives a political context.

Frank McConnell's essay, "Leopards and History:
The Problem of Film Genre," which begins this volume, is
a consideration of this relationship between generic tradition
and individual expression. The essays by Judith Hess and
Jean-Loup Bourget deal with the same issue in its political
context, yet present almost diametrically opposed arguments:
the first sees genre films as conservative propaganda because they are grounded in the predictability of conventions,
while the second claims they gain the power to become sub-
versive statements for the same reason. The three remain-
ing essays in Part One address other theoretical issues involved in film genre study. Andrew Tudor expands upon
some of the problems arising in the attempt to define specific
film genres. Edward Buscombe offers a partial solution in
his distinction between a film's "outer forms" (iconography)
and "inner forms" (themes), and their relationship. In his
essay, Thomas Sobchack analyzes the experience of viewing
any genre film, regardless of its particular genre.

Each of the essays in Part Two approaches a different
genre in a somewhat different fashion. For example, Colin
McArthur explores the gangster film's iconography; Margaret
Tarratt presents a Freudian analysis of science-fiction films
based largely on their narrative conventions; Timothy Scheurer describes the various structures of the musical film; and
D. L. White gives priority to the experience of horror in the
horror film. Jim Leach's essay on "The Screwball Comedy"
is very much concerned with the thematic variations played

by particular directors within that genre.   Three other es-
says--Maurice Yacowar's on the disaster film, Raymond
Durgnat's on epic films, and Nora Sayre's on sports films--
discuss from multiple perspectives genres less immediately
discernible and therefore more often neglected by critics.
The volume concludes with an essay focusing on the Western,
"Genre and Movies," a comprehensive work of film genre
criticism which describes the attributes of the genre, incorporates historical antecedents and concepts of Northrop Frye,
and concludes by offering cogent value judgements of specific
films based on this descriptive analysis.   All of these essays
should be considered in relation to the theoretical frame-
works outlined in Part One.

        Genre criticism is exciting in part because so much
work remains to be done.   That the essays in this volume
define genres by such a variety of criteria underscores this
fact.   Furthermore, genres are amazingly adaptable, and
filmmakers are constantly reworking them to speak to contemporary issues; the critic can only follow, attempting to
explain the new permutations.   By giving careful attention to
iconography and narrative structure, genre criticism perhaps
can help to clarify the nature of myth and uncover specific
contemporary myths--goals also important to the newest critical methodologies.   This book, devoted entirely to film genre criticism, was conceived and is structured largely in the
hope that it might stimulate both the further development of
film genre study and an increased interaction with other relevant areas of critical endeavor.

                                              Barry K. Grant

Brock University
November, 1976

PART ONE

LEOPARDS AND HISTORY:
THE PROBLEM OF FILM GENRE

Frank D. McConnell

Who is the creator of a film? The question, on the
face of it, sounds academic, quite unrelated to any enjoyment,
instruction, or edification we might actually get from a film
or a series of films. But at a rather more serious level,
it is indeed a crucial question. Films are a particularly fascinating mode of art because they call so many of our ordinary assumptions about art into question: neither realistic
nor fantastic, they draw us into a new imaginative world which
is at the same time a real one and a fantasy; neither language
nor silence, they compel us to reinvent a relationship between
the word and the space surrounding the word; neither private
creations nor public acts, they raise again the problem of the
political valence of art. Thus, if we ask, "Who is the creator of a film?" we are in fact asking, not for a single answer, but for a set of answers, for an attitude, that will allow us to take into account the double existence of any given
film as artwork and public dream, as made object and communal expression of the anxieties and hopes of the culture
which welcomes and patronizes it.

The image of Claude Chabrol's The Butcher ... is a
premonitory parable of this question and of the related problem of genre in film. In a thriller set in provincial France,
two people--one a frigid intellectual and one an elemental
sex-killer--face each other across a blackboard on which the
name "BALZAC" is written. In order for us actually to see
the film, that is, Chabrol expects us to understand that it
arises from the intricate interplay of the thriller genre (with
particular relevance to Hitchcock) with the conventions of the
French provincial conte, and of course also with the personal obsessions and idiosyncratic vision of Claude Chabrol.
So that to ask, "Whose film is it?" is not really to seek a
definite answer, but rather to engage ourselves with the

7

forces--personal, historic, and generic--out of which the individual film arises.

        Kafka's short parable of the leopards also has a bear-
ing on the concerns of this chapter because it suggests the
deep relevance of the question of film genre to the parallel
and, in our century, equally complex question of literary genre, the relationships between what T. S. Eliot christened
"tradition and the individual talent." Kafka's statement of
the problem is this: "Leopards break into the temple and
drink to the dregs what is in the sacrificial pitchers; this is
repeated over and over again; finally it can be calculated in
advance, and it becomes a part of the ceremony." The interruption of ritual, the explosive revision of historically established expectation, is of course what constitutes the prophetic moment of art. But, as Kafka suggests, that explosion itself continually tends to become assimilated into the
ritual, necessitating new modes of interruption, new varieties
of creative outrage. History and individuality, Kafka tells
us, create art through their eternal struggle against each
other; and in an art as highly collective, as undeniably historical, and as potentially disruptive as film, we may expect
the paradox of the leopards to operate with special appro-
priateness.

        Recently, two colleagues and I had a conversation
which, through its mutual incomprehension, raised some of
these points in an unusually practical way. One of my
friends was a teacher of English who has also taught and
written widely--and influentially--about film. The other is
a specialist in medieval English and Latin literature and goes
to very few films at all. Friend One was remarking that all
the most interesting young directors in America were self-
conscious genre directors (i. e., Bogdanovich, Coppola, Alt-
man, Lucas). Friend Two then asked, disingenuously, what
we meant by "genre director": weren't all films, in one
way or another, "generic" works, just as all coherent works
of literature establish their coherence through the reestab-
lishment and revision of genre norms? Friend One and I
proceeded to mumble things like "Western ... thriller ...
film noir ... audience expectation," all the while watching
the bemused (or amused?) smile on the medievalist's face
grow more so.

        I am sure we failed to convince the medievalist that
the concept of genre in film criticism has attained anything
like the sophistication with which medieval scholars imbue it.

And we failed, I think, not because of his obstinacy or mis-
comprehension, but because of ours. After our conversation,
I began to realize how very uncertain the idea of genre is,
in both filmic and literary exegesis, and therefore with how
great a degree of subtlety and perspicuity we need to approach
it--whether we are dealing with Piers Plowman or Pickup on
South Street.

It took, I think, a medievalist to remind me of the
real difficulties of talking about genre. For medievalists
deal with a literature and an idea of literature that is largely innocent of the prejudices about individuality and history
which have so profoundly affected later literary criticism and
almost all film criticism. What is especially surprising,
though, is the way in which film, the premiere post-romantic
art form, tends to return, in its actual manifestation of individual and collective vantage points upon reality, to the assumptions of the medieval, rather than of the romantic, poets.
This is not to say, of course, that film is simply a new popular art like the popular entertainments of the medieval period. But it is to insist that in our approach to film as an
heir of the last two centuries of art and poetry, we must
imagine it also as a reconstitution of poetic and generic ideas
far predating those centuries--ideas which return us to the
primal Western concerns of the individual work and its relation to history, of which the individual work is at once the
constituent and the betrayal.

The idea of genre, as commonly used by film and literary critics, is of course an inheritance from the Renaissance, from the rediscovery of the logic of categories during the Enlightenment, and (perhaps preeminently) from the
wedding, during the romantic era, of that logic with the myth
of the poet as prophet, of art as individual negotiation between mind and universe, what Wordsworth calls

                    all this mighty world
        Of eye and ear, both what we half create
        And what perceive.

It is, in other words, a notion involving a kind of adversary
relationship between the creator and the genre in which he
creates. A genre, or type, of writing, of storytelling, of
presentation, is assumed to preexist the individual work in
some sort of Platonic limbo of possibilities; and what we look
for, in judging the particular work of art, is the way in which
individual talent wrestles with tradition, the way the artist

uses--i. e. , rearranges and decomposes--the "rules" of the
form he has selected. This is a distinctively romantic attitude toward genre; we know that the great romantic poets and
novelists, from Blake to Flaubert and Joyce, never used a
form which they did not also parody and invert. But it also
pushes our idea of romanticism much farther back in time
than conventional histories of literature suggest. When John
Dryden faulted Shakespeare's Antony and Cleopatra for not observing the rules of tragic unity laid down by Aristotle, he
was judging like a good neoclassical critic. Yet his judgment
was romantic or modern to the extent that it, too, assumed
that using a genre was a kind of test: can the poet or can
he not fit his genius into the abstract, generic norms governing the work?

While Dryden and his age thought that this fitting was
by and large a good thing, and while Shelley or Gide regarded it as, at best, a dubious achievement, nevertheless all are
in fundamental agreement that the relationship between artist
and form is one of contrariety, and that the artist's individuality (a prime value for Dryden no less than for Shelley)
manifests itself only in tension with the genre within which he
works. And this sense of genre and talent informs what is
still the dominant and most productive form of film criticism,
the auteur theory. To say that film represents the imposition
of individual imagination--that of the director-auteur--upon the
hackneyed and unpromising matter of his conventional subject
is not only the extreme romanticism of film theory, but is also a kind of terminal, absolutist romanticism of literary aesthetics in general. But there are qualifications, if not refuta-
tions.

First, we might note the Promethean overtones in the
word auteur itself. As recently (in the long view) as the
early seventeenth century, Ben Jonson was ridiculed for publishing his collected poems under the title Opera--for claiming, that is, the status of a classical auteur. But romanticism, if nothing else, is the visionary lyricism of chutzpah.
And film, a child of the romantic quest for a perfectly repre-
sentational language, has spawned a theory of interpretation
that exalts the individual personality of the creator beyond any
comparable literary theory precisely because the individual
touch, the signature of a sole creator, is so much less immediately apparent in film than in the novel or the lyric. In
his important essay "La Politique des Auteurs," André Bazin
put it this way: "The evolution of Western art towards greater personalisation should definitely be considered as a step

forward, as a refinement of culture, but only as long as this individualisation remains only a final perfection and does not claim to define culture.   At this point, we should remember that irrefutable commonplace we learnt at school: the individual transcends society, but society is also and above all within him. " Bazin, the founder of the auteurist school, could be less disingenuous than his followers about his final beliefs. And in this crucial passage we see the profoundly nineteenth-century roots of the school: we might almost be reading this as the conclusion to an essay on Byron or Flaubert.   The "personalisation" of the artwork has become not only the point, but the genesis of the impulse to create.   Bazin gives society, history, and genre their due, but only as settings for the consciousness of the auteur, to be subsumed and transcended in his performance.

Of course, the celebration of individual genius does not necessarily imply contempt for the idea of genre conventions.   But there is a tendency--even in studies directly concerned with film genres--to regard them more or less as backdrops for the flaring-forth of individual creative genius. And though this treatment may be an inevitable feature of post-romantic art criticism, it raises problems.   These problems have also been raised, more seriously and with more deleterious effect, in the parallel development of literary criticism.   Every year, thousands of fledgling Ph.D.'s in English are bullied into reading reams of minor Elizabethan tragedies or Victorian novels, precisely so that they can recognize the true glory of a Shakespeare or a Dickens who rose above and transformed the popular generic matter.   I have always found this process confusing, and a little distasteful--not because those minor plays and novels are dull (they are not, really), but just because of the implicit assumption of the method and of its key word, "minor." The assumption is that they are and ought to be dull.

We might say that this sort of criticism of either literature or film is unable to see a genre except out of the corner of its eye, for the genre disappears or fades out in the neighborhood of the single artist's corrosive brilliance. Film critics, of course, have a harder time preserving this myopia than do their literary colleagues, since the art of the film--particularly the magnificent, scandalous art of the American film--is so drenched in the operation of generic, nonindividualistic norms of presentation.   But when the auteur critic comes to the examination of a director who obeys rather than upsets the laws of his chosen genres, he usually runs for

the semantic shelter of that most romantic of concepts, the
"primitive." Whether we read Chateaubriand on the American
Indian or Andrew Sarris on Samuel Fuller or Sam Peckinpah,
the use of the term "primitive" remains essentially the same:
a way of saluting the individual genius of the creator at the
expense of the conventions governing his art, even when those
conventions and that genius are inseparable.

"Primitive" means "prehistoric." And there is a crucial relationship between the ideas of genius we have been discussing and theories of history--not simply those of the history of art, but those of the history of civilization itself. If,
as Bazin, Sarris, and most departments of English believe,
the history of an art is the history of its great figures in a
spiral of ever-growing "personalisation," then the role of genre in art is like the role of society, tradition, or conservative economics in the established liberal view of cultural
change: a shady, primarily negative background for the blood-
lessly revolutionary acts of the enlightened. Bazin's colleagues at Cahiers du Cinéma probably did not recognize how
acute they were in inventing the phrase "politique des auteurs."
As the later careers of Cahiers critics Godard, Chabrol, and
even Truffaut were to make clear, the theory of the journal
presented a particularly traditional (we might almost say a
classically French, Voltairean) transformation of politics and
history into style.

Surely, we can argue that Godard was never more political or more liberally and satirically profound than in his
first film, Breathless, in which the depersonalizing conventions of the gangster film (Belmondo's famous, heartfelt "Bo-
gey!") are systematically corroded and rearranged by the director's anarchic focus on the stereotypical nature of those
conventions. Godard himself plays the anonymous bystander
who tips off the police to fugitive Belmondo's whereabouts,
bringing to birth the film's absurd and predestined catastrophe
--a sure sign of this auteur's adversary relationship with the
primitiveness of his genre. Breathless gives us, with re-
markable purity, the myth of creative genius divorced from
and in conflict with history, with genre. Belmondo's first
words to the audience, after stealing a car, are J'aime la
France: his immersion in the American thriller has turned
him into a tourist in his own country, the first of those alienated hommes revoltés who will become Godard's most important contribution to the narrative traditions of the film.

But--"the narrative traditions of the film"! Is this not

a refutation of the myth which generates Breathless, the myth
of an unstructured, free art, utilizing established conventions
only self-consciously and parodistically? I return to my medievalist friend's ironic smile. Most films are not Breathless: indeed, it is only because they are not that we can
recognize a Breathless for what it is. The myth of genius in
conflict with genre thus becomes a self-fulfilling prophecy.
But there is another way we can imagine the relationship between the specific creation and the historic conditions of that
creation. Who is the author of The Canterbury Tales?
Chaucer or the age? Jacques Maritain, in his famous essay
"Dante's Innocence and Luck," argues that the Commedia is
the product not so much of its creator's genius as of the sublime receptivity of that genius to the total influence of an era.
And, of course, we know a great deal more about Dante and
Chaucer than we do about the authors of most of the great
works of the Middle Ages. In the cases of Piers Plowman,
the Njalsaga, or Sir Gawain and the Green Knight we not only
know nothing about the personality of the creator, but more
essentially, we cannot tell to what degree the excellence of
the work is due to a putative individual creator, or to the accretion of influence, convention, and digressions from the
hands of any number of anonymous contributors, redactors,
and scribes. The analogy between such cumulative production
and the art of medieval architecture is by now hackneyed beyond redemption, though not, I think, beyond repetition, especially if we can see the further analogy to the contemporary
film studio.

    Comparisons such as this have been drawn before.
One of the best early essays on film aesthetics is "Style and
Medium in the Motion Pictures," by the master scholar of
medieval and Renaissance iconography, Erwin Panofsky. And
writers like Parker Tyler, Dwight MacDonald, and Leslie
Fiedler consistently (and perversely, in the view of many film
theoreticians) "read" film as the unconscious projection of
archetypes of the public mind. But this sort of psychic exegesis can scarcely be called a genre approach to film. The
pursuit of hidden archetypes, however valuable, tends to re-
duce even the most formalized characteristics of an artistic
convention to a dead level of Freudian or Jungian sameness.
The same problem results from archetypal approaches in literary or dramatic criticism. Once you have identified the
monomyth at the center of all human imagination, it becomes
ridiculously difficult to discriminate between any two versions
of it, even if the versions are as dissimilar as As You Like
It and Sergeant Pepper's Lonely Hearts Club Band, or The
Trial and Straw Dogs.

A more fruitful approach may be the recently popular "structuralist" analysis of film and literature. Indeed, if there is a point in considering film from a preromantic, medievalist sense of its conventions, structuralism is an attractive candidate for the methodology of that consideration. Itself a product of romantic ideas of language and consciousness, it has evolved into what amounts to a new scholasticism of the imagination. The structuralist attitude is nowhere better epitomized than by Claude Lévi-Strauss, in the "overture" to his study The Raw and the Cooked: "Mythological analysis has not, and cannot have, as its aim to show how men think.... I therefore claim to show, not how men think in myths, but how myths operate in men's minds without their being aware of the fact." If we substitute "genre" for "myth" in this passage, we get a fair idea of where the structuralist critique of literature and film tends. Just as language, the great human structure of structures, not only has a history but is its own history, so the forms of narrative art may be viewed as creating their own masterpieces--operating in men's minds--with a kind of trans- or super-personal determinism which exceeds factors like individual genius or creativity.

Undoubtedly, the structuralist approach I have outlined leads, in its extreme versions, to an obliteration of the idea of the individual work itself, which is just as wrong-headed as the overly romantic auteurism we are trying to escape. But as a corrective to previous trends and as a rich mine of new insights into the operation of myths, it is invaluable. Just as romanticism itself is best comprehended, not simply as the revolutionary myth of personality, but as a tension and contrast with older myths of depersonalization, against which it achieved its moments of maximum power; so our approach to film--particularly to the problem of genre in film--can be illuminated by a set of theoretical considerations whose very contradictoriness ensures that we will not be trapped, in our reading of a specific film, in a single dogmatic and distorting aesthetics.

In his history, Aesthetics and Art Theory, Harold Osborne offers interesting, nonstructuralist corroboration for the idea of film creation we are trying to describe. Osborne remarks that the technologization of art, particularly architecture, in the last two centuries has produced a new kind of artist, for whom traditional aesthetics gives us no very good name: he is the designer, or planner, whose conception of the work is at once realized, transformed, and re-created by the technologists who bring it into being. Osborne's description

of the artist as planner applies equally well to film. One remembers the clever review of Visconti's Ludwig by Pauline
Kael, with its insight that filmmakers are the archetypal mad
kings, manic Master Builders of our era. Insofar as he is
planner or Master Builder, the filmmaker deals, for his raw
materials, not so much in plot, character, or visual effects
--the shibboleths of conventional criticism--as in the sheer
possibilities that generic norms bestow upon art. He deals,
that is, in many-times-told tales which are a result of the
collaboration among the planner's own imagination, the expectations and imaginations of his audience, and the "thinking
which takes place in man" represented by the generic structures themselves. Nowhere, perhaps, is this complex and
difficult relationship between producer and audience, artist
and mass subconscious better caught than in F. Scott Fitz-
gerald's unfinished novel, The Last Tycoon. There, the nar-
rator muses about the career of the book's hero, Stahr, a
driven and tragic filmmaker: "This [Hollywood] was where
Stahr had come to earth after that extraordinary illuminating
flight where he saw which way we were going, and how we
looked doing it, and how much of it mattered. You could say
that this was where an accidental wind blew him, but I don't
think so. I would rather think that in a 'long shot' he saw a
new way of measuring our jerky hopes and graceful rogueries
and awkward sorrows, and that he came here from choice to
be with us to the end." To see "which way we were going,
and how we looked doing it, and how much of it mattered":
if the interplay of convention and originality, cliché and arche-
type that is the narrative film can successfully do that, then
it has achieved no more nor less political and artistic sophistication than the nineteenth-century French novel, or the
eighteenth-century English satire....

GENRE

Andrew Tudor

... Auteur at least originated in film criticism in the
recent past: genre had a lengthy pedigree in literary criticism long before the advent of the cinema. Hence the meaning and uses of the term vary considerably and it is very difficult to identify even a tenuous school of thought on the subject. For years it provided a crudely useful way of delineat-
ing the American cinema. The literature abounds with references to the "Western," the "Gangster" movie, or the "Horror" film, all of which are loosely thought of as genre. On
occasions it becomes almost the end point of the critical
process to fit a film into such a category, much as it once
made a film "intelligible" to fit it into, say, the French
"nouvelle vague." To call a film a "Western" is thought of
as somehow saying something interesting or important about
it. To fit it into a class of films about which we presumably
have some general knowledge. To say a film is a "Western"
is immediately to say that it shares some indefinable "X" with
other films we call "Westerns." In addition, it provides us
with a body of films to which our film can be usefully compared; sometimes, the only body of films. The most extreme,
and clearly ridiculous, application might be to argue that it is
necessarily more illuminating to compare, say, The Man Who
Shot Liberty Valance with a Roy Rogers short than with The
Last Hurrah. Not that the first comparison might not be in-
structive; merely that it is not necessarily the case. Extreme genre imperialism leads in this direction.

Now almost everyone uses terms like "Western"; the
neurotic critic as much as the undisturbed cinemagoer. The
difference, and the source of difficulty, lies in the way the
critic seeks to use the term. What is normally a thumbnail
classification for everyday purposes is now being asked to
carry rather more weight. The fact that there is a special
term, genre, for these categories suggests that the critic's

16

conception of "Western" is more complex than is the case in
everyday discourse; if not, why the special term? But in
quite what way critical usage is more complex is not entirely
clear. In some cases it involves the idea that if a film is a
"Western" it somehow draws on a tradition, in particular, on
a set of conventions. That is, "Westerns" have in common
certain themes, certain typical actions, certain characteristic
mannerisms; to experience a "Western" is to operate within
this previously defined world. Jim Kitses tries to isolate
characteristics in this way, by defining genre in terms of
such attributes: "... a varied and flexible structure, a the-
matically fertile and ambiguous world of historical material
shot through with archetypal elements which are themselves
even in flux."[1] But other usages, such as "Horror" films,
might also mean films displaying certain themes, actions, and
so on, or, just as often, films that have in common the intention to horrify. Instead of defining the genre by attributes
it is defined by intentions. Likewise with the distinction between "Gangster" movies and "Thrillers."

Both these uses display serious problems. The second, and for all practical purposes least important, suffers
from the notorious difficulties of isolating intentions. In the
first and more common case the special genre term is frequently entirely redundant. Imagine a definition of a "Western" as a film set in Western America between 1860 and 1900
and involving as its central theme the contrast between Garden and Desert. Any film fulfilling these requirements is a
Western, and a Western is only a film fulfilling these requirements. By multiplying such categories it is possible to di-
vide all films into groups, though not necessarily mutually exclusive groups. The usefulness of this (and classification can
only be justified by its use) depends on what it is meant to
achieve. But what is certain is that just as the critic determines the criteria on which the classification is based, so he
also determines the name given to the resultant groups of
films. Our group might just as well be called "type 1482/9a"
as "Westerns."

Evidently there are areas in which such individually
defined categories might be of some use. A sort of biblio-
graphic classification of the history of film, for instance, or
even an abstract exploration of the cyclical recurrence of certain themes. The films would be simply defined in terms of
the presence or absence of the themes in question. But this
is not the way in which the term is usually employed. On the
contrary, most writers tend to assume that there is some

body of films we can safely call the "Western" and then move on to the real work--the analysis of the crucial characteristics of the already recognized genre. Hence Kitses' set of thematic antinomies and four sorts of genre conventions. Or Bazin's distinction between classic and "sur-western," assuming, as it does, that there is some independently established essence of the Western which is distilled into Stagecoach. [2] These writers, and almost all writers using the term genre, are caught in a dilemma. They are defining a "Western" on the basis of analyzing a body of films which cannot possibly be said to be "Westerns" until after the analysis. If Kitses' themes and conventions are the defining characteristic of the "Western," then this is the previously discussed case of arbitrary definition--the category becomes redundant. But these themes and conventions are arrived at by analyzing films already distinguished from other films by virtue of being "Westerns." To take a genre such as a "Western," analyze it, and list its principle characteristics, is to beg the question that we must first isolate the body of films which are "Westerns." But they can only be isolated on the basis of the "principal characteristics," which can only be discovered from the films themselves after they have been isolated. That is, we are caught in a circle which first requires that the films are isolated, for which purposes a criterion is necessary, but the criterion is, in turn, meant to emerge from the empirically established common characteristics of the films. This "empiricist dilemma" has two solutions. One is to classify films according to a priori chosen criteria depending on the critical purpose. This leads back to the earlier position in which the special genre term is redundant. The second is to lean on a common cultural consensus as to what constitutes a "Western," and then go on to analyze it in detail.

This latter is clearly the root of most uses of genre. It is this usage that leads to, for example, the notion of conventions in a genre. The "Western," it is said, has certain crucial established conventions--ritualistic gunfights, black/ white clothing corresponding to good/bad distinctions, revenge themes, certain patterns of clothing, typed villains, and many, many more. The best evidence for the widespread recognition of these conventions is to be found in those films which pointedly set out to invoke them. Shane, for example, plays very much on the stereotyped imagery, contrasting the stooping, black-clad, sallow, be-gloved Palance with the tall (by dint of careful camera angles), straight, white buckskinned, fair, white-horsed Ladd. The power of this imagery is such that the sequence in which Shane rides to the showdown elevates

him to a classically heroic posture. The point is reinforced
by comparing Stevens' visualization of his characters with the
very different descriptions offered in Schaefer's novel. The
film "converts" the images to its own conventional language.
Other obvious examples are provided by the series of Italian
Westerns. The use of Lee Van Cleef in leading roles depends very much on the image he has come to occupy over
two decades of bit-part villains. Actors in the series--Van
Cleef, Eastwood, Wallach, Jack Elam, Woody Strode, Henry
Fonda, Charles Bronson--perpetually verge on self-parody.
The most peculiar of the films--Once Upon a Time in the
West--is a fairy-tale collection of Western conventions, verg-
ing on self-parody, and culminating in what must be the most
extended face-off ever filmed. Indeed, the most telling sug-
gestions as to the importance of conventions are to be found
in the gentle parodies of Cat Ballou, Support Your Local
Sheriff, and The Good Guys and the Bad Guys. Without clear,
shared conceptions of what is to be expected from a "Western"
such humor is not possible. One of the best sequences in
Cat Ballou encapsulates the importance of the imagery, the
sequence in which Lee Marvin is changed from drunken wreck
to classic gunfighter. Starting very humorously with Marvin
struggling into a corset, the transformation not only alters
him but brings out a response in us as piece by piece the
stereotyped image appears.

        In short, to talk about the "Western" is (arbitrary de-
finitions apart) to appeal to a common set of meanings in our
culture. From a very early age most of us have built up a
picture of a "Western." We feel that we know a "Western"
when we see one, though the edges may be rather blurred.
Thus in calling a film a "Western" the critic is implying more
than the simple statement, "This film is a member of a class
of films ('Westerns') having in common x,y,z." He is also
suggesting that such a film would be universally recognized as
such in our culture. In other words, the crucial factors
which distinguish a genre are not only characteristics inherent
to the films themselves; they also depend on the particular
culture within which we are operating. And unless there is
world consensus on the subject (which is an empirical question)
there is no basis for assuming that a "Western" will be conceived in the same way in every culture. The way in which
the genre term is applied can quite conceivably vary from case
to case. Genre notions--except the special case of arbitrary
definition--are not critics' classifications made for special purposes; they are sets of cultural conventions. Genre is what
we collectively believe it to be.

It is for precisely this reason that genre notions are
so potentially interesting. But more for the exploration of
the psychological and sociological interplay between filmmaker,
film, and audience, than for the immediate purposes of film
criticism.   (Given that it is not entirely possible to draw a
clear line between the two, this is really an argument for using a concept in one area rather than another.) Until we have
a clear, if speculative, notion of the connotations of a genre
class, it is difficult to see how the critic, already besieged
by imponderables, could usefully use the term, certainly not
as a special term at the root of his analysis. To use the
concept in any stronger sense it becomes necessary to establish clearly what filmmakers mean when they conceive themselves as making a "Western"; what limits such a choice may
impose on them; in effect, what relationship exists between
auteur and genre. But specific answers to such questions
must needs tap the conceptions held by particular filmmakers
and industries. To methodically analyze the way in which a
filmmaker utilizes a genre for his own purposes (at present
a popular critical pursuit) requires that we clearly establish
the principal components of his conception of the genre. But
this is not all. The notion that someone utilizes a genre suggests something about audience response. It implies that any
given film works in such-and-such a way because the audience
has certain expectations of the genre. We can only meaningfully talk of, for instance, an auteur breaking the rules of a
genre if we know what these rules are. And, of course, such
rule-breaking has no consequence unless the audience knows
as well. Now, as I have suggested, Shane may well take on
its almost "epic" quality because Stevens for the most part
sticks to the rules. In a similar way, Two Rode Together
and Cheyenne Autumn are slightly disconcerting, because they
break the rules, particularly vis-à-vis the Indian/White Man
relation. And, most obviously in recent years, Peckinpah's
"Westerns" use such elements to disturb the conventional
Western universe. The much remarked opening scene of Ride
the High Country with its policeman and motor cars; the cavalry charging the French Army in Major Dundee; the car in
The Wild Bunch. Now you, the reader, may agree that these
are cases of deliberate rule-breaking, and such agreement re-
flects that there is, in America and much of Europe, some
considerable consensus on what constitutes the characteristic
"language" of a Western. But this could well be a special
case. To infer from it that all genre terms are thus easily
employed is hardly justified.

This is not to suggest that genre terms are totally

useless. It is merely that to employ them requires a much
more methodical understanding of the workings of film. And
this in turn requires that we specify a set of sociological and
psychological context assumptions and construct explicit genre
models within them. If we imagine a general model of the
workings of film language, genre directs our attention to sub-
languages within it. Less centrally, however, the genre concept is indispensable in more strictly social and psychological terms as a way of formulating the interplay between culture, audience, films, and filmmakers. For example, there
is a class of films thought of by a relatively highly-educated,
middle-class, group of filmgoers as "art-movies." Now for
present purposes genre is a conception existing in the culture
of any particular group or society; it is not a way in which a
critic classifies films for methodological purposes, but the
much looser way in which an audience classifies its films.
On this meaning of the term "art-movies" is a genre. If a
culture includes such genre notions then, over a period of
time, and in a complicated way, certain conventions become
established as to what can be expected from an "art-movie"
as compared to some other category. The critics (the "posh"
critics in this case) are mediating factors in such developments. But once such conventions develop they can in turn
affect a filmmaker's conception of what he is doing. Hence
we get a commercial playing up of the "art-movie" category.

    Let me take an impressionistic example, bearing in
mind that much more extensive work would be needed to establish this in anything more than an intuitive way. At the
beginning of the 1960s in this country the general conception
of an "art-movie" revolved around the films of a group of
European directors. Bergman was already established with,
in particular, The Seventh Seal and Wild Strawberries. The
first year of the new decade had seen Antonioni's L'Avventura,
Resnais' Hiroshima mon Amour, and Fellini's La Dolce Vita.
These four--though perhaps Resnais less than the others--
served to define the "conventions" of the developing "art-
movies" genre. Deliberately and obviously intellectual (there
is nothing more deliberate than the final scene of La Dolce
Vita), with extremely visible individual stylistic characteristics. Bergman's silhouettes, puritan obsessiveness, and grunt-
ing Dark Age meals; Antonioni's minimal dialogue, grey photography, and carefully bleak compositions; and Fellini's self-
indulgent surrealistic imagery (partly in La Dolce Vita but
much more clearly in 8 1/2) circumscribed what was expected of an "art-movie." Increasingly, European films, whether
"deliberate" copies (a sub-Antonioni example is Patroni

Griffi's Il Mare) or later films made by the original directors,
met the conventions which the earlier films had established.
Antonioni's Il Deserto Rosso, Fellini's Giulietta of the Spirits,
Bergman's Winter Light and The Silence, are almost stylistic
parodies of their director's earlier films.   Giulietta of the
Spirits becomes the ultimate in color-supplement "art-movies";
a combination of the earlier films and the newly established
conventions of the genre.

     This should serve to illustrate the way in which genre
notions might constructively be used ·in tapping the socio-
psychological dynamics of film, although it is not designed to
convince anyone of the particular case of "art-movies. "   To
properly establish such an argument would require detailed
research on the changing expectations of "art-movie" audiences (perhaps via analysis of the "posh" critics), on the genre conceptions (and self-conceptions) held by individuals and
groups in various film industries, and on the films themselves.
Now there does not seem to me to be any crucial difference
between the most commonly employed genre term--the "Western"--and the "art-movie" category which I have been dealing
with.   They are both conceptions held by certain groups about
certain films.   Many of the theoretical problems about using
genre terms have, however, been overlooked in the case of
the "Western. "   It has become so much a part of our cultural
patterning that film criticism has tended to use it as if it
were possible to assume common agreement in all the respects on which research would be necessary in the "art-
movie" case.   It may be that there is such common agreement on the "Western"; but it does not follow that this would
be true of all genre categories.   Anyway, it is not at all
clear that there is that much consensus on the "Western. "   It
seems likely that for many people the most Western of Westerns (certainly the most popular if revivals are any indicator)
is John Sturges' The Magnificent Seven.   On the other hand,
in the 1940s the same position might be filled by My Darling
Clementine, in the 1950s by High Noon.   Conventions change,
often for reasons entirely out of the control of filmmakers
and film critics.

     In sum, then, genre terms seem best immediately em-
ployed in the analysis of the relation between groups of films,
the cultures in which they are made, and the cultures in which
they are exhibited.   That is, it is a term which can be usefully employed in relation to a body of knowledge and theory
about the social and psychological context of film.   Any assertion we might make about the use a director makes of genre

conventions--Peckinpah uses the contrast between our expectations and actual images to reinforce the "end of an era" element in Ride the High Country and The Wild Bunch--assumes,
wrongly, the existence of this body of knowledge. To labor
the point, it assumes: 1) we know what Peckinpah thinks; 2)
we know what the audience thinks (a) about the films in question, and (b) about "Westerns"; 3) Peckinpah knows the answer to 2(b) and it is the same as our answer, etc. Most
uses of genre effectively invent answers to such questions by
implicitly claiming to tap some archetypal characteristic of
the genre, some universal human response. This ... depends
on the particular context assumptions employed, and on a
more general notion of film language. To leap in with genre
immediately is to put the cart before the horse....

Notes

1. Jim Kitses. Horizons West (Thames and Hudson/British
     Film Institute, 1970), p. 19.

2. André Bazin, "Evolution du Western," Cahiers du Cinéma
     (December, 1955), reprinted in Qu'est-ce que le Ciné-
     ma? III, Cinéma et Sociologie (Paris: Editions du
     Cerf, 1961). This essay is also available in English
     in André Bazin, What Is Cinema, Vol. II, ed. and
     trans. Hugh Gray (University of California Press,
     1971).

THE IDEA OF GENRE IN THE AMERICAN CINEMA

Edward Buscombe

"Genre" is a term much employed in film criticism
at the moment, yet there is little agreement on what exactly
it means, or whether the term has any use at all.   There
appear to be three sorts of questions one could profitably ask:
first, do genres in the cinema really exist, and if so, can
they be defined; secondly, what are the functions they fulfill;
and thirdly, how do specific genres originate or what causes
them?

It seems sensible to start with a brief review of the
history of genre criticism in literature, since it is in this
context that certain problems first arise.   The notion that
there are different kinds of literature, with different techniques and subjects, was first developed by Aristotle; in his
Poetics he tried to separate out what he called poetry, and
we should simply call literature, into a number of categories
such as tragedy, epic, lyric, etc.   His purpose was to decide what were the particular qualities of each distinctive kind,
what each kind could be expected to do and not do.   He then
tried to establish their relative importance, and after much
debate concluded that tragedy was the highest kind of poetry.

During the Renaissance Aristotle's ideas were taken up
and erected into a rigid system of rules, so that certain precise styles and forms were prescribed for each kind (the
three dramatic unities are the most notorious example).   Such
codification was extended in the Neo-Classical period of the
seventeenth and eighteenth centuries, when literature was divided up into more and more categories, or "species" as they
were called, each with its own proper tone, form and subject-
matter.   As a result of this rather mechanical and dictatori-
al approach, the theory of literary kinds gradually became
discredited.   Even the classical Dr. Johnson was moved to
exclaim: "There is therefore scarcely any species of writing,

24

of which we can tell what is its essence, and what are its
constituents; every new genius produces some new innovation,
which, when invented and approved subverts the rules which
the practice of foregoing authors had established. "

Under the impact of the Romantic revolt against rules
and traditions of all kinds, the idea of literary species, or
genres as they later came to be called, suffered greatly.
The artist was to be free to write in any manner to which
the spirit moved him. It was not until the rise in the late
1930s and early 1940s of a Chicago-based school of criticism
known as the Neo-Aristotelians that much attention was paid
to the influence on the artist of already existing forms and
conventions. The Neo-Aristotelians were consciously react-
ing against the so-called "New Criticism," which had express-
ly repudiated any kind of historical approach to literature.
The famous catch-phrase "a poem is a poem is a poem" sums
up their attitude: that a work of literature exists by itself
and relies upon no reference to any external reality, whether
contemporary or historical.

The Neo-Aristotelians were concerned to rescue literature from such self-imposed isolation, and in attempting to do
so they partially resurrected the theory of genres. But they
did not always avoid what has often been a source of confusion; Aristotle had spoken of literary kinds in two senses:
first as a number of different groups of conventions which had
grown up historically and had developed into particular forms
such as satire, lyric and tragedy; and secondly as a more
fundamental division of literature, into drama, epic and lyric,
corresponding to major differences in the relation between
artist, subject-matter and audience.

More time, in fact, was spent in assessing the natures
and possibilities of these three modes of literature than in exploring the historical genres. As a result, not much of the
work is relevant to the cinema, for these three modes (which
correspond approximately to drama, fiction and poetry), appear to be equally present in the cinema. And, on the other
hand, such work as has been done on the development of particular genres such as the Gothic novel or Victorian melodrama has not ventured far beyond the mere recording of lists
of examples.

Nevertheless, some profit is to be gained from the
literary critics, even if only a warning. Many people wish to
avoid the whole question of genre because it is held that it

will lead to the laying down of rules and regulations which
will arbitrarily restrict the freedom of the artist to create
what he likes, or the freedom of the critic to talk about anything he wants to. But if the theory of genres in literature
has usually been restrictive and normative, it need not necessarily be so. One does not have to set up a Platonic ideal,
to which all particular examples try vainly to aspire, nor
even to say that the closer any individual film comes to incorporating all the different elements of the definition, the
more fully it will be a Western, or gangster picture, or musical. Aristotle's original intention was descriptive, not
prescriptive.

Some positive assistance is afforded by Wellek and
Warren in their Theory of Literature. They neatly state the
crux of the problem: "The dilemma of genre history is the
dilemma of all history: i. e., in order to discover the scheme
of reference (in this case, the genre) we must study the history; but we cannot study the history without having in mind
some scheme of selection."

As they recognize, the problem is only another aspect
of the wider philosophical problem of universals. With regard to the cinema, we may state it thus: if we want to know
what a Western is we must look at certain kinds of films.
But how do we know which films to look at until we know what
a Western is?

For some people the futility of many of the arguments
which arise out of this dilemma (as to whether a film such
as, say, Lonely Are the Brave is a Western or not) is so obvious that they give up in despair. But having posed the problem in such apparently insoluble terms, Wellek and Warren
offer a way out. To begin with, common sense suggests that
it is possible to draw up a list of elements which are found
in films that, for the purposes of the argument, are called
Westerns, and to say that any film which includes one or more
of these elements is thereby held to be a Western, though not
therefore necessarily identical to other examples of the form.
Wellek and Warren go further, however: "Genre should be
conceived, we think, as a grouping of literary works based,
theoretically, upon both outer form (specific metre or structure) and also upon inner form (attitude, tone, purpose--more
crudely, subject and audience). The ostensible basis may be
one or the other (e. g., 'pastoral' and 'satire' for the inner
form: dipodic verse and Pindaric ode for the outer); but the
critical problem will then be to find the other dimension, to
complete the diagram."

This idea of both inner and outer form seems essential, for if we require only the former, in terms of subject matter, then our concept will be too loose to be of much value; and if only the latter, then the genre will be ultimately meaningless, since devoid of any content.

What, then, are the cinematic equivalents of, first, outer form? Not, clearly, rhythm. To the extent to which a film can be said to have rhythm, this depends not upon the conventions of the genre within which it is made, but upon the artistic personalities of the director and editor. [1] Nor does the notion of structure open up many possibilities. It seems extremely difficult to argue that there is any significant similarity between the plots of different Westerns, for example. There are, of course, a number of plot structures which reappear in film after film. There is the one in which a bigoted and usually disciplinarian cavalry officer is narrowly prevented from starting a "full-scale Indian war." Or, again, there is the one in which a reformed gunfighter (or ex-marshal) is reluctantly persuaded to accept responsibility for cleaning up the town. But to use such structures as a basis for defining the genre would mean ending up not with one genre called "the Western," but an almost infinite number of sub-genres. Some may wish to argue that this is the best that can be done. Yet it does seem that these films have something more in common, something which makes the two kinds of story mentioned above part of the same genre.

Since we are dealing with a visual medium we ought surely to look for our defining criteria at what we actually see on the screen. It is immediately apparent that there before our eyes is a whole range of "outer forms." There is, first of all, the setting, the chief glory of many of the films. Often it is outdoors, in very particular kinds of country: deserts, mountains, plains, woods. Or, it is indoors, but again, special kinds of indoors: saloons, jails, courtrooms, ranch-houses, hotels, riverboats, brothels--all places frequented by those who live an outdoor and/or wandering kind of life.

Then there are the clothes: wide-brimmed hats, open-neck shirts with scarves, tight jeans (which have got steadily tighter as the years have gone by), sometimes worn with leather chaps and almost always with spurs and high-heeled boots; or, alternatively, army uniforms, or the wide, but carefully distinguished, variety of Indian costume. There are also certain clothes for specialist occupations: boot-lace ties for gamblers, black gloves for psychopathic hired guns; a man

who wears a watch-chain is often a judge, and a black hat
can denote a preacher; a bowler, a newspaperman. For wom-
en there are usually only two sorts of clothes: wide, full
skirts and tight bodices, or, the more tomboyish jeans and
shirt.   (There is a third costume usually reserved for the
Mexican girl or prostitute--often synonymous--in which the
bodice is looser and the neckline appreciably lower.)

        Thirdly, there are the various tools of the trade, prin-
cipally weapons, and of these, principally guns. They are
usually specifically identified: Colt 45s, Winchester and
Springfield rifles, shotguns for certain situations (such as
robbing banks or facing a numerically superior enemy) and,
in Westerns of an earlier period, single-shot, muzzle-loading
muskets.   Such care in the choice of weapons is not mere
pedantry, nor dictated purely by considerations of historical
accuracy, for an incredible variety of arms were in use.
The weapons employed in the films are there for largely stylistic reasons; consider, for example, the significant difference in the style of movement required to cock a Winchester
and a Lee-Enfield 303.   Other weapons have their place:
knives, often the murderous-looking Bowie type, whips (used
by women or bullies), sometimes cannon for the military,
and assorted Indian hardware, notably the bow and arrow.
Again, there are specialist weapons.   The man who wears a
boot-lace tie should be watched carefully in case he produces
a Derringer.

        Next in importance as tools come horses, also used in
formally differentiated ways.   Indians ride bare-backed or
with only a blanket, a sign perhaps of their closeness to the
animal world.   White and black horses have frequently a symbolic function, and if a woman does not ride sidesaddle she is
no lady, though not always the worse for that.   Doctors and
judges ride in a buggy, unless, like Doc Holliday, they have
ceased to practice.   We know, too, what kind of people travel
in stagecoaches: in descending order of their entitlement to
respect, women, gamblers, corset-salesmen and Easterners.

        Fourthly, there is a large group of miscellaneous
physical objects which recur and thereby take on a formal
function.   Trains are invariably of the same kind: cow-catch-
er in front of the engine, carriages with a railed open plat-
form at the back (useful for fights), and seats either side of
a central aisle.   Mines, general stores and forts also feature
largely, representing the corruption of money, the virtue of
honest industry, and an oasis of strength in a hostile land.

Indians, too, in spite of the more liberal attitudes of the last few years, are still primarily important not as people in their own right but as part of the setting.

All these things operate as formal elements. That is to say, the films are not "about" them any more than a sonnet is about fourteen lines in a certain metre. (Winchester 73 is not about the gun, which is a mere connecting device to hold the story together. The film, like all films, is about people.) Obviously the formal structure is looser than that of a sonnet; not all the elements need be present. But if we say that a Western is a film which includes at least one of them (and of course the list is by no means exhaustive), then we are saying something both intelligible and useful. The visual conventions provide a framework within which the story can be told.

But what is more important is that they also affect what kind of story it will be. Just as the nature of the sonnet makes it more likely you will be successful in writing a love poem of a very personal kind rather than something else, and has so grown up as a genre with both outer and inner form, so too what kind of film a Western is, is largely determined by the nature of its conventions. One can put this more forcefully in a negative way: it is unlikely you will produce a good poem on a large-scale historical theme such as the Trojan War if you first choose the sonnet form. So, too, if you are going to make a Western you will tend not to consider certain themes or subjects (unless, as in High Noon, you are consciously trying to adapt the form to your purpose in an arbitrary way).

In trying to be more specific here, one gets inevitably on to dangerous ground, for unless one has seen all the Westerns ever made (or, to be absolutely logical, all the Westerns that ever could be made) there can not be any certainty that generalizations will hold. Since the object is to stimulate discussion, not end it, however, a start can be made by saying that because of the physical setting a Western is likely to deal successfully with stories about the opposition between man and nature, and the establishment of civilization. As Jim Kitses points out in his book Horizons West, such oppositions are seen from two points of view: for nature, or for civilization. If, on the other hand, you want to deal with the sense of fear, isolation and excitement engendered by great cities, you won't do it very well within the framework of the Western.

This much, perhaps, is obvious.   But it is possible
to go further.   The men in Westerns wear clothes that are
aggressively masculine, sexy in a virile sort of way. [2]   This
in turn determines the character of the hero--taciturn, tough,
uncomplicated, self-sufficient.   It is surely no accident that
the most famous Western heroes are not, by conventional
standards, good-looking.   John Wayne, Randolph Scott, James
Stewart, Gary Cooper, Kirk Douglas, all have their attrac-
tions, but they are not, like Cary Grant, at home in a draw-
ing-room.   Likewise, the clothes of the women determine
that they will be either very feminine or very masculine.
(Part of the interest comes from feminine clothes hiding a
masculine character--Angie Dickinson in Rio Bravo--or vice
versa, as with characters like Calamity Jane, who usually
turn out to be pining for a home and children.)

But either way, because the men are so aggressively
masculine and lead wandering lives and the women are forced
either to stay at home or become the equivalents of men, few
Westerns have a strong love interest.   The formal elements
of the genre make it hard to deal with subjects that presup-
pose in the characters an interest in, and a time for, the
heart's affections.

It's likely, also, that given the arsenal of weapons on
view in the films violence will play a crucial part in the
stories.   This is not to say that there could not be pacifist
Westerns, though they are significantly less common than
pacifist war films, because the kind of weapons used makes
the violence less immediate and unpleasant.   But it is hard
to think of a Western in which there is at least no threat of
violence.   Thus the world of the West is very different from
that of a Henry James novel, where no hand is ever raised
in anger.   Because the guns are there as part of the formal
structure, there will be, characteristically, a dilemma which
either can only be resolved by violence, or in which the violence would be a solution, though a wrong one.   The characters will be of a kind whose virtue resides not so much in
subtlety of intellect, or sensitivity, or imagination, as in their
willingness and ability to stand up for themselves, to be in
some sense, not necessarily physical, strong.

One could go on.   But it might already be objected that
it is the subject matter that determines the outer form, not
the other way round; that the things a director wants to say
will decide the form he uses.   Not enough is known about how
most Westerns were conceived in the minds of directors and

writers to say whether this is the actual process of creation.
One may be forgiven for suspecting, however, that the worst
way to make a Western is to think of a theme and then try
to transpose it into Western form.

If one looks at a cinematic genre in this way, as being composed of an outer form consisting of a certain number
of visual conventions that are, in a sense, arbitrary (in the
same way that a tragedy has five acts), then certain problems
are on the way to being solved. First, we are not bound to
make any very close connections between the Western genre
and historical reality. Of course there are connections. But
too many discussions of these problems fall down over this
point because it is usually assumed that the relationship must
be a direct one; that since in fact there was a West, Westerns must be essentially concerned with it. Kitses, for instance, states that "The basic convention of the genre is that
films in Western guise are about America's past." This is
simply not true of many of the films, including several of the
ones he discusses, for only Peckinpah of his three directors
is at all preoccupied with historical themes. In some of his
films Mann includes such material, though that is not where
the central interest lies; and Boetticher appears quite oblivious to any such considerations. To be fair, Kitses is aware
of other elements in the genre. On pp. 24-5 he summarizes
what he calls "interrelated aspects of the genre," under the
headings of "history," "themes," "archetypes," and "icons"
(which are equivalent to what I have called visual conventions).
But he fails to show in what their interrelation consists; nor,
ultimately, does this first chapter have much to do with his
discussion of particular directors, and for the reason I have
suggested, that history, to which Kitses devotes most of his
attention, is a relatively unimportant part of many Westerns.

There are several reasons why it is necessary to resist the temptation to talk about Westerns largely in terms of
history. First, one usually ends up by talking about Ford,
who is, clearly, more concerned with it than most. But Ford
is not the Western. Secondly, if this is what Westerns chief-
ly present, it is hard to see why half the world's population
should spend its time watching them. Thirdly, and most seriously, to define Westerns as films about a certain period of
America's past is to misunderstand the nature and meaning of
genres, and how they work.

Before going on to deal with this, however, two more
points should be made. Although the Western seems to me

the most important of the genres, the one in which the largest body of good work has been done, there are obviously
others. The same approach could be applied to them; name-
ly, to inquire into the outer form, the visual and other conventions, and to see whether there is the same relation between form and content, whether it could be shown that the
subject-matter dealt with is determined by a series of formal
and given patterns. The gangster movie[3] is an obvious subject of inquiry, though one problem is that it shades off into
the thriller, so that at one end of the spectrum we have, say,
White Heat and at the other Hitchcock. Musicals, too, would
repay attention. Nor need visual elements be the only defining ones, for film is not only a visual art. For example, it
is (or used to be) understood that in Hollywood romantic comedies people do not sleep together unless they are married.
Clearly this is a convention--it never was actually true. And
it cannot be explained merely by referring to the Hays Code,
for that would make it simply a restriction. Although it does
limit the kind of subject that can be dealt with, in the same
way that it does in the Victorian novel, on the other hand a
lot of mileage can be got out of it. The famous scene in It
Happened One Night where Clark Gable and Claudette Colbert
share a room together uses the convention as the basis of its
humor. All the same, the major defining characteristics of
genres will be visual: guns, cars, clothes in the gangster;
clothes and dancing in the musical (apart from the music, of
course!); castles, coffins and teeth in horror movies.

     The second point is that while it is possible to talk of
themes and archetypes in genres, as Jim Kitses does in his
book, it doesn't in the end help very much. He cites archetypes such as "the journey and the quest, the ceremonies of
love and marriage, food and drink, the rhythms of waking and
sleeping, life and death." Not only do these appear in other
genres besides the Western; they exist in films which can
scarcely be classified into any genres, and what is more, they
occur in other forms of art besides the cinema. What we
need is a way of looking at a genre which can make clear
what is distinctive about it and how its outer and inner forms
relate.

     But what functions does genre perform? Or, in other
words, why bother to talk about it at all? Can't we get along
just as well with our present director-oriented theories, while
admitting that some films are like others? The trouble is
that our present theories are so extreme. They assume that
the auteur (who need not necessarily be the director, of

course) is personally responsible for everything that appears
in the film--or that someone is responsible, if only a heavy-
handed producer. This form of over-compensation, a reaction to the critical dark ages when American cinema was dismissed as repetitive rubbish, mass-produced to a formula
(unfortunately all too successful) in the factories of Hollywood,
has led to a situation in which American films are held to be
wholly the expressions of the artistic personalities of their
highly original creators.

There may well be several reasons for this, apart
from the swing of the pendulum. There is a kind of critical
snobbery which assumes that you cannot really appreciate a
film unless you have seen all its director's other films, and
which leads to the more bizarre forms of auteur-hunting. [4]
For if an individual film is good, then it must have an auteur
behind it, and if he is an auteur, it follows that his other
works will be good--or at least interesting. And yet there
are films which are totally successful and which derive their
power from the traditions of a genre rather than from any
distinctive directorial contribution. Casablanca is such a one,
as Andrew Sarris recognizes in The American Cinema. It
doesn't help much to have seen other Curtiz films, but one's
enjoyment is enormously enriched by having seen Humphrey
Bogart and the rest in other films of the period. It may be
objected that strictly speaking this has nothing to do with genre, since the qualities which actors can bring to a film cut
across genres. Yet is it not a fact that Bogart's battered
face instantly communicates a blend of cynicism and honesty,
weariness and generosity, that is genuinely part of a tradition
of the American film noire? What he represents in the film
owes little to Michael Curtiz, much to the other films he
played in.

But the chief justification of the genre is not that it
allows merely competent directors to produce good films
(though one is grateful enough for that). Rather, it is that it
allows good directors to be better. And the main reason why
this has not been more generally recognized is that the auteur
theory is not very well equipped to deal with popular art.
Even in its less extreme forms it cannot really make room
for the contribution of the tradition in which a film was made.
Thus it is not only that, in order to appreciate Casablanca,
we must be prepared to accept Curtiz as an auteur (which is
what Higham and Greenberg request us to do in Hollywood in
the Forties):[5] when we are faced with a genuinely distinctive
artist he is so often considered apart from the genre

background he works in. Robin Wood's book on Hitchcock is
an excellent piece of criticism. But in his discussion of
Psycho he says nothing of the film's obvious relation to the
horror genre. Surely one's sense of fear depends at least in
part on our built-in response to certain stock symbols which
Hitchcock employs. People rarely take Hitchcock seriously
when he talks about his pictures; yet at the head of the section on Psycho Robin Wood has this quotation: "The process
through which we take the audience [is it not significant that
he so often says 'we,' not 'I'?], you see, it's rather like
taking them through the haunted house at the fairground.... "
The house itself, with its vague suggestion of Victorian Gothic,
is straight out of any number of horror films: and when at
the end Vera Miles goes down towards the cellar, we are
terrified not just because we have heard Norman say he is
taking his mother down there (we don't anyway know yet that
his mother is a corpse, though of course we suspect all is
not well); our certainty that something unpleasant will be
found comes from our knowledge that nasty things do come
out of cellars in this kind of film. This is not to deny Wood's
ascription of Freudian overtones to the cellar; but the trouble
with Freudian overtones is that you aren't supposed to be
aware of them. It seems more likely that our conscious reaction to the scene owes more to our having assimilated them
through an exposure to the tradition of the genre.

Most people see films this way. No one would suggest that we must be bound by the aesthetic criteria of the
man in the street. Yet anyone who is at all concerned with
education must be worried at the distance between much of the
criticism now written and the way the average audience reacts
to a film. For them it is not a new Hawks or Ford or a new
Peckinpah; it is a new Western. And to sympathize with this
view is not to deny the claims of these directors to be artists.
Popular art does not condemn its creators to a subsidiary
role. Instead it emphasizes the relation between the artist
and his material, on the one hand, and the material and the
audience on the other. The artist brings to the genre his own
concerns, techniques and capacities--in the widest sense, his
style--but receives from the genre a formal pattern which directs and disciplines his work. In a sense this imposes limitations, as I have suggested. Certain themes and treatments
are, if not ruled out, unlikely to be successful if they work
too hard against the genre. But the benefits are considerable.
Constant exposure to a previous succession of films has led
the audience to recognize certain formal elements as charged
with an accretion of meaning. Some of these I have tried to

isolate, and in some cases their meaning has been suggested.
Some critics like to refer to them as "icons."

All too often, however, discussion has ceased there.
But it is vital to see not how icons relate to the cinema in
general, but to genres in particular, and how in the popular
cinema they may be reconciled to our natural desire to see
films as the expression of an artistic personality.

This can best be done through the notion that a genre
film depends on a combination of novelty and familiarity. The
conventions of the genre are known and recognized by the audience, and such recognition is in itself a pleasure. Popular
art, in fact, has always depended on this; one might argue
that the modern idea of novelty (or "originality") as a major,
even the major, quality to be desired in a work of art dates
from the Romantic period. And, as Raymond Williams shows
in Culture and Society, it is during this period that art began
to move away from its contact with a large, roughly homo-
geneous audience. We have there the beginnings of the present-day division between "mass" and "highbrow" culture. All
too easily this originality degenerates into eccentricity and
communication is sacrificed in the interests of self-expression.
It is one of the chief merits of the American cinema that this
has, on the whole, not yet happened; and because this is so
the popular cinema (which is almost, though not quite, synonymous with the American cinema) offers one of the richest
sources of material for those teaching Liberal Studies to the
culturally unsophisticated. Those who are unconvinced by this
might wish to argue that the opposite of eccentricity is the
cliché. It is true that if a director slavishly copies the conventions rather than uses them, then we get a film which is
just what Hollywood is so often, even now, held to have produced exclusively: a thoroughly predictable string of stock
situations and images. However, this article is not primarily
intended as propaganda for Hollywood. That battle, if not won,
is at least being fought by increasing numbers of people, on
ever widening fronts. Rather, the intention is to argue that
it is a mistake to base the argument for popular cinema exclusively on a case for the auteur.

One of the best examples of the way in which genre actually works is in Peckinpah's Guns in the Afternoon. * Knowing the period and location, we expect at the beginning to find
a familiar Western town. In fact, the first few minutes of the

*In the United States released as Ride the High Country (Ed.).

film brilliantly disturb our expectations. As the camera roves
around the town we discover a policeman in uniform, a car,
a camel, and Randolph Scott dressed up as Buffalo Bill. Each
of these images performs a function. The figure of the policeman conveys that the law has become institutionalized; the
rough and ready frontier days are over. The car suggests,
as in The Wild Bunch, that the West is no longer isolated
from modern technology and its implications. Significantly,
the camel is racing against a horse; such a grotesque juxtaposition is painful. A horse in a Western is not just an animal, but a symbol of dignity, grace and power. These qualities are mocked by it competing with a camel; and to add insult to injury, the camel wins.

Randolph Scott is not just an actor. It is enough to
have seen two or three of his films to know that he represents a quiet, cheerful kind of integrity. Peckinpah uses this
screen image by having him play against it all through the
film; but the initial shock of seeing him in a wig, running a
crooked booth at the fair, does more than upset our expectations about his role in the film. It calls into question our
whole attitude to the heroes of Western legend. Scott dressed
up as Buffalo Bill is an image that relies not only on Scott's
screen personality, but also on the audience's stock response
to Buffalo Bill, for he too is debased by this grotesque im-
personation. This, Peckinpah is saying, is the state that
things have come to, that heroes are exploited for money.

Clearly, then, although Peckinpah is working against
the conventions, he could not do this unless he and the audience had a tradition in common. He needs the outer form,
though in many ways he is making an anti-Western. What is
especially interesting is the relation between this and the inner form. Here I am obliged to take issue again with Jim
Kitses. He believes that Peckinpah's films are essentially
about a search for personal identity. While not wishing to
deny that some such concern may be traced in the pictures,
one must protest that this rather tends to ignore the most obvious fact about them, that they are Westerns. Personal identity can be sought for anywhere, anytime. But the essential
theme of Guns in the Afternoon is one that, while it could be
put into other forms, is ideally suited to the one chosen.
The film describes the situation of men who have outlived
their time. Used to a world where issues were decided simply, on a test of strength, they now find this way of life
threatened by complications and developments they do not understand. Since they cannot, or will not, adapt, all that remains to them is a tragic and bitter heroism.

The cluster of images and conventions which we call the Western genre is used by Peckinpah to define and embody this situation, in such a way that we know what the West was, and what it has become.   The first is communicated through images which are familiar, the second through those which are strange.   And together they condition his subject matter. Most obviously, because the film is a Western, the theme is worked out in terms of violent action.   If it were a musical, the theme might be similar in some ways, but because the conventions would be different, it would probably not involve violence (or if it did, the violence might well be highly styl- ized, and so quite different in effect).   And if it were a gang- ster picture, it seems unlikely that the effect of the film's ending, its beautifully elegiac background of autumn leaves, would be reproduced, suggesting as it does that the dead Judd is at one with nature, that nature which seems at the begin- ning of the film to have been overtaken by "civilization. "

Much of what has been said has been expressed in other ways by recent writers, occasionally more esoterically. What needs to be done now is that our increasing understand- ing of how important semiology is should be put to work, to explore the precise relation between the artist and his given material, in order to explain our intuitive feeling that a genre is not a mere collection of dead images waiting for a director to animate it, but a tradition with a life of its own.   We re- turn to the third question at the beginning of this article. Genres predate great directors.   The Western was going along happily under its own steam well before John Ford, or even James Cruze, came upon it.   We need much more work on the early history of these various forms if we are to fully comprehend their strange power, and how exactly they grew rich enough to attract the talents they did.   Lastly, the ques- tion of the relation between the Western and history, which I have argued is by no means simple, and not always central, can only be answered with certainty when we know how the form began.   It's usually assumed that it sprang, fully armed, from pulp fiction, and yet so much of it is visual that it is hard to believe this is quite true.   And if the Western origi- nates in history and is a response to it, what about the musi- cal?   Or the horror film?   Can we possibly evolve a theory to fit them all?

Notes

1.   Except, perhaps, for the rapid montage sequences of
        many gangster films.

2.   As if to underline this, the gambler, whose clothes are
     flashier, is invariably a ladies' man.

3.   See Colin McArthur's BFI Seminar Paper, "Genre and
     Iconography."

4.   I use the term loosely, to mean the artist awarded credit
     for a film's succession: the distinction between auteur
     and metteur-en-scène has no importance here.

5.   Charles Higham and Joel Greenberg. Hollywood in the
     Forties (London: A. Zwemmer, and New York: A. S.
     Barnes, 1968), p. 19.

GENRE FILM: A CLASSICAL EXPERIENCE

Thomas Sobchack

In their book, An Illustrated Glossary of Film Terms, Harry M. Geduld and Ronald Gottesman define "genre" as a "category, kind, or form of film distinguished by subject matter, theme, or techniques."[1] They list more than seventy-five genres of film, both fiction and non-fiction. There are categories within categories and categories which overlap and are not mutually exclusive. In light of the difficulty of accurately defining the individual genres, I would rather sidestep the problem by considering the Fictional Genre Film as a single category which includes all that is commonly held to be genre film, i. e. , the Western, the Horror film, the Musical, the Science Fiction film, the Swashbuckler, etc. , in order to show that all of these films have a common origin and basic form. Bound by a strict set of conventions, tacitly agreed upon by filmmaker and audience, the genre film provides the experience of an ordered world and is an essentially classical structure predicated upon the principles of the Classical world view in general, and indebted to the Poetics of Aristotle in particular; in the genre film the plot is fixed, the characters defined, the ending satisfyingly predictable.

Because the genre film is not realistic, because it is so blatantly dramatic, it has been condescendingly treated by many critics for its failure to be relevant to contemporary issues, philosophies, and aesthetics. Yet the truth of the matter is that the genre film lives up to the guiding principle of its Classical origins: "there is nothing new under the sun," and truth with a capital "T" is to be found in imitating the past. The contemporary and the particular are inimical to the prevailing idea in Classical thought that knowledge is found in the general conclusions which have stood the test of time. Thus originality, unique subject matter, and a resemblance to actual life are denigrated as values, while conformity, adherence to previous models, and a preoccupation with

39

stylistic and formal matters are held to be the criteria for
artistic excellence.

      The subject matter of a genre film is a story. It is
not about something that matters outside the film, even if it
inadvertently tells us something about the time and place of
its creation. Its sole justification for existence is to make
concrete and perceivable the configurations inherent in its
ideal form. That the various genres have changed, gone
through cycles of popularity, does not alter the fact that the
basic underlying coordinates of a genre are maintained time
after time. From Porter's The Great Train Robbery to The
Cowboys or True Grit, the Western has maintained a consistency of basic content; the motifs, plots, settings, and characters remain the same. What is true of the Western is also
true of the Adventure film, the Fantasy film, the Crime film,
and the Musical, or any fictional genre one can identify. Any
particular film of any definable group is only recognizable as
part of that group if it is, in fact, an imitation of that which
came before. It is only because we have seen other films
that strongly resemble the particular film at hand that we can
say, "Yes, this is a Horror film or a Thriller or a Swashbuckler. " Consciously or unconsciously, both the genre filmmaker and the genre audience are aware of the prior films
and the way in which each of these concrete examples is an
attempt to embody once again the essence of a well-known
story.

      This use of well-known stories is clearly a classical
practice. Homer, the Greek dramatists, Racine, Pope, Samuel Johnson, and all the otner great figures of the classical
and neo-classical periods used prior sources for their stories.
The formative principle behind the creation of classical art
has always been the known and the familiar. The Greeks
knew the stories of the gods and the Trojan War in the same
way we know about hoodlums and gangsters and G-men and
the taming of the frontier and the never-ceasing struggle of
the light of reason and the cross with the powers of darkness,
not through first-hand experience but through the media. For
them it was tales told around the hearth and the yearly ritual
of plays; for us it is the newspapers, television, and the
movies themselves.

      The body of stories is, to use Balázs' terms, the "ma-
terial" out of which the "content" of a genre film can be made.
And it is a strictly delimited area: other films may have the
whole of life experience to choose from, but the genre film

must be made from certain well known and immediately recognizable plots--plots usually dealing with melodramatic incidents in which obvious villains and heroes portray the basic
conflict of good versus evil. No matter how complicated the
plot of a genre film may be, we always know who the good
guys and the bad guys are; we always know whom to identify
with and just for how long. Sam Spade may be considered
by real life standards to be a man of dubious moral character, but in the world of The Maltese Falcon he is clearly the
hero akin to Odysseus threading his way through the obstacles
of a hostile universe, using lies and deceit if necessary to
complete his task.

        Aristotle used the word "mimesis" to describe what it
is a play is about. Supposedly it means imitation. Aristotle
goes on to say a plot is an imitation of a human action, and
there are those who see in this definition the prescription for
a kind of literal realism, holding the mirror up to life. But
Greek drama from which Aristotle drew his conclusions was
never that at all. Very few people in 5th-century Athens
killed their fathers and slept with their mothers. The story
of Oedipus, no matter how rife with Freudian implications for
us today, was after all simply a story, albeit a kind of horror tale of its time, as were most of the stories upon which
Greek writing was based. In practical terms Greek writings
are imitations of prior stories, redone, reshaped, given dramatic form or epic form as the case may be, but nevertheless imitations of fictions.

        Genre films operate on the same principle. They are
made in imitation not of life but of other films. True, there
must be the first instance in a series or cycle, yet most
cases of the first examples of various film genres can be
traced to literary sources, primarily pulp literature. Even
the gangster films of the '30s derive not from life itself, but
from newspaper stories; the musical film from the musical
stage. And once the initial film is made, it has entered the
pool of common knowledge known by filmmaker and film audience alike. Imitations and descendants--the long line of "Son
of 's," "Brides of" and the "Return of 's"--begin.

        One of the paradoxes of a classical approach to form
is aptly demonstrated in the genre film's unrelenting pursuit
of imitation. Classical theory insists upon the primacy of the
original. It is that which must be imitated, and the basic and
fundamental elements must not be changed. Therefore, to
avoid an exact duplicate, subsequent imitations can merely

embroider and decorate, which in most cases destroys the
elegance and simplicity of the original design.   The Doric
column came first, simple, balanced, proportioned, direct.
As the years passed, the Doric gave way to the Ionic, the
Ionic to the Corinthian, the last column so cluttered and intricate that it diluted the original idea.   Classical painting and
architecture give way to the Rococo and the Baroque.   The
decorations increase; the power and the purity of the original
are somehow dissipated.

        We can see the same process at work in the genre
film, and it explains why so often the original version or the
"classic" version seems so much better than any of its followers.   The original Draculas, both silent and sound, Little
Caesar and Public Enemy, The Iron Horse and The Covered
Wagon, Busby Berkeley musicals, The Maltese Falcon.   Not
only were they progenitors of their kind and therefore to be
venerated as examples from the Golden Age, but seen today
they have a sparseness and an economy of means which put
most of the recent remakes to shame.   Christopher Lee cannot compare to Bela Lugosi, and full color blood cannot make
up for the spectral mysteriousness of a Nosferatu.

        A genre film, no matter how baroque it may become,
however, still differs fundamentally from other films by virtue of its reliance on preordained forms, known plots, recognizable characters and obvious iconographies; it is still capable of creating the classical experience because of this insistence on the familiar.   It is that which we expect in a genre film and that which we get.   Other fiction films are not
genre films precisely because they do the opposite; they go
out of their way to be original, unique, and novel.   They appear more realistic, more true to life.   Their characters are
more highly individualized, their actions physically and psycho-
logically more believable, the events of the plot, employing
random events and inconsequential details, well within the
realm of possibility.

        There are grey areas, of course, films which seem
to be closer to genre than others depending on the total effect
of the film, the way in which the realistic elements are emphasized or de-emphasized, the way in which generic elements
are used or abused.   Yet for most films the issue is more
clear-cut.   The ideas and attitudes informing genre films are
diametrically opposed to the other kind of fiction film.   Although there is a detective (the reporter) and a mystery
(What's Rosebud?), it would be difficult to make a case for

Citizen Kane as a detective or mystery genre film. Though
it has certain generic elements, they are not prominent, nor
are they the sole justification for the creation of the film.
On the other hand, Sherlock Holmes films, the Thin Man series, Charlie Chan movies, etc. exist primarily to flesh out
the idea of the detective story on film. They exist as variations on the motif of sleuthing. "Who dun it?" is the primary question raised and answered by these movies. No matter how rich a gold mine of interpretation one may find in
The Maltese Falcon, for example, the basic question dealt
with is still "Who dun it?" not "Who am I?" or "What is the
discrepancy between what a man appears to be and what he
really is?" This is not to say that something of the latter
question is not raised by Sam Spade's character, but certainly the film does not invite the general audience to take the
question seriously, even if critics do.

One of the most important characteristics of the classical complex is a concern with form. Genre films, as suggested, are invariably more involved with formal matters both
in content and in style, since they begin in imitation of other
formal objects and not in imitation of life. In keeping with
this notion, the form of a genre film will display a profound
respect for Aristotelian dramatic values. There is always a
definite sense of beginning, middle, and end, of closure, of
a frame. The film begins, "Once upon a time ... " and ends
only after all the strings have been neatly tied, all major conflicts resolved. It is a closed world. There is little room
in the genre film for ambiguity anywhere--in characters, plots,
or iconography. But even when seeming ambiguities arise in
the course of a film, they must be either de-emphasized or
taken care of by the end of the film.

The most important single aspect of the genre film
which gives it this compact sense of shape is the plot. It's
what happens that's most important, not why. Incident crowd-
ing on incident, reversal after reversal, all strung out like
beads on a string (or a rosary), to be counted one after another until the final shoot-out, the burning of the castle, the
destruction of the fiend, the mortgage is paid on the Big Top,
or the return of the spacecraft to earth has occurred. Inherent and implicit in the beginning of any genre plot is the
end; the elements presented in the exposition at the beginning
are all clearly involved with the inevitable conclusion. Nothing extraneous to the plot can be introduced at random, somewhere in the middle. The best genre films always seem
shorter than they really are. The classical virtue of economy

of means may have been forced upon the genre film because
of its usually low production budget, but it has maximized
this possible defect. Only those scenes which advance the
plot are permitted. Only that dialogue which will keep things
moving is allowed. The adage attributed apocryphally to
Hitchcock, that you should never use dialogue when you can
show it in pictures, is often reversed in the genre film--
even in Hitchcock's films. Whenever it takes too long to
show it, say it instead. Anything and everything to keep the
plot moving, to create the sense of gathering momentum, of
inevitable causality.

To further the speed of comprehension of the plot,
genre films employ visual codes called iconographies, in order to eliminate the need for excessive verbal or pictorial
exposition. Strictly speaking, beyond the use of masks, there
is nothing in Greek drama comparable to the iconography of
the genre film, for as Aristotle pointed out, "spectacle"--
what we see--is the least important element of a play, while
it is obviously a primary aspect of film. A more appropriate analogy can be found in the Greek narrative art--the epic
poems. Homer is an exceptionally visual poet, particularly
when he is describing the armour and weapons of his heroes
in The Iliad; The Odyssey, too, pictorializes costumes, meta-
morphoses, monsters, and settings in a way that brings to
mind the vividness of the modern equivalent--the genre film.

Iconography consists of certain photographed objects,
costumes, and places composing the visible surface of a genre film which creates economically the context and milieu,
the field of action on which the plot will unravel itself. Over
a period of use in many films, these visual elements have become encrusted with shared meanings, so that dialogue and
camera can concentrate on revealing the twists and turns of
the plot. Iconography, like familiar plot situations and stereotypical characters, provides a shorthand of mutually recognizable communications that neither filmmaker nor audience
need ponder: the jungle is treacherous, the castle that towers
darkly over the village is sinister, the flat horizon of the desert is unyielding. Capes and evening clothes create threatening figures unless they are in a musical; laboratories with
bubbling liquids are occupied by men tampering with things no
human should.

Like the epithet--a descriptive characterizing tag-line
in the epic poems (the "wine-dark sea," the "bronze-shod arrows," the "cunning Odysseus")--the icons of genre films

serve to remind the viewer of the internal consistency and
familiarity of the characters and places in the film. These
places and characters do not change in the course of a film,
and very little from film to film. The visual appearance of
a Western town in one film is just about the same as in other
films. The landscape in a sci-fi picture can be depended
upon. The world of the musical is always a glittering unreality poised somewhere between our doughty old world and heav-
en, whether it is set backstage at the Broadway Theater or
high in the Swiss Alps.

As indicated above, characterization in a genre film
often uses the shorthand of iconography. We know a person
by what he wears as opposed to what he says and does. And
once known, the character cannot change except in the most
limited ways. Curiously enough, the Greek word for "character" as applied to human beings was the same as that applied to a letter of the alphabet. That is, the root word
means the "stamp" which imprints the letter on the paper,
or the stamp which imprints the character on to the person.
Right up until the end of the classical era--and the neo-clas-
sical--in the 18th century, the prevailing opinion was that human character was imprinted at birth and that it did not develop or change. Though the subsequent revolutions of thought
in the 19th and 20th centuries have all but wiped out this idea,
the genre film continues to employ this extremely classical
concept.

Frequently generalized and known by his vocation, a
genre character is conveyed through iconographical means--
costumes, tools, settings, etc. The man who wears a star,
whether he is a figure in the crowd or a major character,
has a limited range of responses to situations. The same is
the case with men who wear lab coats, carry sawed-off shotguns, or drink their whiskey straight. These men are their
functions in the plot. Revealed to us through costume, dialogue or physiognomy, they remind us of other sheriffs, private eyes and mad scientists from other movies we've seen.
Type-casting in the genre film is a bonus, not a debit. It is
just one more way of establishing character quickly and ef-
ficiently. John Wayne is the character type John Wayne, his
face no more expressive than the painted masks used in ancient times by the Greeks. Other performers like Bela Lugosi, Peter Lorre, and Vincent Price are instantly "knowable"
as genre figures.

In addition to establishing character with speed and

directness, the use of less individualized characters sets up
the basis for the existence of Aristotelian catharsis by allow-
ing for an increase in empathy by the audience. Being so
much their exteriors, genre characters allow us to easily assume their roles. The fact that we know that they are not
realistic, not part of our real world, lets us slip into their
trenchcoats or boots with ease. We can identify so strongly
and safely with their roles that we leave the theater walking
a little bow-legged or pulling up the collar of a non-existent
trenchcoat to ward off the wind. The genre character, because he is so unrealistic and without depth, because he is
so consistent and unwavering in his purpose, because he is
never forced to come to terms with himself--he has no "self"
in one sense--invites identification with his role or type; that
identification releases us from the ordinary and mundane realism of our own lives. We can say, "I wish I were like him"
--so tough, so hard-boiled, so ruthless, so lucky, so pure,
so wonderfully one-dimensional, so bent on destruction or revenge, or saving the world that eating and sleeping and other
everyday occurrences and responsibilities can never interfere.
While we may all live quiet lives of desperation, genre characters do not. We are all Walter Mittys, and for a few
short hours we can be lifted out of our inconsequential exist-
ences into a world of heroic action.

This difference in level between our world and the
world of the genre film I would regard as fulfilling Aristotle's
dictum that the characters of drama be elevated. Genre characters are certainly far superior to us in what they can do;
they may be limited as ordinary human beings, but they are
unlimited as far as action. They can do what we would like
to be able to do. They can pinpoint the evil in their lives as
resident in a monster or a villain, and they can go out and
triumph over it. We, on the other hand, are in a muddle.
We know things aren't quite right, but we are not sure if it
is a conspiracy among corporations, the world situation, politicians, our neighbors down the street, the boss, the wife;
but whatever it is, we can't call it out of the saloon for a
shoot-out or round up the villagers and hunt it down. Genre
characters inhabit a world which is better than ours, a world
in which problems can be solved directly, emotionally, in action. It is in a sense an ideal plane, a utopia, as far removed from our world as was the world of kings and nobles
and Olympian gods from the lives of the Athenians who attend-
ed the plays and heard the epics.

That we desire to witness such worlds and to experi-

ence classical catharsis is demonstrated by the current phe-
nomenal attendance at Martial Arts films, the newest of film
genres; it would be impossible to count the number of people
who partake of such experiences through the older genres as
offered on their television screens, both in re-runs of theatrical films and the made-for-TV variety. The emotional involvement and subsequent release which Aristotle called catharsis is an obviously desired tonic in our post-Romantic
Modern world. Critics, sociologists, psychologists, and politicians may argue over the social impact of literature and
films which depict violent action--Are they only a reflection
of the times or are they a cause of the violence in our culture?--but Aristotle's position is quite clear: there is a social benefit, a point at which art and the good of the community come together. If the spectator identifies strongly with
the figures of the drama, feeling pity and fear as drawn out
by the activities going on before his eyes and ears, then,
when properly concluded, given the appropriate ending, these
emotions are dissipated, leaving the viewer in a state of calm,
a state of stasis in which he can think rationally and clearly.
Properly conceived and executed, the genre film can produce
this effect.

     The cathartic potentials of the genre film can also be
seen as a way in which the tension of cultural and social
paradoxes inherent in human experience can be resolved.
Freud in Civilization and Its Discontents and Nietzsche in The
Birth and Death of Tragedy discuss the issue at length.
Nietzsche identifies the two poles of human behavior as the
Apollonian and the Dionysian. The Apollonian is the urge to
individuate the self from others and the Dionysian is the urge
to submerge the self into a group, a mob, a clan, family, or
chorus.

     Since the conflict between the individual and the group,
between self-realization and communal conformity, between
the anxiety and loneliness engendered by the freeing of the
self and the security of passive identification with the crowd,
is so all-pervasive an element of human life, it is not surprising to find this tension between individual needs and community needs metaphorically represented in genre films, not
only in Gangster films as Warshow has suggested or in Western films as Cawelti has stated, but in all genre films. This
tension, being so universal, may appear in other films as
well, but because of the classical nature of the genre film,
the resolution of the tension between these two poles will always be in favor of the community. Man is after all a social

animal. Thus--in classical thought--anything which can re-
lieve or diffuse conflicting emotions and purge them from the
individual can only be seen as a social good. Group values
must be continually reinforced in the individual; in the old
days religion did the job, but in post-Reformation times the
burden has moved elsewhere. Patriotic nationalism and world
communism have sought to pick up the standard in real life,
but the only 20th-century art that has consistently reenacted
the ritual of reaffirmation of group values has been the genre
film. Simply enough, it is the form of the genre film, its
repetitive quality, its familiarity, and violent plotting that has
made this work. During the course of a genre film we can
vicariously play out our desire for individuation by identifying
with the protagonist free from the anxiety of group censure.
Personal fears of actually acting out our fantasies of sex and
power are eliminated because we know it is only a movie.
There are no penalties to pay for being either hero or villain
as there are in real life. A short survey of several plot
structures found in various genres will serve to show how
genre plots are the key to the dispersal of the individual vs.
group tension.

In the War film, for example, the most popular plot
involves a group of men, individuals thrown together from
disparate backgrounds, who must be welded together to become a well-oiled fighting machine. During the course of the
film, the rough edges of the ornery and the cantankerous, the
non-joiners, the loners, like John Garfield in Hawks's Air-
force, must be smoothed down to make them fit. They must
all hang together or all hang separately. The emphasis is on
the team. And of course, for the war film the end goal of
the fighting is always the even larger group, the nation. Or
peace in the world, to protect us all from some peculiarly
successful individuals--Hitler or Hirohito or the Kaiser. The
hero's primary function is to mold the group and personally
oppose the idea of individualism whenever it rears its head in
its own cause and not that of the group effort. What better
metaphor than the coward--the man only interested in saving
his own skin, who somehow or other must be forced into
changing his attitude or else destroyed before he infects the
rest of the group. The hero, not just in the War film but in
all genre films, is always in the service of the group, of law
and order, of stability, of survival not of himself but of the
organization, the institution, no matter how individual his activities, while a villain could be defined as a man who ruth-
lessly looks after his own needs first and who works for and
will sacrifice himself for no one or nothing but himself.

In the Swashbuckler, the Errol Flynn character must
restore the true social order, and though he may appear to
be an outlaw now (which allows him to do all sorts of anti-
social actions like killing and robbing), by the end of the film
his crimes against the crown have been pardoned since they
were all done in a good cause. He kneels to his liege lord
and marries the girl (marriage traditionally having connotations of responsibility to the social order).

The Police or Detective film follows the same general
pattern. The cops can do violent anti-social acts (acts which
all of us would like to do) with impunity, for they are fulfilling their primary function to catch the guilty party and restore order. At first glance the Private Eye film doesn't
seem to fit this pattern, but it actually does. Sam Spade and
the police are really on the same side, protecting the mindless masses (who seldom play a central role in the films)
from the evil. True, the police may be corrupt or stupid or
slow to figure things out, yet the end goal is the same. The
ideal of commitment to square-dealing and presumably a community of square-dealers is demonstrated in the moral integrity of the private eye who can't be bought. Hence we may
understand that the particular social order shown, the police
in that city may be stupid or even corrupt, but that there is
somewhere a moral order of community and group benefit as
opposed to personal and material benefit, an ideal vindicated
by the private eye's sending the girl he's fallen in love with
over to prison.

Horror films and Monster films need no elaboration on
this point, nor do Science Fiction films. Though the latter
may leave us slightly wondering if the community shown in
the film will survive in the future, there is the implicit assertion that there is no survival without the group. Science,
that corporate analytical endeavor, will save us if anything
can--not any individual. Westerns are also clearly involved
with the eventual triumph of the forces of civilization, law
and order, even as they are tinged with melancholy for the
loss of individual freedom.

The Musical will often end with a wedding or the promise of one as the boy and girl come together after overcoming
all obstacles. A perfect example of a socially regenerative
action, as Northrop Frye has pointed out in his discussion of
New Comedy in the Anatomy of Criticism. In those Musicals
in which a star is born, in which it seems as though an individual is rising to the heights of individual achievement, it

usually turns out that the star must go on despite personal
tragedy, again emphasizing the group--the Broadway show,
the production standing as metaphor for society.

Any brief rundown of basic plots should serve to dem-
onstrate that the catharsis engendered in genre films is a
basic element of their structure. The internal tension between the opposing impulses of personal individuation and sub-
mission to the group, which normally is held in check by the
real pressures of everyday living, is released in the course
of a genre film as the audience vicariously lives out its individual dreams of glory or terror, as it identifies with the
stereotyped characters of fantasy life. But in the end those
impulses to anti-social behavior (acts of individuation no matter how innocuous or permissible are still tinged with an element of the anti-social) are siphoned off as we accept the inevitable justice of the social order: the group is always
right and we know, in our hearts, that it is wrong to think
otherwise.

In recent years it has become the fashion for some directors to use the elements of the genre film--the plots, characters, and iconographies--to create an anti-genre film.
That is, they will use everything according to the normal pattern, but simply change the ending so as not to satisfy the
audience's expectations of a conventional group-oriented conclusion. If the detective finally gives in and takes the money
and the girl, if the crook gets away with it, if an individual
solves his problems so as to enhance his position vis-à-vis
the world, that is, to increase the distance between his values
and the values of the group--then the film has turned its back
on the idea of genre. It violates the basic principle of the
genre film: the restoration of the social order. Instead of
justification of the status quo, things as they are, these films
intend the opposite. They suggest that individuals can succeed in individual schemes, that separation from the group
can be had without consequences. In this sense they are not
Classical, but Romantic in their tenor.

The genre film is a structure which embodies the idea
of form and the strict adherence to form which is opposed to
experimentation, novelty, or tampering with the given order
of things. The genre film, like all classical art, is basically
conservative: both aesthetically and politically. To embody a
radical tenor or romantic temper in a classical form is to
violate that form at its heart. One can parody the conventions, one can work against the conventions, one can use the

conventions with great subtlety and irony. To hold up individual ideals as superior to group ideals, however, changes
the whole frame of reference. When a seeming genre film
merely changes the ending in a final reversal, catharsis is
restricted. The audience is unprepared by what has come
before. There is no release of tensions, since the inevitable
conclusion for which the audience has come and which could
send them back into the real world smiling, has not taken
place. Rather than stasis, such endings produce agitation,
discomfort, a vague anxiety. The guilt of having identified
with the scoundrel or hero is never dissipated and the viewer must bear the responsibility for his individual desires all
alone.

When Charlie Varrick (in the picture of the same
name, which is otherwise a conventional caper movie) gets
away with a million dollars scot free at the end, he has denied the audience the opportunity of saying, "That's the way
it is. It'll never be any different. Nobody gets away with
fighting against the mob or syndicate." His escape from just
punishment for daring to wrest something of value from the
Olympians of today, the banks, the corporations, the Mafia,
makes him a Prometheus figure who doesn't get caught. It
induces in the audience a kind of irrational radicalism, as opposed to a reasonable conformism: "If he can do it, then
maybe I, too, can fight the system, the institutions, and win."
This is not what the common man fated to a life in society,
relatively powerless to change the course of things, likes to
comfort himself with, and not what a true genre film provides.

For the time that genre characters play out their lives
upon the screen we can safely identify with them, confident
that the group will assert its overwhelming force in the end--
like the chorus in a Greek play, always having the last word,
reminding us that "That's the way it is. Anyone who reaches
beyond his grasp must fall down." We need not feel guilty;
our surrogates will take the blame. We will switch allegiance
by the end and become a member of the chorus. Our split
personality is no longer split. Crime doesn't pay. True love
wins out. The monster is destroyed. The forces of evil and
darkness are vanquished by faith and reason. All is for the
best in this best of all possible worlds. We have achieved
the stasis which Aristotle mentions as the product of catharsis.
A quiet calm. This is not to say that this feeling lasts long
after we leave the theater, but at least we have been internally refreshed by our brief sojourn in a realm of cosmos, not
chaos. If nothing else, the genre film is a paradigm of ritual
and order.

The genre film is a classical mode in which imitation not of life but of conventions is of paramount importance. Just as in the classical dramas of Greece the stories are well known. Though there may be some charm in the particular arrangement of formula variables in the most current example of a genre, the audience seeks the solid and familiar referrents of that genre, expecting and usually receiving a large measure of the known as opposed to the novel. Elevated and removed from everyday life, freed from the straightjacket of mere representationalism, genre films are pure emotional articulation, fictional constructs of the imagination, growing essentially out of group interests and values. Character takes a second place to plot, in agreement with Aristotle's descriptions of drama. And it is this emphasis on the plot that makes genre films the most cinematic of all films, for it is what happens in them, what actions take place before our eyes that are most important. They move; they are the movies.

Note

1. Harry M. Geduld and Ronald Gottesman. An Illustrated Glossary of Film Terms (New York: Holt, Rinehart and Winston, 1973), p. 73.

GENRE FILMS AND THE STATUS QUO

Judith W. Hess

> The ideas of order that [the culture indus-
> try] inculcates are always those of the status
> quo.... Pretending to be the guide for the
> helpless and deceitfully presenting to them
> conflicts that they must perforce confuse
> with their own, the culture industry does not
> resolve these conflicts except in appearance
> --its 'solutions' would be impossible for them
> to use to resolve their conflicts in their own
> lives. --T. W. Adorno, "The Culture Indus-
> try"[1]

American genre films--the western, the science fiction
film, the horror film, the gangster film--have been the most
popular (and thus the most lucrative) products ever to emerge
from the machinery of the American film industry. Critics
have long pondered the genre film's success and have attempted to ferret out the reasons for the public's appreciation of
even the most undistinguished "singing cowboy" westerns. In
general, critics have examined these films as isolated phe-
nomena--as found objects--rather than considering genre films
in relation to the society which created them. Genre films
have been defined as pure myth, as well-made plays, and as
psychodramas bearing within themselves the working out of
unconscious anxieties inherent in the psychological makeup of
us all. Certainly any and all of these explanations contain
some truth; however, none of them explain why American genre films grew and developed and became our most numerous,
if not most artistically significant, film productions.

I think that we may see what genre films are by examining what they do. These films came into being and were
financially successful because they temporarily relieved the

fears aroused by a recognition of social and political conflicts; they helped to discourage any action which might otherwise follow upon the pressure generated by living with these
conflicts. Genre films produce satisfaction rather than action,
pity and fear rather than revolt; they serve the interests of
the ruling class by assisting in the maintenance of the status
quo and they throw a sop to oppressed groups who, because
they are unorganized and therefore afraid to act, eagerly accept the genre film's absurd solutions to economic and social
conflicts. When we return to the complexities of the society
in which we live, the same conflicts assert themselves, so
we return to genre films for easy comfort and solace--hence
their popularity.

Genre films address themselves to these conflicts and
resolve them in a simplistic and reactionary way. Genre
films have three significant characteristics which make such
resolutions seem possible and even logical. First, these
films never deal directly with present social and political
problems; second, all of them are set in the non-present.
Westerns and horror films take place in the past--science
fiction films, by definition, take place in a future time. The
gangster film takes place in a social structure so separate
from the contemporary structure in which it appears to be
taking place that its actual time and place become irrelevant.
Third, the society in which the action takes place is very
simple and does not function as a dramatic force in the films
--it exists as a backdrop against which the few actors work
out the central problem the film presents. As Robert Warshow points out in The Immediate Experience,[2] the westerner
exists in isolation. We have no idea where he gets his money
or washes. His trials and confrontations take place in utter
isolation (the desert or mountains) or in the setting of a tiny,
uncomplicated western town. Horror films present an isolated group of people who live in a tiny village or meet in a
castle or island which they do not leave until the end of the
movie, if at all. Many science fiction films show profession-
als moving away from society--to an island, an experimental
station of some sort, the south pole, outer space--to cope
with alien intruders. Although some science fiction films are
set in modern cities, the cities are weirdly empty and serve
as labyrinths through which the protagonists thread their ways.
The gangster lives in a very limited world populated by a few
other gangsters and their molls.

All of these genre films, science fiction included, present a greatly simplified social structure. However frequently

this kind of very limited social structure may have existed in
the past, it no longer exists in the present. Thus, genre
films are nostalgic, their social structure posits some sort
of movement backward to a simpler world. And in this simple structure, problems which haunt us because of our inability to resolve them are solved in ways which are not possible
today. Genre films reject the present and ignore any likely
future.

The genre films focus on four major conflicts. The
western centers on the violent act and ascertains when, if
ever, it becomes morally right. The horror film attempts
to resolve the disparities between two contradictory ways of
problem-solving, one based on rationality, the other based on
faith, an irrational commitment to certain traditional beliefs.
The science fiction films provide a solution to the problems
presented by intrusion, i. e. , they tell us how to deal with
what may be called "the other. " Gangster films resolve the
contradictory feelings of fear and desire which are aroused
by attempts to achieve financial and social success.

The problems posed by these contradictions are solved
simply. The western decrees that the violent act can become
morally right when it occurs within the confines of a code
which allows for executions, revenge killings, and killings in
defense of one's life and property. In the microcosmic western society everyone's code is the same; thus absolute guilt
and innocence are possible because social and moral goodness
are the same. Horror films present man as fallen, prey to
uncontrollable evil impulses. Only by reliance on traditional
beliefs and the domination of a well defined upper class can
we be saved from doom and perdition. The science fiction
film's answer to the problem of the intruder is sheerest isolationism. No possible advance in knowledge gained from
communication could possibly outweigh the dangers It presents
--the only sane response is to eradicate It. The gangster
film, by implication, opts for happy anonymity. To be successful is to become vulnerable; the successful one becomes
the foe of all who wish to take his place. Gangster films
show the fearful results of attempting to rise within a hierarchical society and thus defend class lines. These simplistic
solutions--the adherence to a well defined, unchanging code,
the advocacy of methods of problem solving based on tradition
and faith, the advocacy of isolationism, and the warning to
stay within one's station if one is to survive--all militate
against progressive social change.

In order to flesh out these assertions it is necessary
to examine each of the genres in some detail. The western
male is dominated by a code of honor which prescribes his
every action; violence by lynching or shooting, amorous advances, or friendships are determined by some fixed rule.
One lynches cattle rustlers but not petty thieves--one runs
them out of town. One sleeps only with bar girls, not eastern school teachers. One never shoots a man in the back;
one is utterly loyal to one's friends, defending them physically and verbally at every possible opportunity. At a certain
mystical point in the interaction between two opposing forces
the western version of the duel becomes morally acceptable;
both the villain and the hero know immediately when this
point comes, as they do not exist as psychological entities
apart from the code--rather, they embody the code. The
earliest westerns afford the clearest expression of the workings of this code. In these movies the heroes and villains
are like chess pieces moved about to depict the code's intricacies. In a great many westerns you will note the eerie oc-
currence of two phrases which are as far as these movies go
toward positing motivation: "I have to..." and "All I know
is...." These phrases express how the code provides motivation, not the person himself. Westerners act together in
absolute, unthinking accord. Westerns examine those aspects
of the code which determine the westerner's response to situations which demand violence. The compartmentalizations of
the code--one treats bankrobbers one way and friends another
--allow for situations which involve contradictory responses.
What happens, for example, in The Virginian (Victor Fleming,
1929), a movie that Robert Warshow calls "archetypal," when
a captured rustler is at the same time a friend? Gary Cooper, a chess piece representation of the code, is caught on
the horns of a moral and social dilemma. Although he must
bow to the will of the other members of the posse, for whom
the situation is not complicated (the rustler is not their
friend), and assist in the lynching, and his friend exonerates
him, Cooper must work within the code to redeem himself--
to rid himself of guilt by balancing the books.

And, there is a single, simple solution. His friend
has been drawn into rustling by the film's real villain, Trampas. Cooper must wipe him out, at the same time showing
the restraint demanded of the westerner. He must wait for
that mystical point in time at which the showdown becomes
morally and socially right. And Trampas, because he is a
villain and thus cannot act any other way, provides Cooper
with sufficient injury and insult, and is thus shot in fair fight.

Several violent actions are condoned in the movie: traditionally sanctioned violence demanded by the group (note that
Cooper never questions the lynching, he only suffers because
he is forced to abandon his friend); violence which is brought
about by repeated attacks on one's character (Trampas indicates that Cooper is a coward) and which redeems the violence Cooper has been forced to do to his friend.   These acts
of violence have complete social sanction.   Only Cooper's
eastern schoolmarm girlfriend fails to condone Cooper's actions; she has not as yet been assimilated into western society.

       In the western every man who operates solely with
reference to this strict code lives and dies redeemed.   He
has retained his social and moral honor.   The code provides
justification; thus it allows for a guiltless existence.   On the
other hand, we do not know ourselves when, if ever, violence
is justifiable.   We have great difficulty in forming a personal
code and we cannot be sure that this code will conform in any
way to the large, impersonal legal code set up to regulate
our unwieldy, decaying economic structure.   The westerner's
code is at once personal and social--if a man lives by it he
both conforms to social norms and retains his personal integrity.   It is evident whence comes the satisfaction we get from
the western.   Momentarily we understand the peace which
comes from acting in accord with a coherent moral and social code and forget our fragmented selves.   Many critics
have seen the western as a glorification of traditional American individualism.   On the contrary, the western preaches integration and assimilation and absolute obedience to the laws
of the land.

       The horror film deals with the conflict between ration-
al or scientific and traditional ways of problem solving.   In
Dracula (Tod Browning, 1930), Frankenstein (James Whale,
1931), The Mummy (Karl Freund, 1932), and The Wolfman
(George Waggner, 1948), the monsters are the embodiment of
human evil.   They are three-dimensional representations of
our uncontrollable will to evil; we must conquer them if society is to survive.   Lawrence Talbot ignores the gypsy's
warnings, is tainted by a wolf bite and becomes dominated by
evil desires--he kills those he cares for.   Dracula, the incarnation of unbridled sensuality, attracts his victims, sucks
them dry, and condemns them to becoming like him.   Before
becoming a mummy, an Egyptian prince has unsuccessfully
pitted himself against the will of the gods.   He, too, represents unbridled sensual appetite, the naked id.   Dr.

Frankenstein's poor maimed creation is a projection of his
own overwhelming will to power and knowledge beyond that
granted man by God. Because he relies totally on scientific
means to ends, he becomes a monster himself--he is redeemed by suffering and by his complete rejection of his
heretical drive to uncover the secrets of life and death.

     Various groups attempt to overcome the monsters.
"Ignorant peasants" (for example, the Egyptian workers or
the Carpathian peasants), who believe in the reality of evil
but who belong to a traditionally oppressed class, are overcome, or, at best, live out a miserable existence under the
monster's sway. The masses are shown to be without sufficient moral strength to overcome the monster themselves.
These monsters are at some point opposed by an enlightened
scientist who, because he believes only in the ability of science to defeat social and physical ills and in rational, demon-
strable means to ends, disregards tradition and thus threatens
the existing social order. Because he refuses to believe in
the power of the irrational will to evil, the monster annihi-
lates him. The monster is finally defeated by a member of
the upper class who abandons scientific training in favor of
belief in the traditional ways in which others before him have
overcome evil forces. Dr. Van Helsing, once he realizes
that medical science cannot save Dracula's victims, does research, finds what traditionally has been used against Dracula
(beheading, garlic, a stake through the heart), and employs
these means. The wolfman is killed by a silver-headed cane,
the mummy is destroyed by an appeal to the ancient Egyptian
gods. Van Helsing makes the required return to tradition
with a commitment to articles of faith, as do all those who
defeat the evil.

     The message is clear; science must not be allowed to
replace traditional values and beliefs. Otherwise, chaos will
result, as humans cannot control their own evil tendencies or
those of the people around them without supra-rational help.
The social order out of which these monsters spring is posited
as good--it must remain unchanged. Only by the benevolent
dictatorship of the hereditary aristocracy can these monsters
be kept at bay; the existing class structure prevents chaos.
Like the German expressionist horror films which preceded
them, American horror films (the first and best of which appeared in the early thirties) may be seen as a reaction to a
period of economic and social upheaval--the films are, in effect, a plea to go back to older methods of coping. This solution works in the horror film's oversimplified world.

The science fiction film, which developed during the
forties and fifties, may be seen as a dramatization of those
fears and desires aroused by the cold war period. "The
other," however strange an alien, has at least some significant relation to those massed hordes of Communists foisted
on the American people by such venomous red baiters as
Joseph McCarthy, Richard Nixon, and Billy Graham. Confronted by "the other," state these films, there is only one
possible response. We must use every scientific means at
our disposal to destroy the invader.

As in the horror film, the social order which exists
previous to the coming of the aliens is posited as good. The
aliens, who are scientifically advanced but who lack emotions
(that is, they do not share our values), invade in frightening
machines. Often non-violent communication is established
between a few scientists and the aliens. However, these scientists invariably learn that these beings aim to take our
bodies (Invasion of the Body Snatchers, Don Siegel, 1956), or
to assume social and political control (Earth vs. the Flying
Saucers, Fred F. Sears, 1956), or to suck our blood (The
Thing, Christian Nyby, 1951). The uneasiness Americans
feel about scientific advance and intellectuals in general is
evident in many of these films--often a wild-haired scientist
is willing to hand over the country to the invaders in order
to learn more about the secrets of the universe. He is either annihilated by the very invaders he has tried to protect,
or he regroups when confronted by the invaders' lack of concern with our traditional values and social structures. Usually, however, the scientists (often they are allied with the
military) are the first to recognize the extent of the aliens'
ill will and band together to defeat them. Great ingenuity and
immediate scientific advance are required to win the fight,
but the scientists discover the necessary materials in the nick
of time and save the world. Although a few films question
the absolute evil of the aliens (20 Million Miles to Earth,
Nathan Juran, 1957; The Day the Earth Stood Still, Robert
Wise, 1951), these films were not well received. It was
those films which gave a single, unequivocal answer to the
problem of "the other" which were the most successful. The
message of these films was that "the other" will do only evil,
no matter what blandishments disguise its true intent. The
only recourse is to destroy it utterly. And, so say these
films, we can. These films build on fears of intrusion and
overpowering and thereby promote isolationism. Also, they
imply that science is good only in as much as it serves to
support the existing class structure.

The best beginning to a discussion of the gangster
film is Robert Warshow's description of our reactions to it:
"The gangster is doomed because he is under obligation to
succeed, not because the means he employs are unlawful. In
the deeper layers of the modern consciousness, all means
are unlawful, every attempt to succeed is an act of aggression, leaving one alone and guilty and defenseless among enemies: one is punished for success. This is our intolerable
dilemma: that failure is a kind of death and success is evil
and dangerous and--ultimately--impossible. The effect of the
gangster film is to embody this dilemma in the person of the
gangster and resolve it by his death. The dilemma is resolved because it is his death, not ours. We are safe; for
the moment we can acquiesce in our failure, we can choose
to fail. "[3]

The world of the gangster is made up of a pyramidal
hierarchy. Only one man can be the top dog. We follow a
single man as he makes his way up the various ranks of the
structure. As in Public Enemy (William Wellman, 1931), he
may start out as a petty thief who sells his loot to a fence a
few steps higher up in the system. He quickly graduates to
stealing liquor supplies, and finally to the rank of boss. Unlike Scarface and Little Caesar, who make it all the way,
Cagney is undone by his own temper and arrogance before he
becomes much more than small time. However, he is in-
trepid enough to attempt to revenge another gang's decimation
of his own hierarchy, and is killed as a warning to others
who might attempt to meddle with the strong. These men are
rebels and renegades, but only within the confines of the existing order. They do not wish to establish a different kind
of structure, but to fight their way to the top of an existing
one. This pyramid is a microcosm of the capitalist structure.
We have a very ambivalent response to the competition necessary to survive in our own competitive society. We know
that we must defeat other people to succeed ourselves. And
because we have reached any worthwhile position through aggression, we are left vulnerable to any competitor who covets
our position. We are left with the choice of fighting with all
comers, and we know we cannot do that successfully forever,
or else failing. As Warshow states, we can exist with our
own economic and social failure as we watch the gangster's
death. For a moment it becomes acceptable to survive, even
at the price of economic anonymity. A gangster film would
never suggest that a different sort of social and political
structure might allow for more humane possibilities. In fact,
the gangster film implicitly upholds capitalism by making the

gangster an essentially tragic figure.   The insolubility of his
problem is not traced to its social cause; rather the problem
is presented as growing out of the gangster's character.   His
tragic flaw is ambition; his stature is determined by the degree to which he rises in the hierarchy.   We are led to believe that he makes choices, not that he is victimized by the
world in which he finds himself.   The gangster film retains
its appeal because our economic structure does not change--
we must commit aggressive acts to survive within the confines of our capitalistic structure.   And, as Warshow implies, when we see a gangster film--be it Little Caesar
(Mervyn Le Roy, 1930) or The Godfather (Francis Ford Coppola, 1971)--we are moved not to struggle out of our class
to question our hierarchical social structure, but to subside
and survive.

    We may trace the amazing survival and proliferation
of the genre films to their function.   They assist in the maintenance of the existing political structure.   The solutions
these films give to the conflicts inherent in capitalism require obeisance to the ruling class, and cause the viewer to
yearn for less, not greater freedom in the face of the insoluble ambiguities which surround him or her.   He or she is
encouraged to cease examining him/her.   He/she is encouraged to cease examining his/her surroundings, and to take
refuge in fantasy from his/her only real alternative--to rise
up against the injustices perpetrated by the present system
upon its members.

Notes

1.   Adorno, tr. in Cineaste, 5:1.

2.   Robert Warshow, "Movie Chronicle: The Westerner," in
      The Immediate Experience (New York: Atheneum,
      1971), pp. 135-154.

3.   Ibid., p. 133.

SOCIAL IMPLICATIONS IN THE HOLLYWOOD GENRES

Jean-Loup Bourget

From the outset, the cinema has been characterized by a certain tension, even a certain conflict, between an apparent content, derived from popular literature, and a number of autonomous stylistic devices (the various uses of actors, sets, camera movements, montage). Strictures traditionally passed on the Hollywood film fail to take into account the basic fact that its conventionality is the very paradoxical reason for its creativity. Conventions inherited from literature have added themselves to social pressures, such as the necessity for self-censorship, and to commercial imperatives, and may well have badly hampered the explicit content and meaning of movies, plot, and characterization frequently tending to become stereotyped. But in many instances the newness of the medium made it possible, even mandatory, to resort to a language both visual and aural, whose implicit meaning was far removed from what the mere script might convey. To give two brief examples: in Griffith's films, we find a tension between the conventional Victorian moralizing of the plot and titles, and the much more subtle meanings of sets, lighting, close-ups of actresses' faces, camera movements, editing.... In Josef von Sternberg's films, there is an open, unresolved conflict between the stereotypes of the plot and dialogues, and the "pure poetry" of the visual elements.

Another point which should be borne in mind is that, whenever an art form is highly conventional, the opportunity for subtle irony or distanciation presents itself all the more readily. The director's (that is to say, the camera's) point of view need not coincide with the hero's point of view; or again, and more generally, since a film represents a superposition of texts, it is not surprising that large segments of an audience (notably including literary-minded critics) should decipher only one of these texts and therefore misread the sum total of the various texts. European directors working

62

in Hollywood developed a technique for telling stories with implicit ironical meanings. For example, Lubitsch's Trouble in Paradise (1932) presents a coherent view of contemporary society under the neat gloss of the sophisticated comedy: thieves are capitalists; capitalists are thieves. Similarly, To Be or Not to Be (Lubitsch, 1942) is not just a farce: it makes the not altogether frivolous point that the historical Nazis were worse actors than the fictitious bad actors of the Polish underground. The point was completely missed by the contemporary audience, who regarded the film as being in very bad taste.

The same remark applies to most of Douglas Sirk's American films. Thus All That Heaven Allows (1956) is not a "weepie," but a sharp satire of small-town America; Written on the Wind (1957) is not about the glamour of American high society, but about its corruption; Imitation of Life (1959) is superficially naive and optimistic, but profoundly bitter and anti-racist.

The conflict between the movie's pre-text (the script, the source of the adaptation) and its text (all the evidence on the screen and sound track) provides us with an analytic tool, because it allows for a reconciliation of two apparently antagonistic approaches: the auteur theory, which claims that a film is the work of one creative individual, and the iconological approach, which assumes that a film is a sequence of images whose real meaning may well be unconscious on the part of its makers.

Elsewhere I have tried to show that the original version of Back Street (John M. Stahl, 1932), while apparently describing a woman's noble and sad sacrifice, is in fact a melodrama with profound social and feministic implications.[1] I also stated that "melodrama" in its traditional sense was born at the time of the French Revolution and reflected social unrest in a troubled historical period. In the context of the description of society, we may therefore distinguish between melodramas such as Back Street, which express a certain state of society, depicting its relative stability and the occasions of potential conflict, and melodramas such as Orphans of the Storm (Griffith, 1922) and Anthony Adverse (Mervyn LeRoy, 1936), which comment on an actual turmoil. It would probably be possible to give a survey of other popular genres in search of similar examples of these alternative approaches: description of an operative system, description of the breaking up of a given structure.

In the first category--films describing the way in
which a given social structure operates--we find many movies
belonging to genres which are often dismissed as escapist and
alienating. While this may well be true in a majority of
cases, it nevertheless remains that escapism can also be used
as a device for criticizing reality and the present state of society. A Utopian world which calls itself a Utopia is not escapist in the derogatory sense of the word; rather it calls the
viewer's attention to the fact that his own society is far removed from such an ideal condition. Many films by such
Rousseauistic directors as Allan Dwan and Delmer Daves belong to this category; they might best be described as "South
Seas adventure dramas": see Allan Dwan's adaptation of Mel-
ville's Typee (Enchanted Island, 1958) and Delmer Daves's
Bird of Paradise (1951); also his Treasure of the Golden Con-
dor (1953), and his Western Broken Arrow (1950). Some of
these films suffer from a stylistic incompetence which somewhat forces the implicit meaning back out of the film itself,
into the director's generous but unrealized intentions. More
to the point are perhaps two films by John Ford, The Hurricane (1937) and Donovan's Reef (1963). The first film implicitly contrasts Raymond Massey, who embodies the oppressive law, with the figure of Lincoln of other John Ford films,
Lincoln being an incarnation of the law which gives life and
freedom. In Donovan's Reef, a brief scene located in Boston
supplies the key to implicit meaning, as we are allowed to
glimpse a caricatural reality of America opposed to the
idealized vision of the Pacific island.

In contradistinction to the legend that in all traditional
Westerns "the only good Indian was a dead Indian," a closer
look at early Hollywood Westerns reveals surprising conflicts
between explicit and implicit meanings. Thus in DeMille's
The Squawman, a subject obviously dear to him since he
treated it on three different occasions (1913, 1918, 1931), an
Englishman who has settled in America is seduced by the
"primitive," and therefore "immoral," beauty of an Indian
woman drying her naked body by the fire. He lives with her
without marrying her, and she bears him a child. Years
later, the Englishman's relatives look him up and insist that
they must take his child to England in order to give him a
proper education. Because of her "primitive" mind (as the
man puts it), the Indian woman does not understand why her
son should be taken away from her, and she commits suicide.
Earlier on, she had already been rejected by her own child,
as he had preferred an electric train to the crude wooden
horse which she had carved for him. In its treatment of the

story, DeMille's point of view is sympathetic to the Indian
woman rather than to the Europeans. To him, she is morally superior. This is made clear less by the plot than by the
lyricism of the sequences devoted to Lupe Velez "seducing"
the Englishman or carving the wooden toy. At the same
time, because of its tragic conclusion, the film could hardly
be accused of being escapist or naively optimistic. In a
much more subtle way, the indictment of white pseudo-civili-
zation is as harsh as in Arthur Penn's Little Big Man of
1970. But these cultural tensions remain implicit and unresolved. Obviously, the "de-construction" of ironical analysis
is not synonymous with "destruction." Is this failure to resolve tensions due to weakness in the creative act? or rather
to the capitalistic mode of film production? In Hollywood,
the director's work, however conscious it may be of social
alienation, is bound by the same alienation.

        Ironical implications of a social breakdown can be em-
bedded in the most highly conventional and least realistic
films. Such a movie is Heidi, starring Shirley Temple and
directed by Allan Dwan in 1937, where Kitsch, as is usual,
verges on parody. Only in a Kitsch film or in a comedy
could servants be emblematically described as holding a feath-
er duster. The Kitsch movie is often located in Central Europe, and the ideal society it tends to refer to is that of the
Hapsburg Empire. There we find a static hierarchized society where everybody is defined by a social function rather than
by individual traits. But the providential architecture of this
social system is so exaggerated that (whether consciously or
unconsciously on the part of the film makers) the effect produced is, in the last analysis, satirical. Stylistically, social
functions are indicated by emblems (folkloric costumes,
pointed helmets, plumes, etc.) which look slightly ridiculous.
For example, in Zoo in Budapest (Rowland V. Lee, 1933),
society is neatly divided between the haves and the have-nots,
between those with some parcel of authority and those without
any. On the one hand, we find certain aristocratic visitors
to the zoo and a multitude of characters in quasi-military uniforms: wardens, policemen, bus drivers.... On the other
hand, we have the peasant visitors in colorful garb, the girls
from an orphanage, and the unsociable hero who seeks the
company of animals rather than that of men. This amounts
to the description of a society so alienated that, in order to
be free, one has to live behind bars in a zoo! The last part
of the film bursts into nightmare, as all the wild beasts escape from their cages--a suggestion that this neatly organized
society is no less prone to explosions and revolutions,

notwithstanding the literally incredible ending which claims to
reconcile the feudal system and the individual's happiness. [2]

Similarly, a turn-of-the-century setting seems to be
very popular in a variety of genres, from literary adaptation
(The Picture of Dorian Gray, Albert Lewin, 1945) to the horror film (Hangover Square, John Brahm, 1945), from the romantic drama (Letter from an Unknown Woman, Max Ophuls,
1948) to the musical: Meet Me in St. Louis (Vincente Minnelli, 1944), Gigi (Minnelli, 1958), My Fair Lady (George
Cukor, 1964). There are probably two reasons for this popularity. For one thing, such a setting has stylistic qualities
of its own which readily lend themselves to artistic effects.
For another thing, it refers to Western society--usually but
not necessarily European--at its most sophisticated, on the
eve of the First World War and of the economic collapse of
Europe. This presumably accounts for the success of the
Viennese film, a genre which has often been wrongly explained
in naively biographical and nostalgic terms. The satirical element which is obvious in von Stroheim's films is implicit in
the works of other European directors. Josef von Sternberg's
Dishonoured (1931) contrasts Marlene Dietrich's amour fou
with the sense of decadence and the collapse of empires, Aus-
trian and Russian. In Anatole Litvak's Mayerling (France,
1936), the lovers are doomed, not by fate, but by the ominous sign of the Hapsburg Empire, the oppressive Eagle of
raison d'état: the ball scene in particular opens with the
camera seemingly tracking through a glass eagle and ends
with the same movement in reverse. In many "Viennese"
films, both European and American, Ophuls uses the device
of a duel, which points out the way in which a particular class
of society goes about solving its private problems when they
cannot be kept private any longer.

Such films therefore enable us to put forward a tentative definition of melodrama as opposed to tragedy: in melodrama, Fate is not metaphysical, but social or political.
Thus melodrama is bourgeois tragedy, dependent upon an
awareness of the existence of society. This echoes Benjamin
Constant's own definition of the new tragedy: "Social order,
the action of society on the individual, in different phases and
at different epochs, this network of institutions and conventions
in which we are caught from our birth and which does not
break until we die, these are the mainsprings of tragedy.
One only has to know how to use them. They are absolutely
equivalent to the Fatum of the Ancients. "[3]

In several respects, the musical is close to the cinematic melodrama, both having developed from forms of spectacle associated with the conventions of the popular stage.
In order to express an implicit meaning, they both have to
rely almost exclusively on stylization, at once visual and
musical (melodrama is etymologically "drama with music"),
for they are both removed from the convention of realism. 4
In the hands of creative individual directors, musicals therefore lend themselves to statements which will pass unnoticed
by the majority of the entertainment-seeking audience and by
critics who judge the explicit content.   Unsurprisingly, some
directors have excelled in both genres, above all Minnelli.
Brigadoon (1954) is an excellent example of what is meant
here: the musical is set against the motif of bustling New
York, and the meaning of the supposedly escapist part of the
movie can only be induced from the satirized madness of the
everyday setting towards the end of the film.

An allegory frequent in the musical is that of Pygmalion, of a member of respectable society raising a girl of the
lower classes to his own level of civilized sophistication.   It
is the particular failure of My Fair Lady to have used Audrey
Hepburn in such a part, because the actress is evidently an
extremely sophisticated one.   Thus the parable rings false;
in order to make it convincing, Cukor should have used an actress of a completely different type, Shirley MacLaine for example, and have her look like a lady by the end of the film.
For the implication should be: there is nothing in high society which a good actor or dancer should not be capable of
achieving through imitation.   Again, it should suggest a reversal of the apparent roles and functions similar to the one
found in Lubitsch's Trouble in Paradise: if dancers are ladies, ladies cannot be far different from dancers.   The whole
oeuvre of such directors as Minnelli and Cukor is based on
this underlying assumption, which, hidden behind a playful
guise, is both a satire of actual social solidity and an indication of possible social fluidity: see Cukor's films starring
Judy Holliday, Minnelli's films starring Judy Garland.

Easter Parade (Charles Walters, 1948) tells a story
similar to that of My Fair Lady, with Fred Astaire and Judy
Garland in roles similar to those of Rex Harrison and Audrey
Hepburn.   But there the allegory works, and goes further, because it has serious bearings on woman's status in society.
At the end of the film, Judy Garland, tired of waiting to be
proposed to, decides that there is no reason why she should
not in fact woo Fred Astaire.   She adopts the man's

traditional role, sends numerous gifts to the object of her
thoughts, and compliments him on his beautiful clothes.   The
musical, like a court jester, is allowed a Saturnalian freedom because it is not a "serious" genre.   Its self-eulogy
("Be a Clown" in Minnelli's The Pirate, 1948; "Make 'em
Laugh" in Donen's and Kelly's Singin' in the Rain, 1952;
"That's Entertainment" in Minnelli's The Band Wagon, 1953)
shows its understandable reluctance to part with such a liberty.

        Another category of films is not content with describ-
ing a system, but portrays its collapse.   Screwball comedies
and Busby Berkeley musicals, connected with the Depression,
can be mentioned in passing. 5   The implicit meaning may be
more difficult to assert (in historical films and epics) because they often refer to revolutions or civil wars whose pattern is given as fact, not as susceptible to an interpretation.
Yet a coherent explanation is sometimes to be found hidden
behind the historical or adventurous plot.   Anthony Adverse,
referred to earlier, is located in the time of the French Revolution and of the First Empire.   It is critical of both the
former aristocracy and of the new classes, depicted as a
ruthless mob aping the former nobility.   The only solution is
found in leaving a doomed continent and sailing for the new
land and the democratic society of America.   A somewhat
similar point of view is expressed in A Tale of Two Cities
(Jack Conway, 1935), where the French Revolution must be
shown as almost simultaneously profoundly justified and profoundly unjust.   This is achieved in a very interesting way.
The first part of the film is, despite a few hints, rather sympathetic to the idea of a revolution, which is shown as inevitable.   Even more committed are the Revolutionary sequences
proper (the storming of the Bastille), which were directed by
a different team--Jacques Tourneur and Val Lewton.   They
are absolutely Eisenstein-like in their depiction of blatant in-
justice and spontaneous union, soviet-like, of people and army.
From there on, it is impossible to think of any adequate transition; the trick consists in skipping over the transition, in
reverting to a title, a pre-text, which claims that the spirit
of liberty had been betrayed even before it had triumphed.
But such is not the evidence on the screen, and the film embodies a strange, unresolved discrepancy between the Jack
Conway-directed sequences (pleasant but traditional in style,
faithful to the source of the adaptation) and the Jacques Tour-
neur-directed ones, formally very original, unambiguous in
their meaning, and telling a tale quite of their own.

Conversely, a perfectly coherent film about the French Revolution is Marie Antoinette (Woody S. Van Dyke, 1937)-- coherent, that is, from a reactionary point of view. Yet, even in this case, we see a tension at work between the explicit argument of the film (as signified by the title: a woman's picture, the sad dignified story of Marie Antoinette) and the implicit political message, according to which the hero/victim is King Louis XVI rather than Marie Antoinette. In the light of the film, she is not much more than a pleasure-loving girl, but he is portrayed as a man of good will, who was betrayed by a conspiracy of Freemasons and the Duke of Orleans.

A sub-genre of the adventure film which almost inevitably acclaims a pattern of social unrest and revolution (always successful in this case, because far removed in time and space; therefore with no apparent direct bearings on present society) is the swashbuckler, the pirate film. The most "democratic" examples of the genre include two films by Michael Curtiz, Captain Blood (1935) and The Sea Hawk (1940). In both, an apolitical man is charged with sedition and actually becomes a rebel (cf. a similar parable in John Ford's Prisoner of Shark Island, 1936). Both films describe the way a colonial system rests on political oppression, slavery, torture, etc.; they both advocate violent revolution as the only means of destroying such a system. The evidence of the genre therefore conflicts with the evidence of colonial films set in the twentieth century, for example in British India or in French North Africa, where it is the outlaw who is supposedly guilty of savagery. It might be illuminating to show to what extent a contemporary, politically committed film maker (Gillo Pontecorvo) has relied on the traditional Hollywood and Cinecittà genre of the pirate film in order to make his Queimada (Burn, Italy, 1968).

As pointed out before, the danger of certain explicit statements about Robin Hood and pirate figures in distant times or remote places is that the remoteness can be emphasized rather than played down. In historical films about outlaws, the viewer is allowed to walk out with a clear conscience and a dim consciousness. This danger was realized and pointed out by directors more sophisticated than Michael Curtiz. In Sullivan's Travels (1942), Preston Sturges satirized the conventions of the social-problem genre which had flourished at Warners under the guidance of Mervyn LeRoy, among others. The bittersweet conclusion of Sturges' film was that a director should not go beyond the camera, that he should

not make social statements when he has but the vaguest notions about the condition of society, and should rather devote
his time and energy to the making of comedies. But his own
film showed that he could somehow do both at the same time:
entertain and make valid comments. Similarly, Vincente
Minnelli's The Pirate underlines the conventions of the swashbuckler. It adds another dimension to the meaning of the
pirate film. Judy Garland, the Governor's daughter, falls in
love with Gene Kelly, an actor who parades as Macoco the
fierce pirate. The point is, firstly, that to make a "revolutionary" and "democratic" pirate film is partly to base the
argument on Errol Flynn's--or Gene Kelly's--sex appeal.
But this is only the first layer of meaning. The actor, not
the pirate, turns out to be the "revolutionary" individual who
is going to achieve social change, for he unmasks Walter
Slezak (Judy Garland's fiancé), the real Macoco who parades
as a respectable citizen. The lesson is therefore that piracy
can be identified with respectable bourgeois society, and that
the artist (whether he be an actor or a Hollywood director)
emerges as the one person with both a sense of individual
freedom and the refusal to oppress others.

Thus the freedom of the Hollywood director is not
measured by what he can openly do within the Hollywood system, but rather by what he can imply about American society
in general and about the Hollywood system in particular. He
can describe in extensive detail how a given social structure
operates, but cannot do so openly unless the society in question is remote in time or space; if he describes the breakdown of a social system, he must somehow end on a hopeful
note and show that both order and happiness are eventually
restored. However, the interplay of implicit meanings, either
subtly different from or actually clashing with the conventional
self-gratification, allows the Hollywood director to make valid
comments about contemporary American society in an indirect
way, by "bending" the explicit meaning (Sirk's phrase). Genre conventions can be either used as an alibi (the implicit
meaning is to be found elsewhere in the film) or turned upside
down (irony underlines the conventionality of the convention).
The implicit sub-text of genre films makes it possible for the
director to ask the inevitable (but unanswerable) question:
must American society be like this? Must the Hollywood system function like this?

Notes

1. "Aspects du mélodrame américain, 1: Back Street," in
    Positif, No. 131 (Paris, October, 1971); English ver-
    sion, "Back Street (reconsidered)," in Take One, III
    (February 1972). The implicit significance of Stahl's
    Back Street is due not to the Fannie Hurst story it-
    self, but to its treatment by Stahl. A confirmation
    will be found in a comparison with the latest version
    of the same story (retold by David Miller in 1961),
    where the meaning is altered, reduced both to its
    mawkish pretext and to very few fulgurant images
    listlessly "borrowed" from films by Douglas Sirk.

2. In Zoo in Budapest, Gene Raymond and Loretta Young
    first find happiness in a bear's den which overlooks
    the town, the outside world. Their situation recalls
    that of Borzage's heroes in Seventh Heaven (1927):
    the "little man" lives in a garret, close to the stars,
    which allows him symbolic "overlooking" of a world
    that crushes him in every other way.

3. Original French text in Benjamin Constant, Oeuvres
    (Paris: Bibl. de la Pléiade, 1957), p. 952. Transla-
    tion mine. Obviously, many cinematic melodramas
    still pretend to rely on the device of superhuman Fate;
    it is only an analysis of their implicit meanings, of
    their sub-text, which makes it possible to unmask such
    Fate and give it its actual name of social necessity.

4. In fact, what is variously termed "romantic drama,"
    "soap opera," "sudser," "woman's film," etc. , spans
    all the gamut from operatic formalism (Dietrich's
    films; Garbo's Queen Christina, directed by Rouben
    Mamoulian, 1933) to the drab realism of the kitchen-
    sink drama. There are some successful examples of
    fairly "realistic" melodramas, notably John Cromwell's
    Made for Each Other and In Name Only (both 1939).
    Nevertheless, even such films are highly unrealistic in
    their catastrophic situations and providential endings.
    The impression of realism is largely due to the actors
    (Carole Lombard as opposed to, say, Joan Crawford)
    rather than to the verisimilitude of plot and setting.
    As a rule, it remains that both the musical and the
    melodrama are more openly formalized and ritualized
    than the realistic guise normally allows. This is due

to their common theatrical origin and to their disre-
gard of subtle, novelistic psychological analysis.

5. See my article on "Capra et la screwball comedy,"
   Positif, No. 133 (December, 1971), pp. 47-53.

PART TWO

THE SCREWBALL COMEDY

Jim Leach

Since Aristotle's thoughts on comedy have not survived, the critical discussion of comedy has tended to concentrate on a definition of the genre rather than on the explication of specific comic works. Theories of comedy abound but none seems universally applicable. The problem is intensified in dealing with film comedy since the very breadth of the genre means that it lacks the precision of the "serious" genres: a genre which encompasses the visions of Jerry Lewis and Ernst Lubitsch is already in trouble (not that there aren't points of contact). One solution might be to develop a more rigorously defined set of genres that work within the comic mode; this approach might even cross the somewhat arbitrary dividing line between comic and "serious" modes since the comic western, war film, and horror film might well be seen as sub-genres of the "serious" genres which they parody. The rudiments of such a theory of comic genres can be found in discussions of the origins of American film comedy which have referred to the slapstick (or crazy) comedies of the twenties and to the screwball (Hawks), populist (Capra), and sophisticated (Lubitsch) comedies of the thirties. [1]

Of these early comic genres, the most enduring have been the slapstick and the screwball, both of which still dominate the American comic cinema, even though few critics have written about them as genres. Stuart Kaminsky deals with them as "two dominant modes" within the genre of comedy, "the mode of the individual, the man out-of-keeping with his culture" and "the man vs. woman type," but he does go on to use the word "genre" in referring to both. [2] The confusion here seems to be related to a basic problem of genre theory: if a genre is defined too loosely (as in the case of "comedy") it ceases to be of any value as a critical tool; if too narrowly, criticism tends to become academic and prescriptive. Slapstick comedy, for example, needs to be defined so that it can

encompass the physical comedy of Sennett, the subtle mime
of Chaplin, the verbal slapstick of the Marx Brothers, the
schizophrenia of Jerry Lewis, and the crude parodies of Mel
Brooks.

Developing from music hall and vaudeville, slapstick
comedy presents a world very close to that of the animated
cartoon, which neatly illustrates Bergson's theory of comedy
as a confusion of the human and the mechanical. In essence,
the comedy depends on the miraculous survival of the human
in a world in which man is treated as a machine. The comic hero may be at the mercy of a hostile world because of
his lack of intelligence, but the intellect is viewed with suspicion because of its identification with inhuman progress and
its separation from human feelings (Modern Times is the
classic example and is closely related to the Frankenstein
cycle of the thirties through its nightmare vision of science
and technology out of control). Slapstick comedy depends on
collision (hence Eisenstein's admiration for Sennett and Chaplin) and that collision may be between man and things (Keaton),
man and inhuman society (Chaplin), or man and word/rules
(the Marx Brothers).

The two key motifs of the genre are the figure of the
little man, who is a victim but whose simplicity is more attractive than the complex society in which he and we live,
and the verbal confusion (a symptom of that social complexity). The former dominates the work of the individual come-
dians of the silent cinema (Chaplin, Keaton, Lloyd, Langdon),
the latter is central to the work of the comedy teams who
came to the fore with the coming of sound. So familiar are
the motifs of slapstick comedy and the comic vision they imply that there can be little problem in establishing it as a
genre expressive of a disquieting sense that the hectic pace
of modern life may have passed beyond human control, and
(usually) a comforting sense that the human will survive.
There is little point in adding here to the large amount of
writing on slapstick comedy beyond isolating it as the basic
comic genre from which most others derive. In the development of a theory of comic genres, the crucial decade is the
thirties and a definition of slapstick comedy is necessary before the (more debatable) genre of screwball comedy can be
discussed.

Screwball comedy certainly does grow out of slapstick
comedy: Andrew Sarris has described Howard Hawks's Twentieth Century (1934) as both "the first of the screwball

comedies of the '30s" and "the first comedy in which sexually
attractive, sophisticated stars indulged in their own slapstick
instead of delegating it to their inferiors."[3] The screwball
vision, like the slapstick, is deeply concerned with the dehumanization of modern society and the apparent disappearance of accepted values. There are, however, several important distinctions to be made between slapstick and screwball comedy. Slapstick comedy usually depends on a comic
performer who maintains his identity intact from one film to
the next; while there was a stock company of screwball actors
in the thirties, very few of them limited themselves to screwball roles and their personalities were always placed within
the context of a world which was obviously, if deceptively,
very close to the "normal" world inhabited by the audience.
(W. C. Fields and Mae West seem to be transitional figures
somewhere between slapstick and screwball.) There is still
a strong element of physical comedy but none of the defiances
of gravity or physiology common in slapstick comedy. The
personality of the comedian does not define the comic vision;
the auteur of a screwball comedy is the director, not the
actor.

     Slapstick comedy is a decidedly misogynous genre:
women are peripheral to its vision (a side-issue to Keaton's
pursuit of his locomotive in The General; a romantic subplot
in the later Marx Brothers films) and are either sentimental-
ized or victimized or both. The only lasting relationships in
slapstick comedy are male (Laurel and Hardy, Chico and
Harpo, Olsen and Johnson, Abbott and Costello, Lewis and
Martin), whereas, as Sarris suggests, screwball comedy is
vitally concerned with the battle of the sexes. Indeed its perspective is essentially feminine, with the absurd logic of the
screwball heroine providing a refreshing challenge to the
mechanical absurdity of male-dominated society. In making
this distinction, of course, "masculine" and "feminine" do not
necessarily refer to actual gender but to the qualities conventionally associated with each sex: in Hawks's Bringing Up
Baby (1938) Susan's influence over David is in conflict with
that of the domineering Miss Swallow; in George Cukor's Holiday (1938) Cary Grant plays the uninhibited screwball who is
in danger of being "civilized" by his fiancée.

     While slapstick comedy remains "innocent" of sex,
sexuality is a central concern of screwball comedy. A key
motif in Hawks's work in the genre is the idea of sex-antagonism: Bringing Up Baby, I Was a Male War Bride (1949),
and Man's Favorite Sport? (1963) all are built explicitly

around the psychological theory that the love instinct in the
male first shows itself in the form of conflict. Yet the male
is sorely tried by frustration and humiliation caused by the
female, and the sexual conflict often develops into a confusion
of sexual roles. The sexual warfare involves a struggle for
dominance, usually with the woman asserting an authority
which society denies her. In both Bringing Up Baby and I
Was a Male War Bride Cary Grant has to wear women's
clothes; in both the woman takes over the active role (Hepburn
drives the car, Sheridan the motorcycle), and in both the resolution is an unsteady balance based on the acceptance of "masculine" and "feminine" qualities in both partners. Transves-
titism is merely the most obvious aspect of a motif which
underlies all screwball comedy and the new factor in the
treatment of this concern is that social standards no longer
provide a satisfactory basis for the working out of sexual
roles.

     Sex-antagonism is also related to the theme of regres-
sion: the difference between the screwball individual and the
social conformist lies in the former's enjoyment of game-
playing. The theme is constant in Hawks but is presented
most clearly in Monkey Business (1952), in which the youth
drug reveals the childishness, savagery, and animal instinct
that underlie the behavior of an apparently mature, civilized
couple. This revelation of the life of instinct beneath the social facade is common to a number of genres: if slapstick
comedy can be related to the horror film (though the monsters
in such films as Frankenstein and King Kong do represent a
clearly sexual threat to civilized society), screwball comedy
is a comic anticipation of the film noir. Both genres grow
out of mixed feelings of fear and desire, presumably related
to the problem of adjusting sexual attitudes to rapid social
change. The relationship between the two is especially compelling in Hawks's Ball of Fire (1941) with its shadowy deep-
focus images (Gregg Toland) and its biting screenplay (Brac-
kett and Wilder), and in I Was a Male War Bride, shot on
location among the ruins of post-war Germany.

     Film noir was, of course, deeply imbued with a heavy
Teutonic angst and was obsessed with the mysteries of female
sexuality, while the key auteur of screwball comedy is Hawks,
a preeminently American director whose work outside the genre is supposedly committed to male camaraderie. Yet Hawks
has never made a film from which women are absent or present merely on sufferance; the women in his films may often
be peripheral to the action (since that action is part of the

male world) but they are always vital to his concerns. Wom-
en function in Hawks's films as a reminder of the absurdity
and limitations of the world in which the men live: their
presence also shows up the limitations of a society in which
heroism has become absurd. The male group does offer a
vital alternative to the sterility of such a society but its full
potential can only be realized when it can encompass the sexual and emotional challenge created by the presence of the
women. In Only Angels Have Wings the absurd heroism of
the fliers gains a new dimension from coming to terms with
the values of Bonnie and Judith (of course, the process is
two-way); in To Have and Have Not Harry throws in his lot
with the Free French only after he has come to accept his
feelings for Slim; and in Red River Tess's interruption of the
final showdown exposes the childish insecurity underlying the
masculine code that demanded the fight (and that demands a
showdown to fulfill the demands of the genre).

    To see Hawks's relationship to the genre of screwball
comedy as being as close as that of Ford to the western il-
luminates both auteur and genre. In both cases, the auteur's
work within the favored genre creates a classic generic framework, while the concerns of that genre spill over into the
auteur's work outside the genre. The effect in the case of
Hawks and screwball comedy is to place absurdity and sexuality at the heart of the concerns of both auteur and genre. As
in the absurdist theatre of Ionesco, there are two kinds of
absurdity in Hawks' screwball comedies--the social absurd
and the existential absurd:

         For Hawks 'craziness' implies difference, a sense
         of apartness from the ordinary, everyday, social
         world. At the same time, Hawks sees the ordinary
         world as being 'crazy' in a much more fundamental
         sense, because devoid of any meaning or values. [4]

Peter Wollen's words apply equally as well to Hawks's adventure films as to his comedies but they also provide a neat
enough definition of the tension in screwball comedy between
life-giving screwball behavior and a life-denying crazy society.

    Bringing Up Baby provides a particularly clear example
of the two kinds of craziness, with the animal vitality of Susan
(Katharine Hepburn) opposed to a society based on inhibition,
possession, and the abuse of language. David (Cary Grant) is
initially associated with the dead bones of the brontosaurus
and has to assert his possession of the golf ball and the car.

In this society, language is not used to communicate but to
obscure, by being transformed into the jargon of experts in
specialized fields. The psychiatrist uses words to "explain"
things: when asked by Susan to explain David's behavior, he
begins, "Knowing nothing of the situation..." and proceeds to
lecture her on the way in which the love-impulse expresses
itself in terms of conflict--a formula which proves accurate
but totally irrelevant to the concrete "proof" to which Susan
puts it. Colonel Applegate is also an expert: he mistakes a
leopard's roar for the cry of a loon because there are no
leopards in Connecticut. The same kind of logic leads the
psychiatrist to assume that Susan is insane and the police
chief to conclude that she is a criminal. Susan sets up an
abnormal environment which exposes the inadequacy of "normal" and "logical" responses.

     According to Robin Wood, Susan represents the "lure
of the irresponsible" and the most successful of Hawks's comedies are those in which this temptation is "adequately coun-
tered by opposition or control. " Both Bringing Up Baby and
His Girl Friday (1940) are flawed because there is no such
control, while Ball of Fire and Monkey Business succeed
since "the disturbing elements that characterise the comedies
are assimilated into an entirely coherent, perfectly proportioned whole. "[5] Hawks himself has regretted that Bringing
Up Baby has no normal character ("Everyone you met was a
screwball") but V. F. Perkins has defended the film by pointing to Hawks's achievement in creating a world in which "the
abnormal is the norm and where, in consequence, the rational
seems outrageous. "[6] Wood's dissatisfaction with "the triumph
of total irresponsibility the film appears to be offering as fitting resolution" points not to moral weakness but to the typical Hawksian use of unbalanced endings. [7] The sabotage of
the traditional western ending in Red River and the violent and
confusing ending of The Big Sleep are key examples from the
"serious" films; the classic example from the comedies is the
ending of Bringing Up Baby, with the collapse of the brontosaurus and the couple literally unbalanced on the swaying plat-
form.

     As Wood points out, the ending of His Girl Friday is
disturbing in that the life that Walter offers to Hildy is "at
least as constricting as the respectability offered by Bruce,"
though Wood claims that the film wants us to feel that Hildy's
choice is satisfactory. [8] Yet the union of Potts and Sugarpuss
in Ball of Fire and the reunion of Barnaby and Edwina in
Monkey Business are at least as problematic: the typical

Hawksian ending is an achievement of balance in which the
possibility of unbalancing is still very much present. In
Bringing Up Baby the social order maintains itself simply by
repressing the "darker" aspects of human nature which might
threaten social stability. As David discovers through his encounter with Susan and Baby, this kind of order is a denial
of life, and he finally opts for challenge, excitement, and a
full life. This is not the "lure of irresponsibility," as Wood
claims, though the danger of a total rejection of the social and
rational is hinted at in the presence of the "mad" leopard
(outwardly indistinguishable from Baby). By its very nature,
the final balance is unstable but at least the dangers have been
recognized. Life, as opposed to death-in-life, is shown as a
complex process of maintaining balance. The anarchy that is
unleashed by the screwball characters is usually dispelled by
the union or reunion of the couple, but the balance is pre-
carious at best and does little to counter the effect of the irrational forces aroused in the body of the film.

     Hawks's comedies are especially pure (and disturbing)
in their treatment of the screwball spirit, but the world-view
that they embody permeates all films in the genre. No other
director identified himself as uncompromisingly with the screwball comedy but effective works were contributed to the genre
in the second half of the thirties by such directors as Jack
Conway, George Cukor, Gregory La Cava, Mitchell Leisen,
Leo McCarey, W. S. van Dyke, and William Wellman. Each
of these directors needs to be investigated to relate the variations he plays on the genre to his work as a whole. Cukor,
for example, in Holiday uses the genre to explore his own
concern with the "double life," screwball qualities coming to
represent the human qualities repressed by the demands of
business and social decorum. Johnny (Cary Grant) has man-
aged to combine both by making enough money in business to
indulge his other self by taking a holiday. When he bursts
into his friends' apartment in the opening sequence to reveal
his sudden romance, the audience (remembering Bringing Up
Baby) expects that the girl will be Katharine Hepburn. The
substitution of a more conventional actress comes as a sur-
prise and the rest of the film depends on the suspense of how
the right couple will get together. Hepburn plays the older
sister who defies the family obsession with business and money. The two sisters represent the alternatives open to Johnny:
a tamed and "successful" existence or the right to find himself by taking a holiday. The comedy derives from the conflict between the pomposity of the nouveaux riches (as at the
official engagement party) and the zaniness of the nonconformists

(as at the rival party in the "play" room). The film ends
with the breaking of the engagement, finally fulfilling the audience's expectations, but Johnny, Linda, and his unconvention-
al academic friends are sailing from the U.S.A. , leaving the
family in charge of the house.

Much more work needs to be done before the exact
place of Cukor and the others within the genre can be finally
defined, and the comedies of later directors like Preston
Sturges and Billy Wilder also need to be examined in relation
to the development of the genre. However, two of the most
important comic directors of the thirties, Frank Capra and
Ernst Lubitsch, do not fit immediately into this development.
My contention that Hawks is the central figure for screwball
comedy would be challenged by Andrew Bergman, whose chapter on "Frank Capra and Screwball Comedy, 1931-41" discusses the genre in terms of Capra's films and fails even to
mention Hawks. Bergman sees It Happened One Night (1934),
made in the same year as Twentieth Century, as "the first of
the screwball comedies" and defines the essence of the genre
as "the process by which mutual cynicism melted before romance. "[9] This description does suit the process by which
Gable and Colbert come together in Capra's film and it certainly can be applied to the sex-antagonism that is developed
in most screwball comedies. But Capra's later films shift
their focus from the sexual to the social implications of the
comedy and would much better be described as populist comedies.

Whether these comedies should be seen as a sub-genre
of screwball comedy or, as Raymond Durgnat suggests, as
part of a larger genre of populist film is of minor importance;
but populist comedy is clearly an off-shoot from the screwball.
As Bergman argues, Mr. Deeds and Mr. Smith are screw-
balls in the context of New York and Washington society but
the triumphant endings of both films present the populist solution to the country's ills as society's willing acceptance of
those allegedly screwball qualities (such as love and faith)
from which it has temporarily been cut off, a simple overriding of the gulf between the existential and social absurd.

Capra's vision is not really screwball at all. Mr.
Deeds is practical enough to tell the trustees of the opera
company that their need for his support suggests that they are
not giving the public what it wants. Whereas the only positive strategy in screwball comedy is to accept the all-pervasive craziness, the populist comedy argues that what society

regards as crazy (Mr. Deeds' attempt to give away his for-
tune) is really a manifestation of the normal human values
with which society has lost touch.   Deeds, after all, is not
throwing his money away but setting up a New-Deal-type pro-
gram to help poor farmers.   Where the endings of Bringing
Up Baby, Ball of Fire, and I Was a Male War Bride differ
from Capra's populist endings is in their ongoing tension.
Capra takes the screwball formula and gives it a political
twist by relating the process by which the screwball wins
over an initially cynical partner to the process by which divi-
sive forces of a corrupt society are ousted by the constructive ability of the screwball individual to realize the American ideal of a classless and egalitarian society.   A momentum is developed at the end of a Capra comedy which, it is
implied, is capable of carrying all before it; the ending of a
screwball comedy is much more tentative, substituting an
openness to experience for a trust in norms or ideals.

      What Capra's films do show, however, is the social
context within which the sexual conflicts of screwball comedy
are to be placed, and many comedies do present an interesting attempt to fuse the populist and screwball visions.   Gregory La Cava's My Man Godfrey (1936) has a wealthy screwball family brought into contact with a bum who becomes their
butler; Capra's You Can't Take It with You (1938) has a poor
screwball family brought into contact with the wealthy son of
a munitions magnate.   While Capra finally has the screwball
family bring out the essential humanity in the industrialist,
La Cava suddenly shifts gears with the revelation that the butler is really a Boston blueblood on the run from a broken
love affair.   Godfrey's experience of the irresponsible screwball family is a negative one but it does help to turn him
from self-pity to social action.   In the final sequence, La
Cava manages to maintain an effective tension between the
screwball and the populist as Godfrey stands in his successful
make-work project but is bulldozed into marriage by the
screwball rich girl to whom he has never once suggested that
he is attracted.

      It is clear that the attitude of Capra and La Cava to
the screwball is deeply ambivalent: on the one hand, it represents an attractive freedom from inhibitions and reinforces the
American distrust of European sophistication; on the other, it
suggests irresponsibility and an alarming lack of social concern.   Films like Conway's Libelled Lady (1936), van Dyke's
Personal Property (1937), and Wellman's Nothing Sacred (1937)
all explore the social aspects of the screwball spirit.   On the

opposite extreme are the sophisticated comedies of Lubitsch,
drawn from a theatrical and European tradition to which slapstick, screwball, and populist comedy are equally opposed.
A film like Design for Living (1933), adapted from a Noel
Coward play, demonstrates the limits of conventional morality
by having the characters ignore it, but the film does not subject the sophisticated life-style to the same devastating as-
sault that it would have received in a screwball comedy.
Lubitsch would join the mainstream of American film comedy
only with Ninotchka (1939), in which Garbo is drawn from the
social absurdity of communism (indicated mainly by serious-
ness and puritanism) to the existential absurdity of romance
and American democracy.

A few films do attempt to combine the sophisticated
and screwball comedies: one of the most successful of these
is Leo McCarey's The Awful Truth (1937). The opening
strongly suggests the sophistication of Lubitsch, with husband
and wife trying to keep up appearances in front of friends who
use their awareness of the marital situation to deliver barbed,
if sugar-coated, remarks. Yet the apparent poise of the husband (Cary Grant), who has been deceiving his wife (Irene
Dunne) with another woman, quickly breaks down under his
suspicions of her. A sequence which begins with sophistication, then punctures the social pretense with screwball zaniness, develops a serious tone as the action, with disconcerting suddenness, leads to divorce (sentimentality avoided, however, by the spectacle of the hen-pecked lawyer expatiating
on the joys of marriage and by the court battle over custody
of the dog). From this point the screwball element takes
over as he tries to win her back from a southern millionaire
and then as she tries to win him back from a rich society
girl. The subsequent confusions owe much to the conventions
of bedroom farce: she is forced to hide her ex-husband and
supposed lover in the same bedroom when she is surprised
by her new fiancé, only to have their voices drowned under
the noise of a brawl in the bedroom, followed by the sudden
emergence of "lover" pursued by "husband." She has already
learned that she loves her ex-husband despite his craziness
and then, in destroying his romance, she comes to realize
that the element of madness is within her as well.

McCarey's ending points to the realization underlying
screwball comedy, that the monster is within (compare the
animal imagery in Bringing Up Baby). Sophisticated comedy
tames the beast by means of artifice, populist comedy by
means of democratic benevolence, whereas screwball comedy

recognizes the impossibility of taming and settles for an un-
easy but exciting co-existence. Just as the film noir inter-
nalizes the monsters of the horror film, so the screwball
comedy presents the psychological aspects of the external
forces at work in slapstick comedy. As we have seen, the
genre does not exclude a social awareness since its sexual
and psychological tensions derive from the existence of a society of the absurd; but it does throw emphasis on the absurd
and the irrational, perhaps implying that a recognition of
these qualities in human nature might lead to a liberation
from the pressures of a society that believes itself to be logical and rational.

        The screwball vision is ultimately at odds with both
the populist (since it condones irresponsibility) and the sophisticated (since it rejects refinement) perspectives. Since populism is Hollywood's dominant ideology and since sophistication
is the ideal of the upper levels of American society, the tensions aroused by this screwball vision dominate much later
comedy. Capra questions the relevance of a screwball approach to the Depression; during the forties its relevance to
the War is similarly questioned. In McCarey's Once Upon a
Honeymoon (1942), O'Hara (Ginger Rogers) moves from irresponsibility and false sophistication to commitment to the
fight against Fascism; but the film questions a commitment
that sends her back to her Nazi husband as a spy, and ends
on a note which is blackly screwball. 10 After the Nazi has
fallen overboard, just a glimpse behind the oblivious O'Toole
(Cary Grant, inevitably), O'Hara gives an account of the fatal
encounter which is both moving and hilarious, O'Toole tries
vainly to tell the captain what has happened (seen in dumb-
show through a window) while the latter tries to concentrate
on a bridge game, and finally the captain decides to turn back
to pick up the Nazi to show that "we" are more humane than
"them." But he cheerfully countermands his order when
O'Hara informs him that the Nazi couldn't swim.

        George Stevens explores the tensions between the
screwball and social conscience in his comic trilogy of the
early forties: in Woman of the Year (1941) Katharine Hepburn's commitment to her feminism and to her job as war
correspondent leads her to the irresponsible neglect of husband and adopted child, while Spencer Tracy represents populism and common sense in his concern with baseball rather
than politics; in The Talk of the Town (1942) and The More
the Merrier (1943) the screwball spirit is tested against, respectively, the need for law and order and the social reality

of a housing shortage. Judy Holliday's "dumb-blonde" persona
creates another set of variations on the screwball: in both
Cukor's Born Yesterday (1950) and It Should Happen to You
(1953) she begins as an irresponsible screwball but is converted simultaneously to romantic love and to a populist rejection of capitalistic corruption. Katharine Hepburn could
draw on the screwball elements of her persona in films from
David Lean's Summertime (1954), where her craziness is seen
as the release from inhibitions of an American spinster on
holiday in Venice, to Bryan Forbes' The Madwoman of Chail-
lot (1969), where her madness saves Paris from the destructive influence of insane businessmen.

The last-mentioned film is not a screwball comedy but
it does carry overtones of populism with its eccentric individual who helps the poor defeat the wealthy and powerful. Despite the attempts to modernize the action, this populist quality belongs rather to the forties of Giraudoux' original play
than to the late sixties. Since the war Hollywood liberalism
has cast a serious eye on its earlier commitment to populism:
in High Noon and Bad Day at Black Rock the weakness of the
people encourages corruption, in The Defiant Ones and A
Child Is Waiting a populist spirit achieves a hard-won but
limited triumph, but society remains hostile or indifferent.
The populist alternative all but disappears from comedy and
the social absurd is seen to have progressed too far to be
cured by an appeal to the essential goodness of heart of the
people. Society and politics seem desperately out of touch
with the people: in Hal Ashby's Shampoo (1975), the 1972
Presidential election takes place as a background to the action,
of interest only to the wealthy Republicans gathered to cele-
brate the victory, and provides a larger context for the failure
of communication and moral vacuum that shape the life of the
hairdresser (Warren Beatty).

Shampoo is a modern screwball comedy but here the
screwball individual has been infected by the sterility of the
social absurd. George's hectic activity and multiple "screw-
ings" reflect the screwball desire to remain free of social inhibitions, but they soon emerge as a desperate attempt to protect himself from his inner emptiness. At one point, he tells
Jackie (Julie Christie) that at least he doesn't screw for money as she does, but only for fun. Money and fun are the
only values that society recognizes, as can be seen from the
two parties which George attends towards the end of the film.
At the first, the establishment spends money freely and has
fun in the conviction that Nixon's victory will enable them to

have more of both; at the other, young people spend money to
get kicks and completely ignore the election. The two simultaneous parties recall those in Holiday, but here neither the
sophistication of the establishment nor the irresponsibility of
the drop-outs offers a positive alternative.

As the parties express a division in society familiar
from the screwball comedy of the thirties, so George is presented with a choice between the sophistication of Felicia
(Lee Grant) and the simplicity of Jill (Goldie Hawn), who is
a populist/romantic heroine despite her neuroses. Neither
of these choices can satisfy him but the film does suggest a
potential for escape in his relationship with Jackie, with whom
he has lived in the past but who is now kept by a rich businessman. They have been separated by their need for fun and
money, expressed in the expensive house she gets from Lester and in the success he has in a job which gives him money
and sexual opportunity for flattering women's vanity. George
loses Jackie because his confusion and frantic lifestyle prevent him from realizing in time his need for her. The down-
beat ending is a dark variant on Hawks's unbalanced endings,
with George perched unhappily on a hill as he watches Jackie
drive off with Lester, whose hair has just been "done" in the
way that George had suggested.

As in Bringing Up Baby, the social absurd is exposed
in its rejection of man's animal nature (in the "liberated"
seventies repression has been replaced by sex as "fun" or as
a business deal), its concern with money and possessions,
and, above all, its abuse of language. The poverty of language in Shampoo is exemplified by George's casual and frequent use of the word "great": once when he tells Jackie that
he feels "great" she forces him to admit that this means "not
too bad." Each character has his own catchphrase, nobody
really listens to anyone else (or to the election broadcasts),
the hairdresser and the banker cannot understand each other's
jargon, George is reduced to incoherence when confronted by
his three women at the election party and when he tries to
justify himself to Jill. Nixon's rhetoric is literally "behind"
this breakdown in language: on TV Agnew speaks of the way
the President can affect the "moral fibre" of the nation and,
after the election, Nixon looks forward to bringing the nation
together. The placing of the TV set between George and Lester during their showdown, stressing their separation, points
to the falsity of the rhetoric and adds to the sense of language
being used to screen out reality.

The comedy has become darker, the tensions more
desperate, but the screwball formula remains strong.   Peter
Bogdanovich's What's Up Doc? (1971), a re-working of Bringing Up Baby, often comes closer to Sennett than to Hawks (as
in the highly improbable chase sequence), but Peter Yates's
For Pete's Sake (1974) does manage to relate its equally self-
conscious use of the screwball formula to the ratrace of capitalism.   Both films offer Barbra Streisand as a new version
of the old Hepburn persona, more frantic, less poised, but
equally oblivious to logic and social decorum.   In Alan Pa-
kula's The Sterile Cuckoo (1969), Pookie's "kookiness" is a
defence against a world dominated by conformists whom she
calls "weirdos"; in Paul Mazursky's Blume in Love (1973)
even romantic love has been driven crazy by a sterile and
materialistic society; in Norman Panama's I Will ... I Will
for Now (1976) the social absurd is all-pervasive and once
more based on the need for fun and money--sex clinics and
marriage by contract are the most prominent examples.   This
last film fails to be a true screwball comedy because, despite
its air of liberation, it cops out at the beginning, since the
couple have already been married, and it cops out at the end
in their easy reunion.   Even its unbalanced ending is a cop
out from its cop out when the screwball (Elliot Gould) admits
that he didn't mean his promise not to chase other girls, and
his inhibited wife (Diane Keaton) carries The Joy of Sex behind her as they walk off to the bedroom in the final shot.

The failure of I Will ... I Will for Now is indicative
of the increased resistance in American society and cinema to
the depiction of strong and free female characters. [11]   Since
the screwball comedy is basically a feminine genre, the opposition to the screwball spirit is correspondingly stronger in
recent films; but the basic structure of the genre remains at
the core of American film comedy and its tensions offer the
most potential in creating a comic vision that would develop
a powerful and disturbing image of modern society.   As in the
case of the "serious" genres, the basic formula will often be
modified by contact with other genres and there are clearly
many more comic genres, sub-genres, and cycles than those
mentioned in this brief survey.   Also the various possible
tonalities need to be explored, especially the "romantic" and
the "satiric."   But there should be no compulsion to classify
every American film as a genre film.   Invention is as important as convention, and the comic in film, as elsewhere,
must always maintain an element of the indefinable and the
surprising.   Breaking down comic films into distinct genres
does, however, offer the possibility of developing an iconogra-

phy of film comedy to complement that already worked out in at least certain areas of the "serious" film.

Notes

1. See especially the discussion by Raymond Durgnat in The Crazy Mirror (New York: Horizon Press, 1970) and the introductory material on genre in his "Genre: Populism and Social Realism," Film Comment, Vol. 11, No. 4 (July-August 1975), pp. 20-29, 63.

2. Stuart Kaminsky. American Film Genres (Dayton, Ohio: Pflaum, 1974), p. 141.

3. Andrew Sarris, "The World of Howard Hawks," Films and Filming (July 1962), p. 23.

4. Peter Wollen. Signs and Meaning in the Cinema (London: Secker and Warburg, 1969), p. 84.

5. Robin Wood. Howard Hawks (London: Secker and Warburg, 1968), p. 78.

6. "Howard Hawks Interview"; and V. F. Perkins, "Comedies," both in Movie, No. 5 (December 1962), pp. 11, 21.

7. Wood, op. cit. , p. 71.

8. Ibid. , p. 77.

9. Andrew Bergman. We're in the Money (New York: Harper and Row, 1972), pp. 136-7.

10. See Robin Wood, "Democracy and Shpontanuity," Film Comment, Vol. 12, No. 1 (January-February 1976), pp. 6-15.

11. See especially the last chapter of Molly Haskell, From Reverence to Rape (New York: Holt, Rinehart and Winston, 1974), pp. 323-71, which analyzes this trend to weaker women's roles in recent films.

THE BUG IN THE RUG:
NOTES ON THE DISASTER GENRE

Maurice Yacowar

Disaster films constitute a sufficiently numerous, old and conventionalized group to be considered a genre, rather than a popular cycle that comes and goes. The disaster film is quite distinct from the science fiction genre Susan Sontag discusses in "The Imagination of Disaster," though like Sci-Fi the Disaster exploits the spectacular potential of the screen and nourishes the audience's fascination with the vision of massive doom.

The disaster genre is older than Griffith's Intolerance. One might argue that the first disaster film was Méliès's happy accident whereby a jammed camera transformed an ordinary autobus into a hearse. There we have the essence of the genre: a situation of normalcy erupts into a persuasive image of death. More obvious examples could be found in Méliès' Collision and Shipwreck at Sea (1898), perhaps in The Misfortunes of an Explorer (1900) and The Interrupted Honeymoon (1899), but certainly in The Eruption of Mount Pelée (1902) and The Catastrophe of the Balloon 'Le Pax' (1902).

I. The Basic Types

At least eight types of disaster film can be distinguished. Of course, there will be overlap between them and even with other genres.

(1) Natural Attack: The most common disaster type pits a human community against a destructive form of nature.

(a) The attack may be by an animal force, such as rats--Willard (Daniel Mann, 1970), Ben (Phil Karlson, 1972). It may be ants, normal--The Naked Jungle (Byron Haskin,

1954), or abnormal--Them! (Gordon Douglas, 1954), Phase
IV (Saul Bass, 1975). It may be fish--Jaws (Steven Spielberg,
1975), or fowl--The Birds (Alfred Hitchcock, 1961), or am-
phibian--Frogs (George McCowan, 1972). It may be rampage
of natural monsters--Elephant Walk (William Dieterle, 1954),
or of giant forms of natural monsters, like King Kong (Cooper
and Shoedsack, 1933), the Giant Gila Monster (Ray Kellogg,
1959), or the giant Tarantula (Jack Arnold, 1955). Or they
can be fantasy monsters, like Honda's Godzilla (1955), Mothra,
Reptilicus, Gappa, Rodan, and the rest of the boys in that
band. In The Lost World (Harry Hoyt, 1924) an aquatic di-
nosaur rips up London Bridge, as Gorgo was to do again for
Eugene Lourie in 1960.

          (b) Or it may be an attack by the elements, as in
John Ford's The Hurricane (1937), or in the ever-popular
flood movie, such as The Rains Came (Clarence Brown, 1939)
and The Rains of Ranchipur (Jean Negulesco, 1955). Volcanoes figure in The Last Days of Pompeii (Maggi, 1908), Volcano (Dieterle, 1953), and of course, Krakatoa, East of Java
(Bernard Kowlaski, 1969), about the volcano Krakatoa, which
is west of Java. The flood and volcano films, wherever they
are set, bear the moral weight of the urban renewal sagas of
Pompeii, Sodom and Gomorrah. Mark Robson's Earthquake
(1974) is a variation on this type.

          (c) A third type of natural attack is by an atomic mu-
tation, as the giant ants of Them!, the giant grasshoppers of
Bert Gordon's The Beginning of the End (1953), The Cyclops,
The Terror Strikes, Yog, Kronos (Kurt Neumann, 1957), The
Creature from the Black Lagoon (Arnold, 1954), The Beast
from 20,000 Fathoms (Lourie, 1953), and It Came from beneath the Sea (Robert Gordon, 1955). Or it may be the disaster of mutation or radioactive effect, as in The Incredible
Shrinking Man (Jack Arnold, 1957), The Amazing Colossal Man
(Bert I. Gordon, 1957) and The Atomic Kid (Leslie Martinson,
1954).

          In all three types, the natural disaster film dramatizes
man's helplessness against the forces of nature. The 1950s'
obsession with atomic disasters showed man diminished by his
own technology, as in the credits of The Incredible Shrinking
Man where the human outline dwindles as the mushroom cloud
swells. The animal films typically dramatize the power of
familiar, small creatures, like ants and frogs, often developing the threat out of domesticated animals, like cats and birds.
In The Birds a complacent society is attacked by birds for no

logical reason. Willard is an impure disaster film, for the
rats' power and malice are at first released under a human's
control. Generally, the animal-attack films provide a frightening reversal of the chain of being, attributing will, mind
and collective power to creatures usually considered to be
safely without these qualities. At the end of Willard, however, the ungentle Ben sniffs smugly in close-up, ominously
free of human control, dominant.

(2) The Ship of Fools: The dangers of an isolated journey
provide the most obviously allegorical disaster films, given
the tradition of The Road of Life. Such Westerns as Stagecoach and Hombre are cousins in another form, where the
savagery of Indians or Outlaws is the threatening disaster.

      The most common Travel Disaster involves flying. So
we have Walter Booth's Battle in the Clouds (1909), No High-
way in the Sky (Henry Koster, 1951), The High and the Mighty
(William Wellman, 1954), Zeppelin (Etienne Périer, 1971),
The Hindenburg (Robert Wise, 1976) and the spawn of Airport
(George Seaton, 1969), Airport 1975 (Jack Smight, 1975), indeed any air-films that involve massive threat of destruction
without the elements of human warfare. Hawks's Only Angels
have Wings (1939) has elements of the disaster film, but not
Tora, Tora, Tora, which belongs in the neighboring genre of
war films. The flying disasters are based on the audience's
familiar sense of insecurity in flight, and upon the tradition
of man's punishment for the hubris of presuming to fly. It's
even hubristic to float: Titanic (Negulesco, 1953), A Night to
Remember (Roy Baker, 1958). The same anxiety is addressed
by the horrors of Underground disaster in Gary Sherman's
powerful Death Line (in America: Raw Meat), and, with the
modification by human malevolence, in The Incident and The
Taking of Pelham One Two Three. Godard works round to a
Disaster vision in his traffic jam at the end of Weekend (1967),
but the fullest extension of the auto mythology into disaster is
the Australian Weir's The Cars that Ate Paris.

(3) The City Fails: Here man is most dramatically punished
for placing his faith in his own works and losing sight of his
maker. So his edifices must crumble about him. This type
dates back to The Last Days of Pompeii, E. A. Martin's War
o' Dreams (1915), Mary Pickford's Waking Up the Town (1925),
Luitz Morat's La Cité Fourdroyée (1924), Lang's Metropolis
(1926), Atlantis (G. W. Pabst, 1932), Earthquake, The Towering Inferno (John Guillermin, 1974), and so on. In The Neptune Factor (Daniel Petrie, 1973) an underwater lab and living

experiment is threatened by giant fish and eels bred by under-
sea volcanoes, so both the forms of Monster and Failed City
converge.

In this type the advances of civilization are found to
be fragile and dangerous. In The Incredible Shrinking Man
the world of commonplace objects overwhelms the hero, until
he resolves in mystic humility to enjoy his disappearance, his
fade into the rich nothingness of God. As we learned from
the coffee-tin he passed, "Use less for best results." In Invasion USA and Red Planet Mars (Harry Horner, 1952) we
enjoy visions of the cataclysmic destruction of America and
Russia respectively.

(4) The Monster: Natural and aberrant monsters were listed
under "Nature, animal" above. But the beast may come from
the vast beyond, as in X from Outer Space (1967). Space
monsters are terrifying even when they are not malevolent:
Twenty Million Miles to Earth (Nathan Juran, 1957), The Day
the Earth Stood Still (Robert Wise, 1951). The monster can
be a vegetable: The Day of the Triffids (Steve Sekely, 1963),
The Thing (Christian Nyby, 1951). It can be man-made: Der
Golem (Wegener, 1920), Frankenstein (James Whale, 1931).
Or it can be bacterial: Shivers (David Cronenberg, 1975). It
can even be a computer: Westworld (Michael Crichton, 1974),
2001 (Stanley Kubrick, 1968), Colossus: The Forbin Project
(Joseph Sargent, 1969). The beast can be a shapeless evil:
The Quatermass Experiment (Val Guest, 1955), The H-Man
(Honda, 1958), X the Unknown (Leslie Norman, 1956), The
Blob (Irving S. Yeaworth, 1958), The Green Slime (Kinji Fuka-
saki, 1969). Even the destruction scenes in The Exorcist
(William Friedkin, 1974) satisfied the appetite for disaster.

Often the monster threatens dehumanization, not death:
Shivers, Night of the Blood Beast, Gwangi, Attack of the
Crab Monsters (Roger Corman, 1957), Not of this Earth (Cor-
man, 1957), It Conquered the World (Corman, 1956), Invasion
of the Body Snatchers (Don Siegel, 1956). Often the monster
is a zombie: Night of the Living Dead (George Romero, 1968),
Plan 9 from Outer Space (Edward D. Wood, Jr., 1956), The
Undead (Corman, 1956), The Plague of the Zombies (John
Gilling, 1966), and Ray Dennis Stecker's The Incredibly Strange
Creatures Who Stopped Living and Became Zombies (1962).
Humans are occupied by alien, dehumanizing forces in The In-
vasion of the Body Snatchers and in The Earth Dies Screaming
(Terence Fisher, 1964). Then we have the host of vampire
films. These all work as black parodies of the mystique of

Christian inspiration/possession. The form shades off into
the Gothic horror tale in the one direction--Nosferatu (F. W.
Murnau, 1922) and Dracula (Tod Browning, 1931)--and into
the science fiction genre on the other--Zombies of the Strato-
sphere (Fred Brannon, 1953)--according to its iconography
(settings, costumes, etc.). Large-scale destruction charac-
terizes the films of the disaster type.

In Forbidden Planet (1956), Herbert Wilcox's clever
variation on The Tempest, the beast is explicitly an externalization of the human id. (The planet Altair was once the empire of the Krell, whose "mindless beast" impulses destroyed
their highly technical civilization.) The monster is often a
projection of or a metaphor for the character's psychological
state. In Willard the rats express Martin's corruption but
Willard's mousiness.

(5) Survival: A respectable variety of disaster films detail
the problems of survival after a disastrous journey--Lifeboat
(Hitchcock, 1943), Marooned (John Sturges, 1970), The Naked
Prey (Cornel Wilde, 1966), Flight of the Phoenix (Robert Al-
drich, 1966), Sands of the Kalahari (Cy Endfield, 1965), The
Savage Is Loose (George C. Scott, 1974)--or after the brawl
is over: Soylent Green (Richard Fleischer), The War Game
(Peter Watkins, 1967), Planet of the Apes (Franklin Schaffner,
1968), The World, the Flesh and the Devil (Ranald Mac-
Dougall, 1959), On the Beach (Stanley Kramer, 1959), Panic
in Year Zero (Ray Milland, 1962), The Omega Man (Boris
Segal, 1971), Zero Population Growth (Michael Campus, 1971),
Teenage Caveman (Corman, 1958).

(6) War: The war film becomes a disaster film when the
imagery of carnage and destruction predominates over the elements of human conflict. Thus The War Game, World in
Flames, Fires Were Started (Humphrey Jennings, 1943), and
the destruction scenes of Gone with the Wind and Slaughter-
house Five could qualify. In the '50s the atomic threat provided a host of visions of the day of judgment: The Day the
Earth Stood Still, The Day the Earth Caught Fire, The Day
the Sky Exploded, The Day the World Ended, Crack in the
World.

(7) Historical: A separate classification should be made of
disasters set in remote times, either past--San Francisco
(Van Dyke, 1936), The Last Days of Pompeii, Cabiria (Pas-
trone, 1914)--or future: Planet of the Apes, When Worlds
Collide (Rudolph Maté, 1951), War of the Worlds (Haskin,

1953), Things to Come (Menzies, 1936). The disaster film
characteristically depends upon the audience's sense of con-
temporaneity, but these films belong by the power and cen-
trality of their doom imagery.

(8) The Comic: There are three types of comic disaster
film.

(a) The disaster can provide a happy ending, as in
DeMille's spectaculars, Samson and Delilah (1949) and The
Ten Commandments (1923, 1956), assuming that one's critical
perspective is not that of the Philistines or the Egyptians.
Here there is a discrepancy between the destruction in the
image and its constructive spirit.   More recent affirmations
through disaster include the balletic explosion of the house
and contents at the end of Antonioni's Zabriskie Point and at
the ending of John Boorman's Leo the Last.

(b) The destruction can be extended into exuberant absurdity, as in the snowballing destruction in certain films by
Laurel and Hardy, in the Mack Sennett smash-ups, and Kramer's It's a Mad, Mad, Mad, Mad World. In Olsen-Johnson,
in Crosby-Hope Road films, and in such oddities as Hopalong
Rosenbloom Rides Again, delight is taken in the violation of
the logic and integrity of the image itself.   This is a comic
kind of violence.   Then, too, there is the comedy among the
ruins that one finds in two brilliant films, Richard Lester's
The Bed-Sitting Room (1968) and L. Q. Jones's A Boy and
His Dog (1976).   In the comic disaster film, the audience's
delight in seeing familiar treasures smashed--an element in
all disaster films--is freest.

(c) The third type of disaster comedy is parody.
Among the various film parodies in Woody Allen's Everything
You Always Wanted to Know About Sex (1972), for example,
is the invasion of an isolated countryside by a giant breast. "I
can handle boobs," the hero confidently avers, but as usual,
the monster is an externalization of the hero's own phobia/
obsession/boobishness.

A genre comes of age when its conventions are well-
enough known to be played for laughs in a parody.   The Big
Bus (James Frawley, 1976) is a full-scale parody of the Trip
Disaster film.   A twelve-million-dollar nuclear-powered bus
is attempting to make the first non-stop journey from New
York to Denver.   No one, of course, asks "Why bother?"

Much of the comedy involves mock-heroic twists. So
the hero's brawl has him wielding a broken milk-carton, sup-
ported by a man with a broken candle. This sends up every
bar-fight ever fought on screen. In Joseph Bologna's ostra-
cized driver the film parodies the ostracism of Richard Barth-
elmess in Only Angels Have Wings. But generally the parody
is of such contemporary films as The Hindenburg and Airport
'75. As Dana Andrews crashes a small plane into the jet in
Airport '75, here a farmer rams his half-ton into the bus.
The bus itself is a ludicrous demonstration of man's technology extended into absurdity: its self-washing mechanism and
exploding tire-changer, its system of jettisoning the soda pop,
its luxurious fittings in wash-room, bowling alley, dining
room, and pool, and the alternately fastidious and sloppy
handling of radioactive matter. The details of the parody in
The Big Bus bring us to the conventions of the genre as it is
played seriously.

II. The Conventions

(1) Except in the historical/fantasy type, there is no
distancing in time, place, or costume, so the threatened society is ourselves. The disaster film aims for the impact of
immediacy. So in the American film of The War of the
Worlds the setting was changed from London to Los Angeles.
When the American No Blade of Grass was set in England, it
was to emphasize the tradition of culture and sophistication
("Keep up your Latin, David; it will stand you in good stead"!!)
that is destroyed by the famine and anarchy.

The device of Sensurround purported to provide the
physical sensation of Earthquake. Significantly, the first
tremor felt was when a character was shown at a movie, i. e.,
when there is a precise continuity between the threatened
character's situation and the viewer's. Similarly, one of the
liveliest frights in Night of the Living Dead is when the zombies attack the girl cowering in her automobile. The movie
was made for drive-in showings, where the subjective shots
here would have had heightened impact. In the horror genre,
Peter Bogdanovich's Targets (1968) works a similar effect.

(2) Given this immediacy, it is difficult to define an
iconography for the Disaster film as one can do for the Western, the gangster film, even the musical and Gothic horror.
The basic imagery of the disaster film would be Disaster, a
general, spectacular destruction, but usually this imagery

occurs only at the end, though often with brief and promising samples along the way. More than by its imagery, then, the genre is characterized by its mood of threat and dread. Thus films as different as the B space monster films and Bunuel's The Exterminating Angel and Bergman's The Seventh Seal can properly be considered Disaster films.

(3) The entire cross-section of society is usually represented in the cast. The effect is the sense of the entire society under threat, even the world, instead of a situation of individual danger and fate. The ads for The Big Bus typically presented a line of head-and-shoulder pictures of its many main characters, each labeled.

Often the stars depend upon their familiarity from previous films, rather than developing a new characterization. Plot more than character is emphasized, suspense more than character development. In Towering Inferno an inherited sentiment plays around Jennifer Jones and Fred Astaire, Robert Vaughn repeats his corrupt politician from Bullitt, and Richard Chamberlain reprises his corrupt All-American from Petulia, itself an ironic inversion of his Kildare. In The Big Bus Ruth Gordon provides both a parody of the Helen Hayes figure in Airport and an extension of her own salty-old-lady act from Where's Poppa? and Harold and Maude.

Similarly, in Earthquake the romantic legend of Ava Gardner keys us to expect that husband Charlton Heston will gravitate towards her in the crunch, particularly when his mistress is lightly accented as an alien (French Canadian Genevieve Bujold). When Marjoe Gortner's amiable grocer turns out to be a sadistic fascist, we're prepared by our knowledge of the actor's career as a duplicitous evangelist. In Airport '75 Gloria Swanson is Gloria Swanson and Linda Blair is a poor little sick girl about to have her kidney exorcised.

(4) The Disaster film often dramatizes class conflict. Thus we have the racial concerns in Arch Oboler's Five (1951), The World, the Flesh and the Devil, and the tensions between John Hodiak and Tallulah in Lifeboat. In The Big Bus posh designer Lynn Redgrave allows her secret new styles to be worn as some vague part of the company's rescue scheme. A hustling businessman is common in the form, like Henry Hull's Rittenhouse in Lifeboat or Theodore Bikel in Sands of the Kalahari. Gig Young acts suspicious in The Hindenburg but only out of his concern for a cunning business deal. The

material concerns--and our differences--of daily life are supposed to pale in the shadow of death cast off in disaster films.
In Earthquake, the villains are the officials of the Seismology
Institute who ignore the graduate student's warnings because
they fear loss both of face and of a possible foundation grant.

(5) Particularly in American films, gambling is a recurrent device. There is a card game in Lifeboat, two sharks
on The Hindenburg, and overall much drawing of straws, flip-
ping of coins, and poetic justice, suggesting the inscrutability
of fate and the pettiness of man's attempts to alter his doom.
Superstition is a fossil of piety. Life is a gamble.

(6) The exception to the cross-section drama is where
a family is beset by the disaster. In The Birds, The Savage
Is Loose, Frogs, and Food of the Gods, one of the central
issues is the family's reluctance to admit an outsider to the
intimacy of the basic unit. In Zero Population Growth the
parents at first refuse to share their parenthood with the
couple who have found them out. The horrific climax in
Night of the Living Dead is when the daughter eats the father,
who had frantically kept outsiders out of the family basement.
In Lifeboat the "family" of Americans must deal with the attempt of Germans to join them, including the German-Ameri-
can Schmidt/Smith. Many disaster films will develop the
image of an inner circle or haven being defended against invasion, with a near-sexual tinge to the entrance (in The Birds,
the pecking through the wood and the invasion of the attic).

(7) The Disaster film is predicated upon the idea of
isolation. No help can be expected from the outside. Further,
the threatened characters are jammed together, without escape,
without relief from each other. The disaster is often directed
at an island community (The Birds, Frogs) or one isolated by
its remoteness (The Thing) or cut off from others by the disaster (The Towering Inferno). Then there are all the survival films set in remote areas. Sometimes even a connection
with someone will heighten the isolation: the separated family talking ship-to-shore in Juggernaut (Lester, 1974), or in
Hindenburg, when the ostensible villain, Boeth, learns that the
Gestapo has killed his girlfriend.

The isolation is an important convention of the genre.
Westerns and musicals both assume strong human community.
But the disaster film draws its anxiety from its conception
of man as isolated and helpless against the dangers of his
world.

(8) The characters' isolation is exacerbated by the various conflicts between them. The basic point of the genre is that man must unite against calamity, that personal or social differences pale beside the assaulting forces in nature.

In Jaws there is a hostility between the noble savage, Quint, and the wealthy college man, Hooper, that is only briefly glossed over by their drunken camaraderie--and by their sharing of wounds! The town knows Amity in its name only. Both in Jaws and in Grizzly, the hero and his political superior quarrel over the danger of the animal threat. In The Poseidon Adventure (Ronald Neame, 1972), the rivalry between the Reverend Scott (Gene Hackman) and the policeman Rogo (Ernest Borgnine) seems like the Renaissance debate between the orders of Grace and Nature.

Here lies the essential relationship between the disaster film and the war film. In both, a society at odds within itself unites against a common threat. In the war film the threat is human; in the disaster film, natural or supernatural. But both genres provide the mimetic harmonizing of a shattered community. War films and disaster films seem to arrive in an alternating cycle, both performing the same general function but with significant shifts of emphasis. War films are at a peak during periods of war and express nationalist confidence. Disaster films express the triviality of human differences in the face of cosmic danger.

The politics of Viet Nam did not find expression in war films, because the climate of opinion about the war was so widely and deeply divided in America; but it did emerge in the cycles of amoral cop and spy thrillers, with their ambiguous myths of militant police action on local or international scale. The disaster cycle of the '70s followed the slow ending of the American presence in Viet Nam. The subsequent cycle of war films was possibly spurred by the fervor of the Bicentennial, but it continued the successful elements of the disaster film: suspense, spectacle, formulaic characterization, and the drama of a divided society seeking vital reconciliation.

In The Big Bus there is a variety of comic reconciliations. At home base Scotty gets his lover/attendant back at the end. The passionate and quarrelling couple, Sybil and Claude, fight, divorce, then are re-married. The driver is reconciled to the woman he abandoned at the altar and to the woman whose father he ate ("Just one foot!", granted).

(9) The war and disaster genres share the further
sense that savagery continues to underlie man's pretense to
civilization. Thus disasters usually breed a lawless anarchy,
as Gortner personifies in Earthquake, or the selfishness of
Ralph Meeker in Food of the Gods, the savagery of No Blade
of Grass; or states of rigorous repression, as in Zardoz
(John Boorman, 1973), 1984 (Michael Anderson, 1955), and
the underworld of A Boy and His Dog. In Sands of the Kalahari Theodore Bikel asks the typical question: "Look at us.
Victims of civilization. Are we lost now or were we lost all
those years before?" Man's technology leads him to disaster,
by plane or ship, by his dominating creations. He builds
towers higher than his fire-hoses can reach (The Towering
Inferno). Often his works survive him, like the Rolls Royce
abandoned on a hilltop in No Blade of Grass, while the soundtrack repeats a car commercial. Man's works are dangerous,
like his robots, his monsters, his transports of delight, even
the earphone transistors which in Towering Inferno deafen the
boy to the danger around him. In The Savage Is Loose the
father systematically rejects the paraphernalia of society: the
pocket-watch, the alphabet, and the guilt-edged family Bible.

And yet. And yet, there is an optimism in the genre.
The center holds even when chaos has broken loose. The
maniacs and fascists are in a minority in the film vision of
anarchy. Gortner's fascist is quickly subdued. Order is re-
asserted. Even in The Savage Is Loose, having tried to kill
his father, the lad still comes to his mother gently, like a
lover, not a rapist. War is hell, but the disaster world is
only an earth of brief disturbance. Pessimistic visions without relief, without hope, are rare: Watkins' The War Game,
for example, and No Blade of Grass. Few films raise a disaster that cannot be survived or that does not bring out the
best in the characters and our society.

(10) Among the recurring character types is the spe-
cialist--the various Edmund Gwenn or Cecil Kellaway scientists or professors, or the amateur ornithologist in The Birds,
whose knowledge provides the basic factual framework for the
drama. Significantly, the specialist is almost never able to
control the forces loose against him/her. The specialist is
there to measure the force of the mystery by his impotence.
For the form serves the principle of the unknowable, the
superhuman, the mystery that dwarfs science.

Usually there is also someone of ominous complacency.
Sometimes he is the scientist, as Carrington in The Thing.

Or he may be a businessman/politician, like the mayor in
the sharkskin grey suit in Jaws. "We are the ugly rich,"
Ray Milland smugly admits in Frogs. This confidence represents the extreme form of the security which the audience
brings into the theatre for playful threatening--and perhaps
the deeper need to be punished for possessing it.

(11) There is rarely a religious figure in the disaster film, because faith would temper the dread, a sense of
God's abiding support would nullify the suspense. In The Big
Bus René Auberjonois plays a doubting priest who wants to
date, who gloats over God's giving him the window seat, and
who finally, his faith recovered, leads them all in a sing-
song, but a secular one. But he is not proof of a common
type. He seems a specific parody of Hackman's priest in
The Poseidon Adventure, whose religion is based on secular
confidence and self-help. He learns a non-religious kind of
humility and sacrifice through the events of the film. The
singing nun in Airport '75 is safely Helen Reddy. Her song--
something about your being your own best friend because no-
one looks after you better than you do--is strikingly oblivious
of Jesus. Moreover, the film turns on the salvation from a
lover from earth. God is no co-pilot in the current disaster
film and probably never was. For only in wars, not in the
upheavals of peace-time, can one claim that God is on one's
side.

Instead of church figures, the form presents evangeli-
cal crackpots, like the drunken seer in The Birds. This co-
heres with the literary tradition of disaster visions, deriving
out of the irregular, outcast prophets of the Old Testament,
proclaiming doom and destruction for man's godless pride and
corruption.

(12) All systems fail in the disaster. Politicians are
corrupt, save the Sam Ervin-type mayor of Towering Inferno.
The church is usually absent, as irrelevant. The police are
either absent or skeptical about anything beyond the familiar.
James Whitmore in Them! is virtually unique as a policeman
hero of a disaster film. George Kennedy is a heroic cop in
Earthquake, but he is disillusioned with and suspended from
the force.

In War of the Worlds the Martians attack the three
basic authorities of '50s America: church, army and science.
The courageous pastor is immediately converted into steaming
ash. The army and science fail in turn to assert their powers

stronger than faith.   The Martians are finally vanquished by earthly bacteria ("For best results use less"!).   Nature alone holds sway in the disaster world.

(13)   The hero is usually a layman with practical sense but without specialized knowledge.   In The Birds Mitch the lawyer can board up a house.   A black handyman is the hero of Night of the Living Dead.   The modest sheriff saves the day in Jaws, when both the savvy of the savage and the knowledge of the scholar have failed.   The specialist in Grizzly, Richard Jaeckel, dies twice, because he presumed to live in the hide of his prey.   In Towering Inferno Paul Newman is a specialist, an architect, but his knowledge is leavened by his rusticity.   Heston plays an industrialized ex-athlete in Earthquake and his achievement in Airport '75 is acrobatic as much as aviational.   Cornel Wilde's persona in his Socially Conscious period reverses his old image of easy, swashbuckling triumph.

(14)   Almost invariably there is a romantic sub-plot. Romance is a vital aspect of the tension between social instinct and selfishness.   So the romance is not just a matter of box-office concession (few things that traditionally work could be!).   The romantic by-play dramatizes the virtue of emotionally responsive humanity.

The romance is risible in Food of the Gods, where the scientist is sexually aroused by Marjoe Gortner from the strain of fighting giant rats.   The theme is worked out most explicitly in The Thing, where the hero's emotional capacity opposes him to the foolish Carrington, to whom the monster is the perfect creature: no heart, no emotions, no pleasure or pain.   For the hero, the icy landscape is a garden spot, for his romantic response to the lady expresses his feeling and joy of life.   The icy landscape is a projection of Carrington's soul.   To Carrington, "Knowledge is greater than life," but to the hero the pleasures and vulnerabilities of the heart are more important than science.   Thus the hero preserves the animal quality of man, against the vegetable values of The Thing and Dr. Carrington.

Similarly, in The Nepture Factor Yvette Mimieux's love for the lost Ed McGibbon causes her to cut the Neptune loose, risking everyone and everything, to recover her lost lover--and the lost laboratory.   Her love opposes the unsentimental logistics of Captain Ben Gazzara.

The romance is a variation upon the primary antithesis between a selfish, fragmented society and a community impelled by other-concern. Libertinism is to be punished by disaster (Pompeii, Sodom, the opening murder in Jaws). In Earthquake Heston must die for his infidelity--and as a reward for his courage and final faithfulness, his death saves him from the long pain of a loveless marriage. The ability to love is the primary virtue of the disaster hero, promiscuity and coldness the main though opposite faults. In The Poseidon Adventure, Rogo's wife, Stella Stevens, is an ex-prostitute. Her early demise is ordained by the same tradition that has the saloon gal intercept the bullet intended for the white-hatted hero, and that claims Heston's life in Earthquake.

In The Andromeda Strain (Robert Wise, 1970) James Olson wears a prophylactic rubber sheath to approach the infected survivors, but to save everyone he must break through his sterile invulnerability. In The Omega Man Heston valiantly fights off plague-riddled inferiors until he falls in love with the negress. His new susceptibility costs him his life but he dies with a fertile and romantic gesture, passing on the serum from his blood to another.

The romantic strain is so familiar that variations can be played by implication. In The Hindenburg the Scott and Atherton characters, a questioning Nazi and a German resistance youth, are kindred spirits for having girl-friends. The nobility of ex-lovers Scott and Bancroft harkens back to the warmth of an earlier Germany. In The Forbin Project we have a romantic attachment between two computers who plot to be reunited when their political masters, the U.S. and Russia, break their connection. The romantic element is introduced when Colossus watches voyeuristically over Forbin's affair and pours his martinis. In The Savage Is Loose the romantic dilemma moves to the center of the film; the incestuous solution is but an extension of the romantic values of the genre. In No Blade of Grass the middle-class daughter must reject the gentleman ordinarily esteemed in her class, in favor of the coarser, rougher man, who can afford her better protection. That slight inflection of the romantic convention speaks volumes in the film.

(15) Often the disasters have a contemporary significance. In The Big Bus there is topical comedy in Stockard Channing's blowsy parody of Liz Taylor, and in the doctor's fear of a malpractice suit. Something of Post-Nixon America is expressed in Airport '75, in the image of an airplane

heading toward the mountains with a hole where its pilots
used to be.   Whether Gerald Ford is played by Karen Black
or Charlton Heston is a matter of party politics, but Larry
Storch as The Press must be an Agnew invention.   The Towering Inferno is a modern Babel, man building to the heavens
without talking to those who might help him.   Earthquake is
an image of a society with its footing shaken out from under
it, both personal and professional responsibilities rent asun-
der.   Its climax of the bursting Hollywood Dam is an image
of what happens when personal codes are abandoned.

In Attack of the Giant Leeches (1959) the monster is
a reasonable squid.   The leeching is done by various interlop-
ing humans, a congenital poacher, and parasitic exploiters of
the merchant's wife and shame.   The hero is a game warden
committed to preserving animal rights and property.

In Frogs the Crockett family is attacked by reptiles
and amphibians, as if to punish them for having tampered
with the balance of nature.   Young Crockett starts the film
by upsetting the canoe of the ecologist hero.   Pioneers the
Crocketts may recall to us, but the animals avenge themselves against them as smug intruders.   The frogs can be
taken as the process of nature; thus one Crockett lady reports
her aging in terms of frog-like bags under her eyes.   The indictment becomes a national one when father Crockett cele-
brates his birthday on July 4.

The film abounds in striking images: a snake in the
crystal chandelier; a frog on the Old Glory birthday cake;
Clint's wife devoured by a turtle (Slow and steady...); a liz-
ard casually upsetting a canister of insecticide to asphyxiate
the grandson; Crockett at the end among his now menacing
hunting trophies, covered by frogs.   In one sly irony, the
daughter who earlier complained that her profits were reduced
by the cost of anti-pollution devices is lured by a butterfly into the swamp, then bled by leeches.   The large close-ups of
the frogs suggest they sit in judgment of man for his arrogant
abuse of nature, with a force hitherto restrained.   The film
articulates the '70s concern with the abuse of the environment.
So does Food of the Gods, where nature itself provides a dangerous food that will turn small creatures into monsters, once
catalyzed by human greed.

Walon Green's The Hellstrom Chronicle avoids the fictional form in favor of a documentary pretense, but it has the
effect of a disaster film, dramatizing man's smallness and

vulnerability in the context of the smaller creatures of nature.
Its science and pseudo-science give the film the air of newspaper factuality, as the atomic dramas seemed to have amid
the Red- and Bomb-scares of the '50s.   The anxiety fostered
by "Dr. Hellstrom" recalls the dislocation Gulliver suffers in
going from Lilliput to Brobdignag.   The film achieves that
kind of reorientation of the viewer's senses.

        Both The Hellstrom Chronicle and Fantastic Voyage
were produced in the early years of the L. S. D. phenomenon,
when society was excited with prospects of revolutionary perception.   So Hellstrom makes a gigantic, compelling world
out of the insect-close-ups.   And Fantastic Voyage sets an adventure story in "inner space," the body providing the kind of
eerie spectacle previously found in interplanetary travel.   The
final danger in that adventure is the explosion of the heroes
into full size while still within the host body.   Premature explosion is a danger that is not remote in any dream that exploits the presence of Raquel Welch.

        (16)   Poetic justice in disaster films derives from the
assumption that there is some relationship between man's due
and his doom.   Hitchcock's The Birds is distinctive in not
providing a cause for the birds' attack, but typical in present-
ing the characters as selfish, complacent figures who generally deserve to be shaken up.   So do we all, or we wouldn't go
to disaster films.

        Specific flaws need not cause the disaster, but some
inference of guilt by association may be drawn.   In San Francisco the earthquake is not just due to the San Andreas Fault,
but seems at least partly a response to the moral atmosphere
in which Clark Gable could knock down priest Spencer Tracy
for banning a scantily-clad performance by Jeanette Macdonald.

        In one respect "poetic justice" breaks down in disaster
films.   Often the good die with the evil.   In The Poseidon
Adventure, prostitute, priest, and generous swimmer die alike.
No logic dictates who will live and who will die in the crash
of The Hindenburg.   The mortality rate among stars and heroes is higher in the disaster film than in any of the other
didactic popular genres.

III.   The Application

        The main purpose in defining a genre is to establish a

context for the approach to an individual work. David Cronenberg's Shivers might serve as an example of a film illuminated by the sense of the disaster genre.

Shivers opens with a media-sell voice-over, oozing with the complacency that in disaster films is doomed for downfall. It is an assured voice of brittle normalcy, selling the joys of the Starliner apartment building on an island in Montreal. The company prides itself on the apartment's self-containment. The setting is thus developed into an image of the enislement of the sensually obsessed. The facilities cater to nothing but the appetites and the image of the beautiful life. Yet the inhabitants are lonely, insular people, condemned to sad privacy until the disaster frees them for unbridled lust, a horrible parody of community and love.

The disaster is an attack of red, phallic little critters that have been bred by the mad Dr. Emil Hobbes, combining the effects of V.D. and aphrodisiac. To save man from having tragically lost contact with his physical nature, Hobbes would convert the world into a gigantic orgy.

The "Starliner" presents life as a trip, a new, exciting ultra-modern exploration. The film is about the "sex-trip," about the use of free sex as an escape from the ostensible stasis of the responsible and restrained life. The film works against the romantic conventions of the genre, and against the liberated sensuality of its day, by making the sexual connection between people the horror, not the cure. The parasite is spread by figures representative of the current sexual liberation: a precocious nymphet, an adulterer, the old swinger with his megavitamin virility, the Swedish couple, the bachelor swingers, hetero and gay.

Cronenberg's Emil Hobbes has a connection to the real world, the philosopher Thomas Hobbes who in Leviathan argued the primacy of the physical nature of man and his universe. As Hobbes provided the rationale for Restoration libertinism, Cronenberg reverts to his name for his reversal, a horrific vision of our exalted libertinism. Our sensual togetherness Cronenberg makes more horrifying than the initial loneliness of his characters. The parasites appear as a cross between your standard red phallus and miniature whales, to confirm the Hobbes connection.

As so often in the genre, the monsters are only partly threats from the external world, and partly projections of the

characters' mental or emotional states.   In this case the
parasites are images of the characters' sexual compulsions.
So when they attack Barbara Steele they come up from within
the drainage system, through the plugged drainpipe of her tub,
sexually to enter her.   She has been moping around in a pre-
masturbatory lethargy, lying open in her tub, loosening up
with a large brandy, as if in unconscious hope for sexual engagement.

The hero is a young doctor (Paul Hampton) who re-
strains his sexual responses.   He chats coolly on the phone
while his nurse strips for him.   The audience, both out of
vicarious appetite and by its acquaintance with the conventional romance of the genre, expects, wants him to curtail his
call and make love to the nurse.   But Cronenberg's hero puts
science and duty ahead of casual lust.   That is the central
moral thrust of the film.

Cronenberg makes the lusting creatures his zombies,
against the tradition of the genre.   His orgiasts' hyperactivity
belies their void in will, soul and sense.   Cronenberg dramatizes the depersonalization of "liberated" sexuality.   It is un-
settling to find that the zombies are the characters fulfilling
our fondest fantasies--sex unlimited by law or capacity.

The film closes with a completion of the media-sell
frame.   A disc jockey assures his audience that nothing dangerous has happened.   While the beautiful people drive out in
their performance cars to infest the world with debilitating
appetite, all in the name of love and freedom, the disaster itself is hushed up by the loud confidence of the announcer.

Shivers is a powerful, unnerving film.   Even its sup-
porters are repelled by it.   Much of its anxiety derives from
the effective way that Cronenberg has inflected--and in some
cases radically reversed--the conventions of the disaster film,
the cultivated but unwritten expectations of his audience.   That
is one of the things that a genre is supposed to do.

EPIC, EPIC, EPIC, EPIC, EPIC

Raymond Durgnat

An epic, according to the Concise OED, is a poem
"narrating continuously achievements of one or more heroes,
as the Iliad or the Odyssey," and a "poem of any form, embodying a nation's conception of its past history." Most early
literary epics are glorified battle-scenes, but this militarism
carries both epic essentials: a sense of heroism, and a
sense of history. But we must extend the dictionary definition. History is international now, and Communists and
Americans alike see their own history in that of other nations
(Spartacus). There is even the epic of history-yet-to-be (in
intention, at least, Things to Come). In the Iliad, the Odyssey and later the Aenead, religion, history, battles and individual heroism formed one indivisible whole; for mythology
and history were not separated, and history was mainly kings
and battles, the latter depending on individual courage and
skill. The same sense of one vast cosmic action on which
grand destinies hinge invests Milton's Paradise Lost. Today,
though, this primal grandeur is less easy to obtain, for our
thought is broader and more compartmentalized. No longer
are religion and patriotism, kings and countries, battles and
history almost synonymous. Nations today are so large and
complex that the individual feels lost. Only in times of great
crisis can he wholly identify himself with his country.

But the mythological, historical and heroic stress of
the epic all seem to point to a deeper underlying meaning.
Stories of heroes and gods are epic, suggesting as they do
the cosmic scale--man measuring and exerting himself against
the greatest forces in the universe. In mythology as in history, human activity finds its largest scale; man matches, in
action, the hugeness of the world. Today the real equivalent
of the "battle-epic" is the story which integrates a wide range,
richness and maturity of experience into one action, one mission. For example, Fuller's Merrill's Marauders is a battle-

108

film, but though its mood of tight-lipped heroism is brilliantly evoked and maintained, its range of experience is too narrow, it remains a "war lyric" rather than an "epic." Particular, limited actions may indeed carry an epic "weight";
the story of Scott of the Antarctic could have been handled on
an epic scale, for man's challenge to his own powers of endurance has an epic quality. Above all, today, we are far
more aware of the diversity of factors which make history.
It may be made by the passive endurance of footsloggers en
masse (Dunkirk), or by the arts of peace rather than war
(Wilson, King of Kings). A few films (Rocco and His Brothers) tell stories of men in the street in such a way as to
suggest the immense weight of social history; others, though
impersonal in emphasis, imply individual strength and suffering (Grass, Strike). Despite attempts at the epic of modern
generalship (The Gallant Hours), the epic of the individual
warrior is almost always a costume film (El Cid). Hence
the popularity of costume epics....

But the epic is always connected with action, with effort, with extroversion. "Tragedy" and "epic" were distinct
Greek genres. "Tragedy" comprised all serious drama (including happy ends), and the emphasis lay on the qualities of
emotional experience, on family and personal stories, on
moral issues; the "epic" concentrated on the large-scale en-
terprises and actions, of which the smaller themes were only
part.

If the epic has a bad name among discriminating filmgoers, it is for a variety of reasons. The word is often de-
graded to mean "expensive," "spectacular" or "action-packed."
The stress on action and the lingering prestige of classical
times result in a weird misuse of the "epic" label: if Buck
Jones waves six-guns and heads 'em off at Eagle Pass, that's
a horse-opera, but if Maciste stands on Thermopylae and
throws cardboard rocks at Golaith, that's an Italian "epic."

Further, as we have seen, the epic unity is obstructed
by the range of modern thought. The older sense of enterprise and grandeur runs counter to modern man's feelings of
having too many of his choices imposed on him by routine, by
bureaucracy, by rubber-stamps and byelaws. War is commonly waged on a scale so huge that few soldiers even see
their general, and the human scale is humiliatingly puny when
ten times as many heroes as Alexander needed to conquer the
Western world are butchered to gain a yard of Flanders mud
--for a day or so.

Further, the bourgeois preoccupation with individual psychology ("motive," "characterization") means that our artistic standards are usually far more appropriate for drama than for the epic. Thus, our more sensitive artists hesitate or feel ill at ease in the "epic" genre, whose prestige attracts the naïve or the pretentious or lures the film-maker to abandon the experiences he knows for the sake of some empty academic "grand style."

Lastly, there is the trade sense of the word "epic"-- any film which has cost x million dollars. Yet even here something of the original sense of the word survives--for big budgets are usually devoted to what is hoped will be "big" subjects. However, Gone with the Wind and Duel in the Sun (for example) are not epics in our sense of the word; they are relatively intimate dramas which happened to be very expensive to make. Indeed, they both began with medium-large budgets, and grew with Selznick's enthusiasm; they are as good as they are because they remained essentially intimate in emphasis and scale. Similarly, DeMille's Samson and Delilah is, in emphasis, a drama about a warrior and a femme fatale, conforming to the American mysogyny of the '40s. It has some epic ingredients (Samson's feats of strength) but they are subsidiary; indeed, what epic scale it has comes from its biblical association. The Bible is the best, the greatest, the most significant book, the epic of man's relationship with God; everything in it has "cosmic" significance. This indirect stature is more fully present in Wyler's Ben-Hur, whose hero's renunciation of revenge is matched against the huge, significant presence of Christ.

It is almost impossible for any two critics to agree on which films are epics and which aren't, for epic stature depends on a certain emotional and moral weight; and different spectators' minds work in different ways, give weight to different things.

Currently the word "epic" conjures up a costume spectacle, with a few historical or mythological characters, and at least one big battle. National characteristics still count for a great deal, despite Italy's increasing expertise in the "international," Hollywood style. Though all nations have produced epics, the Americans and Italians, now as always, dominate the genre.

In the '30s, Britain produced one or two films which, almost accidentally, qualified as epics (e.g., as The Iron

Duke [1935], George Arliss defeats Napoleon and dominates
Europe's history. But most of the scenes are conversations
in stately homes or huge palaces). Similarly, most British
historical films, from The Private Life of Henry VIII (1933)
to The Young Mr. Pitt (1942), dwell cosily on their hero's
social round and political intrigues. Korda's "royal" series
(The Private Life of Helen of Troy, The Rise of Catherine
the Great) are really boudoir comedies crossed with historical spectacles. They combine two genres which Lubitsch had
alternated in Germany before going to Hollywood; his Passion
and Lady Hamilton alternated lavish crowd scenes with aristocratic personages seen less as leaders than as haughty victims.

Gabriel Pascal's Caesar and Cleopatra resumed the
same "royal boudoir" mixture. Handicapped by its utter fidelity to Shaw's amusing, chilly transliteration of wise, witty
George Bernard Caesar charming the sex-kittens of 1899,
Pascal's film mixed spectacle and intimacy even more awk-
wardly than Fox's Folly. As for Korda's last, sadly tatty
Bonnie Prince Charlie rubs it in: the English are too re-
fained for epic; they shrink from brash grandiosity, but have
nothing much to put in its place, bar Shakespeare. Apart
from its battle and the odd soliloquy, Henry V, being the
fourth part of a serial, is almost completely incomprehensi-
ble (who on earth is that fat man who dies at length, for no
reason, early on?). Richard III was perfectly summed up by
two phrases: "In Vistavision!" and a ten-year-old lad's "Cor,
there's four 'Sirs' in that picture!" Today, if the British
reach the epic spirit it is through the emotional self-efface-
ment of the near-documentary.

Nor, surprisingly perhaps, have the Germans showed
themselves at home with the epic spirit. Perhaps Fritz Lang's
Nibelungen films, Seigfrid and Kriemheld's Revenge, are
epics, translating into expressionistic terms the murky fatali-
ty, the turbidly tragic, atmosphere of Teutonic legend. Yet
their sense of positive heroic energy is not very strong, and
a certain static-ness, even passivity, seems nearer the para-
lytic post-Versailles angst than the spirit of epic tragedy.
Nazism was too highly mobilized in the present to bother much
with historic precedent; history was exploited only to vilify the
Jews and the British; Nazi "idealism" betrays its mechanized
brutality in every image of Triumph of the Will, which might
almost have been an epic of athletics; and the last pale glim-
mer of Prussian heroism may be seen mumbling pathetically
before a Nazi court in Leiser's Mein Kampf, and died hanging
on a butcher's hook in 1945.

Russia's costume epics are mainly an outcrop of Stal-
inism. The new Bolshevik spirit, proletarian and international, renounced Russia's past which was nationalism and tyran-
ny. Historic films were transparent to present preoccupations. Petrov's Peter the Great was virtually a justification
of Stalin the Great; the purges of the '30s are tacitly compared to Peter's brave bullying of the corrupt old boyars and
the cunning monks whose bronze bell he melts down to make
a big, big cannon. As the Nazi menace loomed, Stalin ap-
pealed increasingly to the almost Messianic undertow of nationalism in the Russian soul. In Eisenstein's Alexander Nevski the heavily armored Teutonic knights are lured into fighting on a frozen lake whose ice cracks beneath their weight.
Russian heroism and General Winter will win, by their usual
recibiendo. Perhaps the most deeply moving Russian "epic"
is the John Ford-like Chapayev, whose melancholy moral is
that the day of the old, heroic, revolutionary leader is gone;
he is too slapdash, the quiet cold Commissar at his side is
always right.

In Italy, Mussolini's Abyssinian enterprise inevitably
produced a crop of "Roman grandeur" epics, but the Italian
epic has deeper roots. Whether mediated through Catholicism,
through the classical strain in Renaissance secular art, or
through Italy's archeological and architectural richness, the
past is alive there with an informal vividness which shames
Britain's traditionalism, filtered as it is through middle-class
notions of what good little schoolchildren ought to know. By
1913 the Italians had tackled most of the epic perennials--
Nero, Spartacus, Distrozione di Cartagine, Gli Ultimi Giorni
di Pompeii (twice!), La Gerusalemme Liberata, Marcantonio
e Cleopatra. The poet d'Annunzio deigned to lend his name
to the script of Cabiria, to which he contributed only the basic
idea, and not a very original one at that; still he gave the
world Maciste, and it is ironical that this hunk of muscle-
bound cinema should have sprung from the pen of a celebrated
poet. Guazzoni's Quo Vadis incurred the skyrocketing budget
of £7,000 and grossed ten times its cost. With its sister
epics, it smashed its way across the American market, dwarf-
ing the puny efforts of a still shaky ragged Hollywood.

The next fleet of Italian epics set sail about 1924, when
the newly Fascist studios vainly attempted to recapture their
pre-war position. d'Annunzio co-directed Emil Jannings in
Quo Vadis, and Carmine Gallone remade (what else?) The
Last Days of Pompeii. (It was later filmed, disappointingly,
by the King Kong team in 1935, with Preston Foster; academi-

cally, by Marcel L'Herbier, in 1947, with Micheline Presle; and, comic-strip-ically by Paolo Moffa in 1959, with Steve Reeves.) Their failure doused the epic spirit until Carmine Gallone's Scipio L'Africane obliquely glorified colonialism by poison gas, though Blassetti's 1860 (1933), now seems democratic enough, celebrating the common people's role in supporting Garibaldi.

The post-war Italian cinema has epics galore: only Blassetti's Fabiola (1947) strove for the "prestige" air of the first epics; most "muscleman" epics are Westerns in togas; but the post-war Western's streaks of bitterness and highly moralized, vicious violence are replaced by the Mediterranean sun, bright pagan temples, softly pretty Princesses, slave-girls galore, and a jollier, naïver tone.

Guazzoni's Quo Vadis inspired the American cinema, previously intimate and realist, to Griffith's Intolerance and the grandeur that was Cecil B. If DeMille had had a coat-of-arms, a cross and a bathtub would have been equally prominent thereon, and this moral dichotomy is characteristically Victorian. The prosperous, expansionist, puritanical Victorian bourgeoisie was fascinated by Imperial Rome, which, they felt, rose through its ascetic virtues and fell through its very enviable opulence. Even DeMille's floggings and general sadism are a Victorian taste. As Grierson remarked, DeMille's epics are Jewish rather than Anglo-Saxon, Jewish in their enjoyment of physical sensuousness--asses' milk baths, glittering silks, fur rugs and opulent jewelry--while the action sequences are sheer G. A. Henty, but with a second helping of gore.

DeMille apart, the American epic forte is in sheer size and in big battles. The spectacle often encumbers the storyline, which is frequently paralyzed anyway by simple goodie-baddie moralizing, while the battles generally lack the tactical clarity of Peter the Great, Alexander Nevski and The Seven Samurai. It's a pity that by sheer weight of budget the epic has come to be thought of as an American specialty, for the Americans are rather bad at them.

Occasionally the battles are fine (DeMille's The Crusades, Intolerance, of course); the debauches are always innocuous dancing turns, sometimes with inspired flashes (Vidor's Solomon and Sheba excelling Wyler's Ben-Hur). In general, though, American epics depend on their moral intensity, and so are simply more diffuse than their ordinary dramas.

There are exceptions--notably Spartacus and, if it's an epic,
Barabbas.   But Kirk Douglas and the American writers
spoiled Camerini's Ulysses (1955) by reducing the myth to
terms of the sheer, fierce will to succeed; the original has
a much greater emotional spread.   Even the sophisticated
Aldrich's Sodom and Gomorrah boringly opposes the virtuous,
hard-working, patriarchal Hebrews and the rich, corrupt,
Lesbian-dominated Sodomians.   Stewart Granger tries to get
the Israelites to control Sodom by means of their virtual salt-
monopoly, and the ethical dilemmas of fighting capitalist
greed by capitalist means are honestly stated.   Aldrich's film
is vitiated, however, by its stilted style and by the Israel-
Sodom antithesis, based as it is on the contrast, too often
made by old-fashioned American puritans, between rural America (hardworking, frugal, virtuous) and the big city (rich,
pleasure-ridden, corrupt).   Aldrich has the courage to attack
the audience--Granger denounces all those who have come to
enjoy watching Sodomian tortures--why else did we come to
see Sodom and Gomorrah?   But one can't admire the moral
courage of a film which paraphrases male homosexuality by
Sapphism (more obvious in the Italian version than in the English one), and only very vaguely hints at the plain Bible truth
that Lot and his daughters committed incest with impunity.

        Howard Hawks's Land of the Pharaohs is visually dul-
ler, but has a more interesting moral.   Hawks uses the
Pharaohs' obsession with pyramids and tombs as a target of
attacks on religion (much of the dialogue is aimed sardonical-
ly against the policy of making sacrifices in this life for benefits dubiously attainable in the next) and against conspicuous
consumption (the pyramids, monuments of necrophilia, parody
present-day California's super-de-luxe, piped-music Gardens
of Rest).   Hawks's film (which might be entitled The Big
Sleep) is an attack on the pointless amassing of riches, and
attains a brooding authenticity in its study of a prehistoric
Kane numbly wavering between his pyramidal Xanadus, his
colorless family life, and a sexy, perfidious gold-digger (Joan
Collins).   But the plot is rather inert, and, as Hawks himself has said, he hadn't a clue as to how Ancient Egyptians
behaved.   Also, Cinemascope is a terrible shape for pyramids.

        Guazzoni's Quo Vadis, despite the charms of its green,
lemon and, for Rome's burning by night, purple tints, is almost "invisible" today--the semaphore-style acting of the
period, not to mention the piston-like "Fascist" salutes, re-
duce it to a hilarious Ballet Mécanique of eyeball-rolling,

arm-flinging and fast, frantic posturings. But the pathos and
violence of the Italian primitives often survive today--the
blind girl wandering, miraculously unscathed, through the destruction of Pompeii, and then wading out into the sheltering
sea, to be drowned; the woman of La Nave, proudly anticipat-
ing her torturers, and kneeling to press her face into a bra-
zier of glowing coals; the slow death of St. Sebastian, rolling
his eyes in prayer and agony, with arrows in his stomach,
throat, breast and thigh; the lions in Quo Vadis, advancing on
mothers with babies at the breast, and, later, disgruntledly
pawing bundles of clothes wrapped round what by now are
lumps of raw meat. Above all, the films survive as spec-
taculars--marching armies, panic-stricken mobs rush, flow,
cascade, hither and thither, on several levels, in several di-
rections, like torrents of humanity, creating visual patterns
dramatically far more exciting than Hollywood's static masses
of extras.

Because epics are not primarily "psychological" they
often suggest a highly developed pictorial style, whether theatrical (as in the case of Max Reinhardt-style films) or painterly. But here is the trap. A director who simply repro-
duces the stage pose, or the ideas and compositions of great
paintings, is certain to finish with a slow, static, visually
naïve film. He may even come to feel that grandiose visuals
require a simple plot--yet the epic's extroversion can accom-
modate decisions and moral issues as subtle as anything in
drama (Kubrick's Spartacus is a good, if not a brilliant, example). The creative problem is to reconcile a strong, subtle
narrative with genuinely filmic terms.

A characteristic solution is found by Eisenstein. Alexander Nevski breaks down into a succession of "canvases"--
Nevski Defies the Mongols; The Sacking of Pskov; Troops Don-
ning Armor; The Battle on the Ice; and so on. Each sequence
corresponds to a painting, by Uccello or Delacroix, whose
separate details and configurations are "clipped out" into close-
ups, medium-shots, and so on, and reassembled, not in space
but in time. The track and pan are further ways of transpos-
ing space into time.

For some reason, film aestheticians rarely take the
study of screen visuals further than talking about movement,
light, and composition; but Eisenstein's films are models of
the cinema's legitimate borrowings from painting--supremely
in Ivan the Terrible, the director puts to emotional use the
weight and volume of the human body, the tension of muscles,

the surface and flow of draperies and dresses, the orchestra-
tion of space and shape, stance and depth. Italian culture is
saturated in painterly sensibilities (hence, perhaps, the fi-
nesse and brio of Italian cameramen), but their epic visuals
too often remained as academic as Blassetti's--though 1860
has several very beautiful shots, as of an exhausted oarsman
lying slumped in his gently rocking boat. But throughout
Fabiola the academic stilts the dramatic.

        Riccardo Freda's battle-scenes (a current French fad),
as in The Mongols and Vengeance of the Gladiators, are no
more than competent. But color and Cinemascope seem to
have liberated the Italian eye. Many a dramatically banal
Italian epic is a real pleasure for those who enjoy the riotous
richness of color, decor, costume and flesh: the zooms into
the blazing sun, the wine-dark sea, the glint of coppery light
on the hero's brawny flesh, the trajectory of blazing torches
hurled against the night sky ... for sheer visual-sensual
pleasure, I warmly recommend, in order, Guns of the Black
Witch, Sons of Thunder, Hercules at the Centre of the Earth,
Hercules Conquers Atlantis, The Giant of Marathon and even
Warrior Empress. In most cases these effects are notations
for an epic, which isn't, alas, in the film--though the Hercules films are imperfect, minor, beautiful, poetic myths.

        This isn't altogether to dismiss the second part of the
Steve Reeves Thief of Baghdad and the laboratory scenes of
The Wonders of Aladdin, though only to be recommended to
addicts. My epic-going has some lamentable omissions, but
I would warn the reader against (in descending order of bore-
dom) Ursus in the Valley of the Lions, Vengeance of the
Gladiators, Warlord of Crete, Duel of the Titans and Golaith
Versus the Giants.

        A second problem with 'Scope is that it sometimes
overemphasizes background and tempts the director to pretty
patterns at the expense of dramatic content; together with a
relative neglect of cutting.

        How many of these faults might be remedied is sug-
gested in, oddly enough, a magnificent semi-comic epic, Sons
of Thunder (alias Les Titans, alias My Son the Hero). Its
send-ups of the genre are hilarious; the people join in the
hero's cries of "Long live liberty!", then look at each other
blankly and mutter: "But what is liberty?" (never mind, they
have the sense to overthrow the tyrant anyway). When a
hunted Negro rips a wooden bridge to pieces with his bare

hands we hear the march from The Bridge on the River Kwai,
when the prehistoric Princess longs for a man her feelings
are expressed by a smoochie samba, when the hero's buddies
come to his aid we hear "Anchors Aweigh," and the tyrant's
battalions march into battle to the strains of "Deutschland
über Alles." There is a friendly parody of a John Ford
Western and a deaf mute who talks in Harpo Marx sign language. Like Hercules Conquers Atlantis, the film is anti-
racist. The twin heroes are a demoniacally exuberant, Teu-
tonic-Prince-looking blonde, and a surly, burly Negro. The
film makes a great show of exalting brain (the former's) at
the expense of dumb-ox brawn (the latter), but the heroes
win, in effect, by magic, dash and cold steel. When the
Negro breathed in deeply, the magnificence of his torso wrest-
ed a gasp, almost a scream, of admiring shock from lasses
and lads alike in the front row of my local Odeon; while the
Titans, after we have been led to expect a sort of super-
magnificent-Seven, turn out to be shaggy dimwits who come
shambling in like out-size ancestors of the Bowery Boys.

The Gorgon isn't very frightening, and Hades is a
candy-gloss and marzipan-colored grotto, but Antonella Lualdi
is succulent beyond words in wigs of purple, mauve and plati-
num, and a Zaroffian manhunt of the Negro leads to a bit of
cutting as slick as the run of the arrow in Fuller's brilliant
film. The whole thing is overflowing with vitality, so flexible an amalgam of the Italian and American styles, and so
often so beautiful to watch, that I was almost disappointed
that Duccio Tessari hadn't struck out to make a "straight" romantic epic. The moral is that the truest epics are produced,
not by an inflated, "prestige" style, but by treating a "big"
subject with the same intimacy and variety of mood which one
would bring to a little one.

The "epic" can be art; indeed, art should have an
epic strain, and it's a criticism of our self-conscious, doubt-
ridden age that the epic doesn't come to us naturally as an
expression of man's fullness, vigor and sense of mission.

THE ICONOGRAPHY OF THE GANGSTER FILM

Colin McArthur

In Little Caesar (1930) a police lieutenant and two of
his men visit a nightclub run by gangsters. All three wear
large hats and heavy coats, are grim and sardonic and stand
in triangular formation, the lieutenant at the front, his two
men flanking him in the rear. The audience knows immediately what to expect of them by their physical attributes,
their dress and deportment. It knows, too, by the disposi-
tion of the figures, which is dominant, which subordinate. In
The Harder They Fall (1956) a racketeer and two of his men
go to a rendezvous in downtown New York. As they wait for
the door of the building to be opened they take up the same
formation as the figures in the earlier film, giving the same
information to the audience by the same means. (The fact
that they are, in the first case, policemen, and in the second
case, racketeers, is an interesting ambiguity which will be
examined later.) In On the Waterfront (1954) and in Tony
Rome (1967) there are carefully mounted scenes in which the
central figure is walking down a dark and deserted street.
In each case an automobile drives swiftly towards him; and
the audience, drawing on accumulated experiences of the genre, realizes that it will be used as a murder weapon against
the hero. Both these examples indicate the continuity over
several decades of patterns of visual imagery, of recurrent
objects and figures in dynamic relationship. These repeated
patterns might be called the iconography of the genre, for
they set it off visually from other types of film and are the
means whereby primary definitions are made.

The recurrent patterns of imagery can be usefully divided into three categories: those surrounding the physical
presence, attributes and dress of the actors and the characters they play; those emanating from the milieux within which
the characters operate; and those connected with the technology at the characters' disposal. Among Hollywood leading
men, Edward G. Robinson and James Cagney dominate the

gangster films of the thirties; Humphrey Bogart the thrillers
and Richard Widmark the gangster films of the forties; and,
though not in such a clear-cut way, Richard Conte has a good
claim to this role in the gangster films of the fifties.   In addition to these major icons of the genres, there are other
players of the second rank such as George Bancroft, Barton
MacLane, Joe Sawyer, Paul Kelly, Bob Steele, Ted de Corsia,
Charles McGraw and Jack Lambert, to name only a few, who
have become inseparably associated with the gangster film/
thriller.   The American cinema has traditionally achieved its
effects with the utmost directness, and never more so than in
the casting of gangster films and thrillers.   Men such as
Cagney, Robinson and Bogart seem to gather within themselves the qualities of the genres they appear in, so that the
violence, suffering and angst of the films is restated in their
faces, physical presence, movement and speech.   By the curious alchemy of the cinema, each successive appearance in the
genre further solidifies the actor's screen persona until he no
longer plays a role but assimilates it to the collective entity
made up of his own body and personality and his past screen
roles.   For instance, the beat-up face, tired eyes and rasp-
ing voice by which we identify Humphrey Bogart are, in part,
selections we have made from his roles as Sam Spade, Philip
Marlowe and others.

   It is not only the actors playing the roles who recur,
but the roles themselves.   Genres become definable as such
by repetition until fairly fixed conventions are established,
and this is particularly apparent in the spectrum of characters in the gangster film/thriller; racketeers with brains who
rise to the top, gangsters without who remain as hoods, gangsters' women, stool pigeons, cops and bent cops, crusading
district attorneys and legal mouthpieces for the mobs, private
eyes and heroes forced by circumstances to be such, nightclub owners and their sadistic strong-arm men; and the count-
less secondary figures on the fringes of this dark world,
newspapermen, pool-room and gymnasium owners, news-
vendors and so on.   The interpretation of these roles may
develop.   For instance, James Cagney's particular physical
dynamism was interpreted, in the gangster films of the thirties, as necessary ruthlessness in getting to the top, but in
the gangster films he made in the post-war period, especially
White Heat (1949) and Kiss Tomorrow Goodbye (1951), this
physical dynamism was interpreted as psychotic.   A touch-
stone of normality is usually present, often centered on the
figure of the gangster's mother.   This is apparent in the earliest examples of the genre such as Little Caesar (1930), The

Public Enemy (1931) and Scarface (1932); it is present vestig-
ially in The Big Heat (1954) and achieves almost pristine re-
statement in The Brothers Rico (1957).

But the figures in the gangster film/thriller proclaim
themselves not only by their physical attributes and their
roles but also by their dress. The peculiar squareness of
their hatted and coated figures is an extension of their physical presence, a visual shorthand for their violent potential.
Clothes have always been important in the gangster film, not
only as carriers of iconographic meaning but also as objects
which mark the gangster's increasing status. Scenes in tai-
lors' shops are frequent (The Public Enemy, Al Capone
[1959]), and both Rico (Little Caesar) and Tony Camonte (Scarface) invite comments on their clothes ("How do you like it?
Expensive, huh?"). Alec Styles, the gangleader in The Street
with No Name (1948), tells a new member of his gang, "Buy
yourself a closetful of clothes. I like my boys to look sharp."
Characters in Baby Face Nelson (1957) ("Get rid of that gun-
ny-sack") and Murder Inc. (1951) ("Burn that tent you're wearing") are instructed to change their clothes as a mark of their
rising status, and Tolly Devlin's ascent within the syndicate
in Underworld USA (1960) is marked by syndicate boss Gela's
comments on his clothes.

Following The Naked City (1948), several gangster
films and thrillers appeared carrying the word "city" in their
titles: Dark City, Cry of the City, City Across the River,
While the City Sleeps, The Sleeping City, Captive City and so
on. Alongside these came other films featuring the word
"street" in their titles: The Street with No Name, Race
Street, Side Street, Down Three Dark Streets, The Naked
Street, not to mention Where the Sidewalk Ends and The As-
phalt Jungle. This development simply made explicit what
had always been an important element of the gangster film/
thriller, the urban milieu. [1] Robert Warshow, in his essay
"The Gangster as Tragic Hero," writes:

> The gangster is the man of the city, with the city's
> language and knowledge, with its queer and dishon-
> est skills and its terrible daring, carrying his life
> in his hands like a placard, like a club ... for the
> gangster there is only the city; he must inhabit it
> in order to personify it: not the real city, but that
> dangerous and sad city of the imagination which is
> so much more important, which is the modern
> world. [2]

Thus the city milieu serves both as a background for the activities of the gangster and the hero of the thriller, and as a kind of expressionist extension of the violence and brutality of their world. The sub-milieux of the gangster film/thriller are, in fact, recurrent selections from real city locales: dark streets, dingy rooming-houses and office blocks, bars, nightclubs, penthouse apartments, precinct stations and, especially in the thriller, luxurious mansions. These milieux, charged with the tension of the violence and mystery enacted within them, are most often seen at night, lit by feeble streetlights or more garish neon signs, such as the Cook's Tours sign "The World Is Yours" in Scarface, or the flickering signs which cast threatening shadows and half-disclose mysterious visitors in the offices of Sam Spade (The Maltese Falcon) and Philip Marlowe (Farewell, My Lovely). Fritz Lang, in his German film Metropolis, created a huge city embodying his expressionist fantasies. When he came to America he had no need to recreate his city; it already existed.

The gangster and the hero of the thriller, being modern men of the city, have at their disposal the city's complex technology, in particular the firearms, automobiles and telephones which are recurrent images of the genre. It is fitting that the Western hero, moving balletically through his archaic world, should bear graceful weapons such as the Winchester rifle and the Colt pistol. The weaponry of the gangster film/thriller is much more squat and ugly: the police .38, which forms the title image of Kiss of Death and the opening image of The Big Heat; the Luger; the sawn-off shotgun; the sub-machine-gun which becomes an object of veneration in Scarface and Machine-Gun Kelly. Andrew Sinclair, in his book Prohibition: the Era of Excess, describes the role of the automobile in the Prohibition/repeal debate:

> The armour-plated cars with windows of bullet-proof glass, the murders implicit in Hymie Weiss's phrase 'to take for a ride,' the sedans of tommy-gunners spraying the streets of gangland, all created a satanic mythology of the automobile which bid fair to rival the demonism of the saloon. The car was an instrument of death in the hands of the crook and drunk, and prohibition was held to have spawned both of them.

The automobile is a major icon in the gangster film/thriller. It has a twofold function in the gangster film: it is the means whereby the hero carries out his "work" (Tom and

Eddie in The Public Enemy, waiting orders from Nails Nathan, stand beside their car like the crew of a Panzer about to go into action); and it becomes, like his clothes, the visible token of his success. Eventually it becomes the symbol of his unbridled aggressiveness, and it seems perfectly logical that the automobile should be used regularly as a lethal instrument in both thrillers and gangster films (see The Dark Corner, Underworld USA, The Moving Target and others). [3] So powerful a symbol has it become of the gangster's presence that characters may respond with fear to an automobile without seeing the men within it (see Kiss of Death, The Garment Jungle, Assignment to Kill and others).

The telephone has, on occasion, been used as a murder weapon in the gangster film/thriller and this, too, seems logical. The physical environment, an expressionist representation of the violent potential in the genres, becomes the instrument of violence. More often, however, telephones are used to intimidate the weak, as in the threatening calls to Mrs. Renato in The Garment Jungle and to Mrs. Bannion in The Big Heat.

It is, of course, an artificial exercise to discuss individual iconographic elements when they exist in dynamic relationship within the fabric of particular films. Now and then several iconographical elements combine in singular purity and there are found the sequences most characteristic of the genres. For instance, the opening sequence of The Harder They Fall, showing several figures (Bogart, racketeers and others) entering cars and hurtling through the empty New York streets to an early morning rendezvous, evokes brilliantly the ugliness of the milieu and the ruthlessness of the racketeers before disclosing the squalid operation they are embarked upon. Again, the sequence in Little Caesar when Tony, the gang's driver, is shot down on the steps of the church by Rico from a speeding car, brings dynamically together several iconographical elements. The same elements are interestingly used in the French gangster film Le Deuxième Souffle, in which the trademark of the central figure is to shoot his victims inside a car which he himself drives. Perhaps the iconography of the gangster film is presented most strikingly (and, incidentally, the non-realistic quality of the genre most clearly exemplified) in the characteristic montage sequences of thirties gangster films where the outbreak of gang war is chronicled. The films at these points prise themselves free from their inhibiting narrative structures and present the pure imagery of aggression: speeding cars, screaming tires, figures blasting each other with revolvers and sub-machine-guns. A frozen frame from such a sequence would look like a pop art poster representation of the essence of the gangster film.

But to define the gangster film/thriller solely by its iconography is to suggest that the genre is static and unchanging, that the gangster film of the thirties is indistinguishable from that of the fifties, or the forties thriller from its counterpart of the sixties. In fact, both thrillers and gangster films, especially the latter, are in constant flux, adding a new thematic dimension here, a new moral emphasis there.

Notes

1. There is within the gangster film a sub-genre beginning with Dillinger (1945) and culminating in Bonnie and Clyde (1967), in which the action does not take place in the city, but in the small towns of the rural mid-West. Even within the gangster films of the thirties (G-Men [1935], for instance) the conventions allowed the city milieu to be forsaken for a final shoot-up at the gangsters' mountain hideout. Thrillers of the last decade have tended to move from the city to more exotic locales such as Florida and the Californian coast.

2. Robert Warshow, "The Gangster as Tragic Hero," in The Immediate Experience (New York: Atheneum, 1971), p. 131.

3. The menace of the automobile is not, of course, confined to the gangster film and thriller. Cars are used as blunt instruments in, for example, the black comedy It's a Mad, Mad, Mad, Mad World.

THE POETICS OF HORROR:
MORE THAN MEETS THE EYE

D. L. White

The concepts commonly associated with and used to describe the horror film may not be enough to explain horror or how films produce it. This is not just to say that horror films are more than the sum of their parts--that can be said of any good film and most bad ones--but that what makes a good film, no matter what its genre, is something which cannot be entirely accounted for by its parts or elements; it is something within the identities of the pieces from which the film is constructed and within the nature of the ways in which they are combined.

Since horror films are usually considered B-movies and are seldom the product of prestige studios, it is particularly easy to think of them as entertainments, as examples of a certain director's, producer's, or actor's skills, or as souvenirs from film history. As a result their analysis is apt to be unusually superficial and specious, too often consisting of little more than a summation of their plot or a listing of their credits. The possibility that a horror film may be, or may have to be, a work of art, although one of the stock reflections of film criticism, tends to go unexplained and undeveloped.

The linking of horror and art, in fact, goes back to Greek tragedy. The word "horror" itself is found in Aristotle's Poetics: "fear and pity may be aroused by spectacular means; but they may also result from the inner structure of the piece ... even without the aid of the eye, he who hears the tale told will thrill with horror and melt to pity at what takes place." Shots of Gothic manors lit by lightning, of shadows glimpsed under doors or of a hand gliding along a banister are examples of the "spectacular means" of horror; they are the kinds of devices that have been used so often

124

that they have come to define the genre of the horror film.
Free of the broader context of the films of which they are a
part or of our memory of similar images in other films,
however, such shots may not necessarily produce fear and
dread.   What is essential to horror may be something else.
Films such as Bava's Nightmare Castle (1966) and Kenton's
House of Frankenstein (1944), that are nothing more than a
stringing together of every horror cliché from dark castles
and mad scientists to the return of the dead to terrorize the
living, provoke only laughter, while a film such as Frankenheimer's The Manchurian Candidate (1962) that has none of
the traditional surface characteristics and gimmicks of the
horror film, or Hitchcock's Psycho (1960), with its obvious
elements of humor, become something profoundly hideous and
shocking.

If a film has anything to do with the supernatural,
cults, monsters, mad scientists, graveyards, old castles, or
uncharted islands it is classified as a work of horror, while
films not dealing with such particulars are apt to be classified as something else.   Any genre whose assumed characteristics are so superficial is easy to affect and easy to abuse
--from carelessness, from overconfidence, from a filmmaker's inability to bridge the gap between what he wants to
say and do, and what he thinks he wants to say and actually
knows how to do.   The test of a film must be the film itself,
not the blanket of terms used to explain or describe it.
When judged in terms of its acting, photography, or direction,
or in terms of the relevance, significance, or contemporary
nature of its content, the horror film is probably no better
and is often a great deal worse than the ordinary western,
melodrama, or comedy.   Such traditional concepts may not
touch what is the real essence of some films.   Likewise, a
film is not a horror film only when it contains certain elements common to the genre; certainly the number of these
elements is no measure of a film's horror or of its quality.

A film succeeds if it provokes emotion, and the more
meaningful the emotion the better the film; one emotion a
film can produce is that of horror.   The outward appearance
of horror films may not even indicate the right direction for
their production or their criticism to take.   By ignoring the
emotions associated with horror such an approach could just
as easily point in the wrong direction.   It is hard enough to
find words and syntax that begin to represent our reactions
and our opinions about a film, but it is even harder to express the beliefs and the logic that lead to that opinion or are

responsible for that reaction. A critic's attempt to simply
describe a film, for example, is apt to be just as much a
rationalization for the underlying, but unstated, assumptions
he brings to bear in his analysis of films and works of art
generally as it is a statement of what he actually saw or
heard in the film in question. Anything more than a plain
positive or negative response may require an argument that
implies more than a critic intends to imply or more than he
actually knows. Unfortunately, the more elegantly the criticism is written the more reasonable it appears and the more
persuasive and potentially misleading it is apt to be.

Moreover, like any work of art a horror film, when
successful, generates some of its power by its confounding
of analysis. The existence of often seen films such as
Weine's Cabinet of Dr. Caligari (1920), Murnau's Nosferatu
(1922), Julian's Phantom of the Opera (1925), Whale's Frankenstein (1931), or Browning's Dracula (1931) can make analysis even more difficult. That these films are better distrib-
uted than others may imply something about their quality,
when in fact it proves nothing. On the other hand, seldom
seen films such as Ingram's The Magician (1926), Curtiz's
Mystery of the Wax Museum (1933), or Weine's Hands of Or-
lac (1925) can also confuse the issue by becoming the justification for elitist attitudes on the part of critics and film buffs.
When those on the outside of the I've-seen-it clique finally
have a chance to see the film for themselves they are apt to
be more interested in it as their ticket into the cognoscenti
than in seeing it for what it is or is not. As a result, the
sprocket-worn classics, regardless of their merits, easily
maintain their reputations while rarer, more esoteric movies
attract followings that are, perhaps, not justified by their
questionable or tangential interest.

In a field such as the horror film, in which the same
story may be filmed again and again, this attitude can distort
our historical and aesthetic perspective to such a degree that
it may be difficult for film-makers setting out to remake a
classic to either learn from its mistakes or duplicate its suc-
cesses. Even more difficult is the creation of a work of horror independent of the subjects and patterns of the genre's
established classics; The Cabinet of Dr. Caligari, for instance, may have had an influence on the German films of
the twenties, but it seems also to be a case of a popular and
acclaimed film having little serious influence on films generally. Its characters and the style of its sets show up in an
incomplete sort of way in subsequent films, but duplicating

these elements alone does not even suggest what gives Caligari its power.   What is essential in Caligari is not even
recaptured by its maker, as Weine's ludicrous Genuine (1920)
testifies.

What Is Primary?

        Any successful film-maker in any genre must turn a
concept or script into a series of images and sounds that expresses the essence, as well as the surface, of the source.
To make a successful horror film a film-maker must decide
what is primary to the production of horror, and if the characteristics found in existing horror films are the best or the
only way to achieve it.   Why, for example, is a film such
as Psycho generally labeled a work of horror and not a detective or crime thriller?   Anyone who has seen Psycho
would agree that it inspires fear and dread and therefore de-
serves to be called a horror film.   Its success in producing
horror in spite of its de-emphasis of many of the elements
common to the horror film and its accentuation of detection/
crime material is an indication that the essence of horror results from other more subtle elements in its make-up.   From
the first shots our attention is on Marion, played by Janet
Leigh, and her frustrated love affair.   Throughout her stealing of the money and her attempt to reach her lover the camera stays either on her or on the envelope containing the
cash.   The details of her behavior and of her handling of the
envelope center our interest on her state of mind, resulting
in a sense of security and inevitability in our following of her
life that is shattered by her murder; yet the killing, surprisingly, does not alter the inertia of the film.   One story does
not stop and another begin; Marion is more than a way of
leading us to Norman Bates.   Instead we see Norman only as
the detective sent to recover the money; Marion's lover or
her sister see him in their search for her.   The rainy night,
the hint of something odd about Norman and his mother, the
Gothic house on the seldom traveled road--these similarities
to other horror films are there, but they are not obtrusive
or fitted into the plot to give a superficial illusion of horror;
they are used because of the qualities they actually possess,
the indications they actually make, and because they are the
most practical narrative devices.   In fact, if analyzed not in
terms of impact, but in terms of genre icons and plot patterns, Psycho would seem to be more a crime film than a
work of horror.

Ulmer's The Black Cat (1934), on the other hand, openly uses what amount to horror clichês, but uses them to set
up a contrast for some departures from tradition that are to
follow. It begins with a young couple's midnight journey
through a strange country, adds a mysterious and menacing
stranger, and ends up stranding the three of them in the middle of a fierce storm. But instead of a dark castle, the film
reverses the cliché and has their refuge be a spotless mod-
ernistic estate; the storm clears to reveal a beautiful spring
day; the stranger becomes the couple's protector; and instead
of the usual stark high-contrast photography we get the soft
patterns of grey usually associated with Sternberg. The
Black Cat, in comparison to Psycho, is not a complex or profound work, but it does achieve horror. Its success in spite
of plot or technique further suggests that it is something else
in the film to which we respond.

If the majority of films achieve anything it is the illusion that they are a phenomenon of our times, that they tell
us something we have not been told before, or that they are
the latest, and therefore the best, examples of film as art.
When such reasons are tempting enough we can fool ourselves
into seeing what we have been led to expect, even if it is not
there in the film at all. Unfortunately, if we can respond to
what is not there, we may fail to respond to what is. The
Kremlin Letter (1970) is an example; its horror, and as a result, its quality, is overlooked. That it stars Bibi Anderssen,
Richard Boone, Patrick O'Neil, George Sanders, Max Von Sy-
dow and Orson Welles, and that it is written and directed by
John Huston have not made it a critical or popular success.
Being on the surface a '60s spy film, it doesn't quite meet
the standards of the art house audience; not being pure-Bond
or pure thriller it doesn't quite meet the entertainment demands of more general audiences. That The Kremlin Letter
is already an overlooked, underrated film demonstrates how
judgments based on cast, plot, director, formal qualities or
social relevance can not help but be arbitrary, inadequate and
misleading when perceived genre is based on the superficial
instead of the subtle.

It is unfortunate that few people have been motivated
to see The Kremlin Letter and that few critics have been able
to describe it as what it is, because besides being essentially
a work of horror it is an impressively good film. It treats
the complexities of its plot as an artistic problem the solving
of which gives each line of dialogue, each shot, and each cut
more concentrated meaning than if the plot had been conven-

tionalized instead of the film's technique and point of view
stylized.   In lieu of the usual unities of time, place or theme,
the film unifies itself and produces its subtle qualities by establishing a peculiar and ever-building momentum in the nature and progression of its episodes.   When not seen as a
composition of these episodes in time the film looks as if it
were just a conglomeration of sex, sadism, and torture.   But
in context such elements are neither blatant nor obtrusive.
We do not see a series of sensationalist scenes passing before us but experience the feeling of being trapped in a world
of perversion, violence, and death.   Seeing only this threatening world, but not the usual characters and trappings we have
come to expect from either spy or horror films, The Kremlin Letter is more than most are willing to take.   It is not a
study of espionage or of political corruption.   These elements
are there but only as a pretext for the film itself.   It is the
film's design, the way its elements are combined in time that
makes The Kremlin Letter horrible, disturbing, and yet beautiful.   However, this perfection of form is hard for people to
accept since they are neither accustomed nor willing to see
something as beautiful when its primary purpose is to capture
ugliness, evil and misery.   What is needed is not a generic
framework based on subject matter alone, but one based on
emotional intent and effect.

The Structure of Horror:
Uncontrolled Causation

     The murder melodrama, the black comedy, the Chand-
ler-Hammett school of detective story, and the spy film are
obvious examples of films that employ much the same methods and devices as does the horror film.   It is the form
these films give their content, however, that determines if
they contain elements of horror, or whether, in the case of
films such as Psycho or The Kremlin Letter, they become
exclusively works of horror.   Mysteries, secrets or evil do-
ings in an old house can be a beginning, but by themselves
can never provoke horror.   A murder or detective story such
as Leni's The Cat and the Canary (1927), West's The Bat
Whispers (1931), or Brahm's The Lodger (1944) is structured
with an end other than horror in mind. Some scenes may
achieve horror, and some characters dramatically experience
horror, but for these films clues, motives and a logical explanation, at least an explanation plausible in hindsight, are
usually crucial, and should not be sacrificed for atmosphere
or dramatic effect.

A horror film, on the other hand, is not just a sequence of certain events: it is the unity of a certain kind of action. It must be more than just the unity of a life, such as that of a mad doctor; of an act, such as his crimes or experiments; of a place, such as the castle where he conducts his experiments; or of a period defined by the prejudices of his colleagues or of the society that drives the doctor to misuse his discovery. Likewise, perfect characterizations, plots with no loose ends, the perfect rendering of atmosphere, elegant camera work or editing may offer the possibility of evoking horror, but by themselves are secondary to its creation. It does no good if a film has no faults in these areas, if at its core it has no cardinal virtue. Psycho and Siegel's Invasion of the Body Snatchers (1956), in fact, use would-be flaws as means of achieving horror. It does not subtract from Invasion of the Body Snatchers that the girl's personality is destroyed and replaced before our eyes whereas all the preceding victims had had their bodies replaced as well. We see that this variation does not destroy the film's believability or quality; it adds to its horror. Neither does it subtract from Psycho that Janet Leigh, the supposed star, is killed in the first third of the film; the fact that the film goes on without her teaches a great deal about what and what not to be concerned with in a film.

No matter how many or how few shots, scenes or episodes make up a work, each such unit and every instant of each unit must communicate the motivations and relationships of the whole of which they are all part. Shots, for instance, may be taken from fresh camera set-ups that force on us specific points of view, or within a single shot a traveling camera, shifting lighting, moving actors, or changing sound or content of some kind may be used to emphasize distinct actions or elements within a more general action. In a successful film, however, each shot must also contribute to the integrity, the character of the larger composition that holds the shots together. I am not implying that each shot in a horror film must show a severed limb or a vampire stalking a victim, but that a pervading sense of horror, like a pervading sense of suspense, comedy, or drama, is a fundamental way of providing the causation in terms of which the many elements of a film, like the events of its plot, are unfolded. Similarly, I do not intend to imply that each shot or unit must maintain the integrity of a single such force. Hitchcock's most suspenseful films, such as The 39 Steps (1935) or North by Northwest (1959), are highly comic; the comedy in Preston Sturges' Sullivan's Travels (1941) or The Miracle at Morgan's

Creek (1944) depends on suspense; Whale's The Bride of
Frankenstein (1935) and The Invisible Man (1933), or Freund's
Mad Love (1935), in addition to being works of horror, em-
ploy both comedy and suspense as well; Dracula, Schoedsack's
The Most Dangerous Game (1932) or Frankenheimer's Seconds
(1966) are highly dramatic.

   Horror, like drama, comedy, or suspense need not be
an obvious component in a film's composition to be the major
factor behind that composition. In the case of Psycho or of
films not usually classified as works of horror, such as The
Kremlin Letter or Huston's A Walk with Love and Death (1969),
Gance's J'Accuse (1938) or Fleischer's The Boston Strangler
(1967), the element of horror is subtle and comes from the
peculiar progression and cumulative impact of the narrative.
No one, for example, in The Kremlin Letter is ever in control of his life or environment; no one is ever sure that his
allies or enemies are what they seem; unknown forces plot
everyone's fate and, eventually, force them to give up those
they love. Like pawns, people move from one insecure position to another and, very soon, we too begin to feel isolated
and defenseless. Such films are best described and, therefore, best criticized as works of horror because of the continual revelation of random, but at the same time, inevitable
forces asserting themselves within their events and characterizations. The lack of comprehensible causation is crucial.

The Psychological Base: Fear of Powerlessness

   The two most popular subjects, not only in films of
all types but in art in general, are probably love and death;
ironically, the two are often linked. The horror film is particularly fond of violent death and bizarre love. Because we
all fear death and try to protect ourselves from it, even the
most clinical and seemingly repellent presentation of, say, a
murder is apt to interest us. But the arousing of our fear
of death by itself is not enough to produce horror; horror requires a certain manipulation of that fear. Psycho provides
a good example; without suggesting that Psycho's murder sequences are not both emotionally and aesthetically compelling
to watch, I wonder how much narrative and, perhaps, even
formal interest they have on their own, apart from the total
film? The film is a composition in time; its purpose is much
more than to establish a framework for these scenes. Psycho
is not shot and edited to match these highly stylized sequences.
Although these scenes are startling, it is significant that they

are not out of place because they are part of a total composition and are linked in a network of causes and effects with
each part of the film.   If a film is to frighten us it must use
elements that are genuinely frightening: in the case of Psycho, not just an old dark house, but the madness of a man
like Norman who lives in that house--not just murder, but
the kind of death from which there is no protection, no warning and no escape.

        The fact that audiences tolerate, even seek out and
enjoy, a film designed to horrify them can tell us a great
deal about what it is in these films that makes them inspire
fear or dread.   Conversely these films can tell something
about those who enjoy them, and, by induction, about people
in general.   Beneath the castles, creatures, and the supernatural elements of successful horror films are less obvious,
but equally as prevalent themes.   Like the forces behind a
dream, these themes appeal to, and as a result gain power
from, basic psychological forces.   An aesthetic of horror is
almost a materialization of psychology--not just an abnormal
psychology, but a psychology of all man's behavior and experiences.   To analyze horror films is to examine them in
terms of the causes and effects, the links that exist between
them and the world that surrounds them, between mechanisms
within them and mechanisms within us.

        Generally the force at work in a horror film might be
defined as the triggering of our basic fear of the unknown,
our fear of being unable to deal with our environment.   Obvious embodiments of this fear are monsters and nightmarish
situations beyond our comprehension and control.   But there
is no reason to assume that horror is synonymous with the
supernatural.   It is not necessary to go beyond conventional
situations to find ingredients for horror.   Although the pre-
ponderance of supernatural themes in horror films and the
fact that it is traditional to associate horror only with the
supernatural indicates the richness of such a source, we must
be careful not to neglect films that have employed other subjects and circumstances to produce horror.   Equally effective
as a situation beyond reason and explanation is that in which
the protagonist understands the dynamics that are at work and
can predict what is going to happen to him as a result, but
still can do nothing to change his fate, as in Seconds or The
Kremlin Letter.   Characteristic of horror is a continual loss
of means of escape until there is no safety and no hope of
safety.   The fear of the panicked man in the opening scene of
Tourneur's The Curse of the Demon (1958), for example, is

easily transmitted to us even though we have as yet no justification for sharing his fears.   Unforeseeable elements in a
situation thought to be under control can also embody horror.
The tightrope walker in Browning's Freaks (1932) thinks she
has successfully hidden her crime from the freaks, and Dr.
Moreau in Kenton's The Island of Lost Souls (1933) thinks he
has his island and his creations hidden from the world and
under his power.   But a combination of insight and accident
proves them both wrong and in the process produces horror
for them and for us.

    Art has always shown that the destructive forces of
man's life are as much a part of his personality as they are
of the world in which he lives.   Almost unintentionally, a
horror film is apt to dramatize this abstraction through a
kind of counterpoint.   For example, there are two kinds of
men contrasted in The Black Cat, two schizoid states of mind
in Psycho, Murnau's Faust (1926) or Mamoulian's Dr. Jekyll
and Mr. Hyde (1932), and in Dracula or The Island of Lost
Souls two kinds of beings--men and those less than men.   In
each case there are two forces at odds with one another, that
through their conflict define one another.   Although horror
films may appear to be politically, sociologically, and philo-
sophically simplistic their point of view is usually highly ambiguous and, one could argue therefore, highly realistic.
They tend to dismiss the possibility of making simple moral
judgments on their content or characterizations, the result
being that they are left with the more general but also more
profound themes of guilt and responsibility, and of life and
death.   This is, ultimately, the genre's claim to fame.   Even
the most simple-minded horror film, as if by accident, asks
the same questions as do the greatest works of art.   The
fact that many of us find horror films so intriguing may indicate that they also provide an answer of sorts.

    In films such as Faust and Seconds the fear of power-
lessness is so all-embracing that it even subordinates the
fear of death, forcing us to recognize that it is more than
just our biological lives we are trying to protect.   A creature
such as King Kong or a man such as Zaroff in The Most Dangerous Game can be frightening, but not as horrifying as the
threat of something seen but not comprehended, as are the
phenomena in Invasion of the Body Snatchers, Dracula, or
Tourneur's I Walked with a Zombie (1943), or the power of
"the company" in Seconds or of the espionage network in The
Manchurian Candidate.   The physical possession of someone
else's body in The Black Cat, Psycho, and The Most

Dangerous Game symbolizes this fear; in Mad Love such possession is represented by a wax statue, in I Walked with a
Zombie by a voodoo doll; in The Island of Lost Souls or Fran-
ju's The Horror Chamber of Dr. Faustus (1960) it is symbolized by mutilation. The dread of not possessing one's self
is so recognizable that in a film such as Dryer's Day of
Wrath (1943) it needs no physical manifestations at all, only
its suggestion through dialogue. These possibilities express
every man's concern for his physical and psychological safety
and individuality. When we see this integrity violated it is a
threat to our ego's ability to protect itself because it dramatizes the failure of another ego to preserve itself.

Threats of Animalization, Fear of the Id

        The horror film offers the possibility of carrying to
its most effective extreme a process common to many genres
of film: it is the same process at work in an individual's dehumanization as in Losey's The Servant (1964) and Accident
(1967), in a family's drift to barbarism as in Visconti's The
Damned (1969), and in a symbolic society's fall from civilization as in Hitchcock's Lifeboat (1943) or Brook's Lord of the
Flies (1962). In the horror film, however, the process becomes one of animalization. It results in ape men and were-
wolves, of people turning into something more primitive than
man, or in Island of Lost Souls and Schaffner's Planet of the
Apes (1968), animals becoming more than animals.

        The problem of making the distinction between an ani-
mal and a perverted member of our own species is generally
solved in one of two ways. The first involves having a man
change from a conventional well-socialized being to a beast,
as the result of some spell as in The Cat People (1942), drug
as in Dr. Jekyll and Mr. Hyde, or disease (be it physical or
mental) as in Dreyer's Vampyr (1932), Nosferatu, or Dracula.
In their normal lives these people are capable of resisting the
destructive impulses to which they freely submit in their other
form. The second solution is to emphasize the sexuality of
the beasts, a common pattern being a human woman threatened by an animalistic male. Although monsters are not always male--e. g., the girl in The Cat People who becomes
the animal personification of the ferocious female--their threat
is almost always sexual. In Nosferatu and Dracula the vampire's threat is more of seducation than of death; in Dr. Jekyll
and Mr. Hyde, Hyde is physically ape-like and abnormally sexual; in Frankenstein the villagers seem to fear not so much a

murderer or a monster as a child molester. The horror-
producing element here is the simultaneous presence of both
a desire to gratify and the fear of losing control of the id--
a fear that the id will become one's whole personality.

A more subtle, but in its way even more disturbing
variation of this fear is that of being under someone else's
power, of losing control over not just the id but the entire
self. Often in films this fear is part sexual, but it is more
than just the desire for sex; it is the conscious or unconscious perversion of sexual or romantic attraction. In the
world of Day of Wrath, for example, sexuality and love are
to be feared; the misinterpreted forces of sexuality become
as threatening as any creature or monster when they are defined as witchcraft. When a man feels a sexual attraction,
as did the old husband for his young wife, he accounts for it
in terms not of something within him, but of something beyond his control, something for which he need accept no responsibility; in short, as his coming under someone else's
power.

What might be called God-mania is also a common
element in the horror film. Zaroff in The Most Dangerous
Game, Moreau in Island of Lost Souls, and Dr. Pretorius in
Bride of Frankenstein literally state their desire to play God.
The theme is just as prevalent, however, in The Magician,
The Cabinet of Dr. Caligari, The Invisible Man, Fisher's
The Man Who Could Cheat Death (1959), or in the actions of
the mother in The Manchurian Candidate or the old man in
Seconds. Of course, there is nothing horrifying in the desire
for power; it is a normal, if not always attractive, human
trait. It is only when someone is accused of being mad with
power and the desire for undreamed of freedoms, of sinning
against nature, or of dealing with forces beyond the reach of
man that the issue of power becomes perfect material for horror. The issue then becomes one of loyalty or resistance to
a set of beliefs; it becomes a matter of faith. We are usually so socialized that we are not aware of the viewpoint or the
orientation by which we live. We tend to be insulated from
criticism of our assumptions and prejudices, and blind to the
potential validity of the assumptions of others. As a result,
a direct attack on something such as our society's political or
religious beliefs is apt to be ineffective. The horror film,
however, can dramatize the frailty and arbitrariness of such
assumptions in its characters and institutions, and can let us
see our assumptions in a more critical way than is comforta-
ble. In a film such as Bride of Frankenstein the result is

humorous; the film's personalities are nothing more than a
lumping together of ludicrous prejudices.   In a film such as
Island of Lost Souls, on the other hand, the result is true
horror.   When the beasts' society crumbles it carries its
laws and beliefs to their logical conclusion, releasing a sort
of mass animalization.

The orientation of the society of Day of Wrath is so
enclosed and self-perpetuating that the destructiveness of its
assumptions becomes visible only through its distortion of sex.
The satirical metaphor of Victorian sex codes of Nosferatu,
Dracula, or Island of Lost Souls represents similar sexual
world views.   Misinterpretations of sex, however, can also
be shown through a single man's perverted point of view.   In
The Black Cat Karloff's preserving the bodies of his dead
wives and marrying his daughter is a shocking but at the
same time intriguing breach of conventional taboos.   Whereas
this character builds his own isolated world to hide his madness, Dr. Gogol in Mad Love constructs a socially acceptable
facade that both disguises and satisfies his fixation with the
mutilated--he becomes a plastic surgeon and habitué of a theater specializing, like him, in the sadistic and physically grotesque.   Norman Bates in Psycho, on the other hand, builds
an interior wall to hide one half of his personality from the
other.   The frustrations behind the actions of his two selves
become apparent because they parallel the frustrations of
Marion and her lover.   Marion's stealing of the money springs
from the healthy and normal desire to be able to marry and
be independent of her family.   Next to her crime, however,
are Norman's murders, that are a perverted and abnormal
working out of the same personal conflicts and sexual drives
that motivate Marion.   He wants sex, but he is afraid of it.
In lieu of it he kills and gains both a sexual release and an
excuse for abstinence.   In short, all that is represented by
Norman's life and all that is represented by Marion's are
paralleled as well as contrasted.   Such counterpoint is characteristic of the way that horror films inadvertently define
what is supposedly madness, or heresy, and what is not.

Fears of Rejection and Perfection

Perhaps the least obvious fear to be found in horror
films, but also the most pervasive, is that of being cut off
from others, of being rejected by those around one.   Like the
fear of death, which centers attention on things which could
destroy life, this fear of alienation draws our attention to those

things in us and around us by which we define ourselves as
living, functioning human beings. As compelling as any scene
in film is the sequence in Invasion of the Body Snatchers in
which the girl's personality changes before our eyes and those
of her lover, in fact changes during their kiss. In a more
straightforward but still moving scene in Vampyr one sister
already infected by the vampire must be restrained from at-
tacking her sister. In both cases, within a single shot all
that is meant by trust and love is shattered. The projection
of this fear of estrangement is also effective. The young
couples in The Black Cat and in The Most Dangerous Game
are cut off from the society they know and can deal with;
they are forced into a strange world without knowing the rules
of that world and, until they learn them, they are under the
power of forces they do not understand. In Day of Wrath it
is the fact that one person does understand more than his
peers that isolates him, or in the case of Invasion of the
Body Snatchers and The Cat People compels him to go to a
psychiatrist. Because someone knows more than the conventional viewpoint allowed by his society he is declared mad or,
in Day of Wrath, a witch. Just seeing that such mechanisms
exist is enough to provoke horror. The threat is always there,
that even knowing the rules or carrying the correct assumptions is no guarantee of understanding or of being a part of
the world into which you are born. The monster in Bride of
Frankenstein and the doctor in The Invisible Man are rejected
by their worlds because they personify the unknown; they gain
our sympathy because of this rejection and cease to be a
threat. It is the bloated villagers, the shrieking women, and
the police in their ignorance that become the monsters. That
such people can sanctimoniously intimidate and even kill those
who deviate from their codes of behavior forces us to recognize that similar threats can be made on us.

        The fears in horror films rise from sociological as
well as psychological themes. Count Dracula's power over
the villagers, or Dr. Moreau's authority over his creatures,
is, for example, the result of social stratification. Typically
the villains of horror get away with their crimes because they
are, like Dracula or Baron Frankenstein, aristocrats, and as
such must be unquestioningly obeyed; because they have
achieved a respected status as professors or scientists like
Jekyll or Gogol in Mad Love; or because they are rich like
Moreau and can buy the complicity they need and employ men
rejected by the respectable world. In contrast, the scientist
in The Invisible Man fails in his plan to capitalize on his experiments because he cannot establish authority over the

convention-bound man.   Characteristic of horror is the theme
of unrestricted freedoms for the few and too many covert
regulations for the many.   In Invasion of the Body Snatchers
the fear is specifically that of a perfectly regulated society,
perfect in the sense that each of its members is free of disruptive individuality and inescapably locked in his sociological
niche.

        No matter how bizarre or twisted the world of a film,
it still must co-exist with our memory of the larger non-film
world; in short, it must be credible.   The problem in Psycho,
for example, is to create the appearance of a friendly, health-
y, although troubled young man while at the same time showing in his actions the menacing base beneath the appearance;
it is the same problem as that in The Manchurian Candidate
and in Seconds, and the reverse of that in The Black Cat,
where the hint of a friend must exist beneath Bela Lugosi's
menacing surface.   Because of the potential contrasts between
a character's appearance and his actions, or because of the
abrupt changes possible in his behavior through time, the horror film builds a degree of unpredictability into its view of
human personality and, as a result, nullifies the usual clues
and indicators we use in judging people and in what to expect
of them.   We are constantly reminded that there is a potential for evil in some and we are constantly warned that we
can never protect ourselves from evil in us or in someone
close to us.   The fact that horror films are not bound by convention to dwell on the good in man only emphasizes this fear.

        It is in films employing relatively simple plots, few
characters, and a limited range of themes and techniques that
it is easiest to construct parallels, references, and a structure that fully utilizes all the elements possible in this over-
laying of a fantastic and a realistic world.   This simplicity
can result in a kind of perfection, but it is the perfection of
a design and not a composition; I Walked with a Zombie, Bal-
con's production of Dead of Night (1945), Island of Lost Souls,
and The Black Cat are works of this kind.

Chaos of the World and of Dreams

        When a more complex conception with more elements
to interrelate achieves perfection, the result can be levels of
meaning not possible in the simpler work.   It is the adding of
profound statement to perfect design that makes such films as
Vampyr or Day of Wrath, Freaks, Dr. Jekyll and Mr. Hyde,

Invasion of the Body Snatchers, Psycho, The Manchurian
Candidate, or The Kremlin Letter such achievements. The
best horror films create something that stands for the chaos
of the world. Mad Love, Psycho, and Bride of Frankenstein
create parallel worlds of confusion in their characters' minds;
Vampyr, Island of Lost Souls, and Day of Wrath create so-
cieties that stand as microcosms for that confusion. The
Manchurian Candidate or Invasion of the Body Snatchers do
both. They may present a simplified, stylized view of the
world but they never take the world for granted.

A successful horror film forces us to suspend our reliance on the conventional frame of reference of normal life;
we are forced to function on its terms. We do not have to
believe that people can turn into panthers as in The Cat People, into birds as in Freaks or wolves as in Dracula. We
only have to give up for a time facts we bring into the theater with us, and accept that some of the film's characters
believe that such occurrences are facts. If the film's propositions do not refute each other and are not dependent on
each other in such a way that if we reject one we must also
reject those that follow from it, then the horror of a film
can expand to include every element and every scene. Like
the musical, the horror film is not expected to conform to
the conventions of traditional plot patterns or of daily life.
It is free to translate everything from psychoanalytic theory
to the whimsical intuitions of its makers into images, sounds
and events of film, to become an objective presentation of
subjective human experiences. In this sense films such as
Mad Love and Bride of Frankenstein are the extreme examples not only of their genre, but of film in general. Each
contains so many elements at odds with each other that they
effectively cancel one another out to reveal something of what
lies beneath. Their mixture of comedy and tragedy, reality
and fantasy, captures something of the chaos of the world and
some of the ways men go about giving that chaos the illusion
of order. Such films show that normal society, and normal
people and their lives, are not as rational as they seem, and
that abnormal people like Gogol in Mad Love or Norman in
Psycho are not as irrational or their acts as unintelligible as
they, at first, appear.

Horror films come in black and white and in color;
they can be highly stylized as is Caligari or pseudo-documen-
tary as is Watkins' War Game (1967); they are made by both
good and bad film-makers. There seem to be no particular
camera angles or movements, editing techniques, acting styles,

make-up methods, or set designs common to all horror films
or essential to the production of horror. However, there is
a technique, as distinct from theme, that is found to some
degree in all works of horror. It can result from the way a
writer describes a shot or a cut, from the way a cameraman
frames a shot or lights a scene, from the way an editor as-
sembles that scene or from the way the sound mixer manipu-
lates its sound, or it can result from the way a director
places and moves his actors and props. We all dream, and
as a result can see elements or scenes in films as having
the quality of a dream, or psychological aberrations or hallu-
cinations. The horror of Polanski's Repulsion (1965), for example, does not come just from the theme of the girl's fear
of sex. Instead it results from film's ability to make her
real life and her fantasy life look and sound the same, and to
manipulate the physical appearance of both to capture her increasing isolation and madness by literally making the ceil-
ings increasingly nearer, the corridors longer, the rooms
larger, the lighting darker, and the sounds more distant.

In Preston Sturges' comedy Unfaithfully Yours (1947),
there is a dream sequence for the length of which the film
becomes a work of horror. An orchestra conductor suspects
his wife of adultery, and while conducting a concert visualizes
a grotesque plan to kill her and blame her death on the sus-
pected lover. He dreams of making a phonograph record of
what sounds like his wife's screams calling her lover's name,
of killing his wife, placing the record player in the room with
her corpse, and inviting the boyfriend to wait for her in the
next room. When the record comes on the fake screams attract the innocent man into the adjoining room where he is
confronted with the woman, her throat cut, yet apparently
naming him as her murderer. Horror depends on the linking
or superimposition of events, objects, or sounds that may
have no conscious or logical meaning, but contain a subconscious, irrational association. The horror of this sequence
in Unfaithfully Yours comes from the contrast of the film's
images and sounds, and the ability of that contrast to communicate the incongruity of the boyfriend's knowing the woman
is dead, but hoping she is alive, coupled with the husband's
simultaneous desire to see her dead, yet also alive. Incorporating such a grotesque sequence in a comedy is a highly am-
bitious undertaking; the probability of failure is far greater
than if a comic sequence were used in a horror film. If this
scene had not been handled as a fantasy, if it had been identified as a dream only when over, not only would its potential
for comedy within the context of the film have been lost, but
the film itself would have become, not charming, but hideous.

As the dream can express what a character would not normally express consciously, the aberration elements of the dream can become confused with normal life, providing a character with a way of doing what he wants to do while denying that he has done it or desired to do it.   The husband's aberration in Day of Wrath, that his wife is a witch, for example, lets him avoid the responsibility of his lust.   In Mad Love Gogol's belief that the statue, like Pygmalion's, has come alive is the illusion he constructs to deal with the pressures of a world he cannot overcome.   The murderer's belief in Florey's Beast with Five Fingers (1947), that the severed hand has come alive, is his way of hiding from himself that he, not the hand, is the killer.   Each of these men has suppressed forces within himself and transferred the threat to objects or to other people; for them a dream has become reality.   Each film shows their insanity by distorting the world in terms of their point of view.   Horror depends on sensing, but not knowing, what to believe or who is or is not mad.   Seeing the brain-washed veteran kill his wife in The Manchurian Candidate, Perry kill the family in Richard Brooks' In Cold Blood (1967), or the plumber skillfully and randomly kill in Fleischer's The Boston Strangler is a threat to us because we see the vulnerability of the victims and the inevitability of the crimes in light of the killers' twisted yet sympathetic personalities.

Films may also harness the dream's potential for communicating abnormal mental processes, not by incorporating a dream sequence or a character's dream-like aberrations, but by the film itself becoming like a dream or, in the case of horror films, a nightmare--Hitchcock's Vertigo (1958) or Marnie (1964), or Dead of Night.   The effects of confusion, misinterpretation or prejudice are often a concern in art, and are of necessity always a theme in works of horror.   The dreams of the hypnotized soldiers in The Manchurian Candidate, for example, provide a way to project elements of their personalities as well as their plight.   Each soldier sees in his dreams the conference at which the extent of their suggestibility is demonstrated to Russian and Chinese officials; but each remembers the conference in a jumbled way, sometimes as it was, sometimes as the garden club meeting they were told it was, but more often as a jumbled merging of the two.   For example, the voices of the officials come out of the mouths of the lady members of the garden club.   At other times the lady lecturing about begonias is seen before portraits of Stalin and Lenin; one black soldier sees the odd-sounding ladies as black.   In Marnie a childhood dream blends with the present. A shot begins at night in a shabby room with a hand tapping

on the outside of a window, then pans to show Marnie sleeping during the day in her expensively furnished room.

   In Dead of Night sets, characters, and dialogue from
the film's half-dozen independent episodes merge into a pro-
gressively more complex and horrifying finale that ends by
repeating the film's beginning as a déjà vu experience; each
of these dreams becomes a recognizable whole only when it
depicts a murder, repressed in the case of Marnie, committed under suggestion as in The Manchurian Candidate, or
not yet committed, but foreshadowed, as in Dead of Night.
Many films not usually thought of as works of horror can be
described and analyzed in terms of their dream-like qualities,
Bunuel's El (1952), Bergman's The Silence (1963) or Fellini-
Satyricon (1970), to suggest a few. In each of these films
there is the chance and sometimes the inevitability that the
dream will become a nightmare, and that like the characters
in the film we will be trapped in that nightmare. The degen-
eration of the beggars' banquet in Bunuel's Viridiana (1961),
Juliet's worsening neurosis in Fellini's Juliet of the Spirits
(1965), or the interrogations in Bergman's Shame (1968) or
Welles' The Trial (1963) are in essence scenes of horror that
taint the entire films of which they are part.

Extensions of Everyday Fears

   Horror should not be considered an exotic emotion,
but rather one based on the common fears of everyday life.
Like the fears expressed and resolved through dreams, the
fears found in horror films often take exotic and barely recognizable forms so that they will not be unbearably threatening while being resolved. Films such as The Kremlin Letter
and The Boston Strangler, however, do not disguise their horror producing elements. They do not create a safe emotional
distance for the viewer, and as a result, are often seen as
depraved, repulsive, and unrealistic even though they themati-
cally parallel the popular horror films of the past. The Boston Strangler, for example, explores the consequences of the
fear of death, fear of powerlessness, fear of alienation and
fear of mutilation; it dramatizes man's ability to see threatening forces in himself as evil in others; it is the extreme example of a man who has lost control of himself and who is
both overpowered by his society and in revolt against it; and
it is a good example of film's ability to capture the confusion
of reality, memory, and dream. The only way to reveal the
forces at work, and the implications of the events and tech-

niques, in such films as The Boston Strangler, A Walk with
Love and Death, or Seconds is through the use of the concept
of horror. As a critical tool, horror should not be restricted to films employing the same devices, plots or actors as
the standards of the genre. Anyone not willing to apply the
concepts of horror to any work that employs its themes and
forces has little chance of appraising the total value of many,
perhaps most, works.

     Is it always necessary to draw a line between the fic-
tional world of the film and the real world? Seconds is one
of the most realistic horror films. It is set in the recognizable present and deals with the problems of contemporary
American society; its central character is bound, defined, and
frustrated by the conventions, ambitions, and standards of our
times. Through surgery, falsified documents, and relocation
he is offered a second life, a chance to be free of the re-
strictions with which he has lived so long. His change of
perspective, however, besides letting him recognize the assumptions and prejudices that make up his personality, lets
him see that the organization that sold him his new life has
assumed the same role in that life that the pressures and institutions of society took in his old one. First society, and
then the organization that has replaced it, become like monsters. Society and the omniscient organization know all about
him and can control the most subtle details of his behavior.
In contrast, he knows nothing about their workings and is powerless to influence any of their decisions concerning him.
One by one, the indicators he has used to judge people, situations, and emotions are shown to be useless, leaving him
helpless to deal with the most mundane events. Out of the
ordinary events of life--meeting a girl, having a cocktail party, talking to an old friend--comes horror. He is told to ad-
just to his new surroundings and to find a personality to match
his new appearance. But he has no way to justify the assumptions of his society or to determine his position within it. Instead of gaining a new personality he loses his old. His ego
is confronted with the most horrifying realization possible--
that it is nothing. The arbitrariness, efficiency, and inevitability of his death are consistent with his impotence and un-
importance in the world around him.

     The horror of impotence in the face of overwhelming
authority, expressed traditionally through figures such as
Caligari, Moreau, or the sorcerer in The Magician, is no
more and no less powerful than when expressed more realis-
tically by the Inquisition-like threat of Day of Wrath, the

computer in Sargent's <u>Colossus</u> (1970), the feudal system in Mizoguchi's <u>Sansho, the Bailiff</u> (1954), or the organization in <u>Seconds</u>. The fears of modern life are essentially the same as fears found throughout history and art; if they differ it is only in form, as the threat of mass annihilation from plague differs from that of nuclear war. More realistic, more contemporary horror films can do everything the traditional horror films do, and achieve something more. They can help people deal with such fears, can help both those who make the films and those who experience them to face and, as a result, see more clearly not only the nature of the fears brought on by contemporary society but the nature of that society itself.

THE AESTHETICS OF FORM AND CONVENTION
IN THE MOVIE MUSICAL

Timothy E. Scheurer

What do you go for----Go see a show for?
Tell the truth, you go to see those beautiful Dames.   --Al Dubin and Harry Warren

In the scene from Ray Enright and Busby Berkeley's
Dames (1934) from which the above lyric is taken, the ener-
getic young producer (Dick Powell) and his "backers" involved
in "putting-on-the-show" are discussing what makes a show
popular with an audience; oddly enough, after forty years the
question is still being discussed among aficionados of the Film
Musical and popular film in general. In spite of the facts
that critical response to the Film Musical has been traditionally less than edifying and that film scholars have only touched
on it tangentially, large crowds have flocked to see musicals
since movies first learned to talk. Unfortunately, most of the
criticism of the Film Musical has run along one track, an essentially historical one, and its primary thesis has been similar to one offered by Roy Paul Madsen, who echoes an ostensible consensus opinion by opting for the "escapist" argument:

> Although escapism can be used to justify anything,
> the thin stories and minuscule messages of the aver-
> age musical make it clear that the only reason it
> thrives during days of ordeal is that it offers the
> national audience collective pleasure, relaxation and
> escapism. Film and television musicals really find
> their social value, if they need one, in giving the
> viewer something to sing about and in providing a
> respite from continual confrontation with The Prob-
> lems. [1]

It's a familiar argument--one at least as old as Dubin and

Warren's lyrics for Dames: the Film Musical offers entertainment for entertainment's sake and in this way it serves
some cryptic utilitarian purpose.

The "escapist" theory is ultimately too confining, even
though it seems to have the popular culture in mind. Neither
should it be assumed that Madsen's argument is invalid--one
need only look at the great proliferation of musicals during
the Depression, World War II, and the Korean conflict to understand that--but it really only treats one side of the popular response to the Film Musical. For in examining the so-
cio-historico-cultural tableau shrouding a popular art form we
tend to dismiss the question of what sort of inherent aesthetic
appeal a film genre as genre may have. Perhaps, then, it
would be useful to suspend the prevailing critical tide and examine the forms and conventions of the Film Musical and how
they function, discussing briefly its aims on a broad structural plane, and then (reversing yet another prevalent critical
trend)[2] moving into a discussion of the major components intrinsic to the genre and its form: music, dance, and libretto,
and how they function and distinguish the Film Musical as a
whole.

The whole idea of the Film Musical is predicated on
the concept that music and, in the majority of cases, dance
are used in part to tell a story. There are a few instances
where a story is rendered entirely through the medium of
music, as in Jacques Demy's The Umbrellas of Cherbourg
(1964), but for the most part the musical is distinguished by
its finely balanced interplay and synthesis of non-musical and
musical sequences. In the context of the musical as a whole,
music is the most important governing principle in the style,
structural unity and movement of the film. The use of music
in drama as such first of all forces us to reexamine, on a
large contextual basis, the mode of reality presented by the
Film Musical.

Louis D. Giannetti has noted that "realistic film theo-
rists either ignore the musical, or make an exception of it";[3]
the reason for this is that the musical is a highly stylized
representation of life where the reality is not revealed through
the actions we normally associate with everyday living, but
where a different mode of reality, the inner reality of feelings, emotions, and instincts are given metaphoric and symbolic expression through the means of music and dance. The
musical is not so much a reflection of life as it is an interpretation of life; it dispenses with normal dialogue or soliloquy

in favor of the more metaphoric medium of music where elements like harmony, melody, and rhythm coupled with a lyric
phrase become manifestations of the inner feelings and motivational impulses of the characters, and which, consequently,
control the action and impel it forward. To understand the
Film Musical demands that we understand the roles stylization
and expression play in the song and the dance sequences which
in large part determine the structural movement of the film
as a whole; as Rouben Mamoulian notes, "Stylization, integral-
ly and properly carried out, conveys a deeper reality to the
audience than everyday kitchen naturalism can. "[4] Thus it is
essential that the audience not only understand--or better,
perhaps, accept--the mode of reality presented in a musical,
but that the director and other artists involved in the musical
create a world where it is natural to sing and dance about
something when the feeling arises or is demanded. If an
audience is to become involved in or derive any sort of aesthetic experience from a Film Musical their sensibilities must be
engaged on this level and the elements of music, dance, and
libretto must be directed toward this end.

How well a Film Musical works as a whole, how well
it creates a specific mode of reality, is heavily incumbent
upon how well musical numbers are varied, coordinated and
integrated. Music is capable of expressing many emotions or
underscoring any variety of moods and actions;[5] a song with
a tendency toward repetition of notes has, depending to a certain extent of course on rhythm, an aggressive quality;[6] while
a song written, let us say, stepwise and at a slower or mod-
erate tempo often flows and is capable of vacillating between
poles of elevation and calm. Both types of song, and the
variants of these two types, serve as important structural
components in the musical. On The Town (1949), for example, is a tremendous success because it begins on a note of
aggressive intensity with the song "New York, New York"
which the three sailors (Gene Kelly, Frank Sinatra, and Jules
Munshin) sing as they begin their quest for love and laughs
during their leave in New York. The film maintains that
same intensity through Ann Miller's song and dance in the museum ("Prehistoric Man"), to the number performed atop the
Empire State Building by the sailors and their girls ("On the
Town"), and into the dream ballet, "A Day in New York" (a
modification of the Jerome Robbins and Leonard Bernstein
ballet Fancy Free), which rhythmically, melodically, and the-
matically underpins Gaby's (Gene Kelly) problems in trying to
establish a permanent romantic relationship with Ivy (Vera-
Ellen). The ballet is particularly effective in light of an

earlier sequence, a charm song, "Main Street," performed
by Kelly and Vera-Ellen which sheers off some of Ivy's stolid
and pretentious veneer to reveal her real self and her affection for the love-struck Gaby.

Another film, It's Always Fair Weather (1955), begins,
like On The Town, with a rather aggressive song and dance
number performed by three servicemen (Kelly, Dan Dailey,
and Michael Kidd) just returned from the war, but it does not
sustain this feeling throughout. The most obvious omission in
the film, however, in terms of thematic and musical structure
is the absence of a good romantic love ballad and accompanying love dance which should be performed by Kelly and Cyd
Charisse, his romantic interest; throughout the film Kelly has
been struggling with his inability to commit himself to anything, but by the film's end he is firmly committed to Charisse. A dance performed by the two would have established
a solid medium of expression for their somewhat ambiguous
feelings, reinforcing the theme of the film and at the same
time answering the conventional exigencies of the genre. In
the latter film a lack of varied songs is clearly a weakness
because it has not, through song, offered the viewer the opportunity to experience and understand the multifaceted natures
of the different characters and their relationship to one another.

It is exactly this implementation of a balanced and yet
varied score which makes the Astaire-Rogers musicals so
successful. In Top Hat (1935), for instance, there are two
rhythm numbers ("No Strings" and "Top Hat, White Tie and
Tails") which help delineate Jerry's (Fred Astaire) character;
there is a "charm song" ("Isn't This a Lovely Day") which
sustains an optimistic mood at a crucial point; there is a
"love ballad" ("Cheek to Cheek") which, with its unusual 64-
bar chorus, offers Jerry a perfect opportunity to woo and win
Dale (Ginger Rogers); and, finally, there is a musical scene
number ("The Piccolino"). A well rounded musical score is
essential in a good Musical for more than just entertainment's
sake: it is our direct encounter with the characters' way of
looking at the world and life.

In creating effective musical numbers for a Musical
the film medium commands a special power because it can
complement and explore the melodic, rhythmic, and lyrical
possibilities of the music through a variety of cinematic techniques. This, of course, is more evident in dance sequences,
but it is also important in filming the simple rendering of a

song by a character. During the singing of a love ballad, for
instance, the camera can not only register the feelings of the
singer through close-ups, but also, with, perhaps, the small-
est most fluid movement, can record the reaction of the partner as a particularly melodious or lyrically meaningful phrase
is sung. Or through inventive editing it can capture the joy-
ful rhythm of one man's statement about himself and life, as
in Norman Jewison's filming of "If I Were a Rich Man" in
Fiddler on the Roof (1971). In any case, what the director
must do is complement in filmic terms what is being sung
and said in musical terms; he must capture that element which
all good songs have in common: the neat fusion of the general (or familiar) and the particular. [7]

For a song to function effectively in a Musical it must
not only capture and communicate the total mood of the dramatic situation, but it also must be familiar enough to the
audience, both musically and lyrically, to engage their attention. A song of any type written in a twelve-tone row will
probably detract more from the situation than further it, no
matter how relevant the lyric may be to the situation or to
the people's lives in the audience. Popular music lends itself well to the Film Musical as, generally, the dramatic situations depicted are meant to communicate something not only
within the film but to the audience, who can apprehend more
readily the basic song structures of popular music as well as
the native language idioms characteristic of the musical's song
lyrics. In a song situation, then, the melodic, harmonic, and
rhythmic elements of the music do the most in establishing a
"general" feeling for the situation; music should serve as a
metaphor in a song situation: it should match and develop the
meaning, mood, and rhythm of the dramatic situation through
appropriate musical structure. The filmmaker must, in turn,
complement this general feeling established by the song in
filmic terms. While keeping his eye on the general structure
and movement of a scene, the filmmaker must also be aware
of the degree of particularization presented in the lyrics of
the song; the lyrics of a song serve as the bridge between
various sequences by helping us keep a finger on the spoken
story line. The lyric is also the verbalization of a particular
feeling or idea (underlined by the music) that a particular character is attempting to express. Lehman Engel states: "One
element all best lyrics have in common is directness and precision of idea and image. "[8] The filmmaker must complement
the lyric with a similar eye toward precision of idea and image. A good example occurs in Cover Girl (1944) when Rita
Hayworth sings the Ira Gershwin-Jerome Kern ballad "Long

Ago and Far Away" to Gene Kelly in the nightclub. The director, Charles Vidor, begins with a medium shot of Hayworth reassuringly singing to Kelly of her love for him; the next shot is a close-up of Kelly with a troubled look on his face but at the same time resolutely set in rejecting her plea; back to a close-up of Hayworth, now more saddened, singing rather ironically, "The dream I dreamed was not denied me." Vidor then opens the scene to take in both the principals while Hayworth sings: "Just one look and then I knew/That all I longed for, long ago, was you." At this point Kelly changes mood (a two-shot inserted here) and as he goes to her the camera pulls back and the dance begins. In this scene Vidor has captured not only the evocative longing sort of quality in Kern's melody but has also reinforced the specific message of the lyrics through specific film techniques. It is this sort of treatment of songs that enables the Film Musical to transcend what is normally done on the Broadway stage, and, consequently, makes it a special form of art.

The lyrics of a song clearly help identify and particularize character in a song situation, but it is the dance which strives further to bring to the surface the complexity of emotions residing within a character. Just as the appropriate lyric phrase must be welded to the given musical phrase, so the dance must also work closely with the music but in a much more sophisticated fashion. Dance, in the majority of cases, evolves out of a song situation; it extends and amplifies through bodily and, essentially, non-verbal movement what was stated in the lyric, and, at the same time, it attempts to move the degree of expression and interpretation onto a more elevated or, at least, more metaphoric plane. Peter Hogue, in an article on The Band Wagon (1953), illustrates this principle in his discussion of Fred Astaire's "By Myself" number from the film: "Though piqued by neglect, his vigor and sense of purpose are quickly renewed as his walk from the station inevitably (because of the genre) yet spontaneously (because of Astaire) elicits a song and dance. The song tells us of Hunter's determination in live in 'a world of my own' and the dance reveals his inner resources for self sustenance. In the early scenes in particular, dance is more than entertainment and more than art; it is both a catalyst for, and an expression of, the quintessential vitality which is itself the meaning of Hunter's life."[9] The dance situations in a Film Musical, then, should, in the context of the film as a whole, bring us to a closer understanding of the characters as individuals and how they stand in relationship to one another and their environment.

Within this broader context the dance serves more specific functions. Bob Fosse says, in John Kobal's Gotta Sing
Gotta Dance: A Pictorial History of Film Musicals,[10] that
the dance can "set the environment or atmosphere or character behavior of a particular locale or particular set of characters...." This type or function of dance enables the audience to get a general feeling for a place in the musical and
it also serves to reinforce the basic texture and mood of the
musical as a whole; a dance of this sort is also instrumental
in establishing basic conflicts among and motivational patterns
in different characters. The opening sequence of West Side
Story (1961), for instance, serves both ends. The high aerial
shot moving into a more specific view of the Jets on the play-
ground and the unfolding dance illustrates and delineates not
only the dismal surroundings of New York's west side but also,
through Jerome Robbins' marvelous jazz ballet choreography
and Robert Wise's crisp camera work, the intensity of the
basic conflict between the gangs.

Another end dance should attempt to achieve is to
"Move the story and character along. Further the action...."
This, of course, is the most obvious of all criteria for effective dance numbers; in essence the dance should be of such a
nature that it seems all of a piece with the action preceding
and following the number. A good example of a song and
dance which fulfills this end is "Goin' Courtin'" in Seven
Brides for Seven Brothers (1954), where Jane Powell gently
initiates the bumbling brothers to the "glories" of wooing and
dancing to a point where they are joyously involved in their
new-found ability to dance and are ready to go to the forth-
coming barn-raising. Still another fine example of this type
of dance is the "Dancing in the Dark" sequence from The
Band Wagon. In the film, prior to the dance sequence,
Astaire and Cyd Charisse believe they cannot work together,
but as they are walking together late one evening the sounds
of Arthur Schwartz's melody drift in and they find themselves
dancing to the music and subsequently with one another; tensions are resolved.

Fosse states that dance can also be employed to "Express a particular emotion. This does not necessarily move
the story along but does elaborate on a particular feeling of
the moment. Dances of 'love' would fall into this group. Also dances of elation...." In this type of number the dynamic
fusion of music, dance, and cinematography is of the utmost
importance because so much of what is to be expressed is
reliant upon the type of melody used in conjunction with the

combined rhythms of song, dance, and camera work. The
most notable examples of this type or function of dance are
the ballad or love dances in the Astaire-Rogers films ("Night
and Day" from The Gay Divorcee [1934], "Cheek to Cheek"
from Top Hat, and "Let's Face the Music and Dance" from
Follow the Fleet [1936], to name but three). Another real
classic of this type is Gene Kelly's "alter ego" dance in Cover Girl, in which Kelly dances with his own image by means
of double-exposure photography. In deference to Fosse, most
dances should, and oftentimes do, advance the story. Because emotions are so important in character motivation,
dances of this nature enable us to understand better why a
character acts as he does and where his emotions will eventually lead him or her in the total movement of the story.

"The last group that comes to mind," Fosse states,
"are really what could be called just 'entertainment'...."
Here Fosse cites his own "Steam Heat" number from Pajama
Game (1957). The most obvious dances of this type, however,
are Busby Berkeley's playlets ("42nd Street" from 42nd Street
[1933], "By a Waterfall" from Footlight Parade [1933], "I Only Have Eyes for You" from Dames, etc.) and the large production numbers from revue Musicals (Ziegfeld Follies [1946],
etc.) and those in musical biographies (Till the Clouds Roll
By [1946], Three Little Words [1950], Night and Day [1946],
etc.). In entertainment numbers the dance is filmed almost
exclusively for effect, with the camera eye directing all its
attention on the form. By the same token, however, entertainment numbers can be neatly integrated into a film's structure. For instance, in backstage musicals like 42nd Street
the entertainment numbers are designed to show us how well
the show (which has been a "blood and guts" effort to put together) is going; we should, in a sense, get a feeling of being
"wowed" much as the fictional audience supposedly watching
the number in the theatre is.

An effective dance number in a Film Musical should
attempt to achieve all the above ends, and, in fact, most good
numbers do so without seeming pretentious or too caught up in
their own art. Dance, by its nature, is a stylized reflection
and interpretation of reality; thus, as the audience views a
dance they should be aware of the element of communication
being expressed by the characters, either internally or between
one another. The filmmaker's and choreographer's tasks are
to engage their audience's interest and involvement in this abstract mode of reality being presented in the dance, and to do
this they have a multitude of cinematic techniques at their

disposal. The principle concern, however, in filming dance
sequences is choreographing the camera to suit the individual
dance routine. As Walter Sorell points out: "Filmed dance
must ... be a compromise. The movement of the camera
must serve the movement of the dance, and the dance must
be choreographed with an eye to the camera."[11] In essence
what this "compromise" means is that the director not only
turns an eye inward toward the form and movement of the
dance itself, but that he also turns his eye outward toward
how the audience will and should perceive the action. By
choreographing the camera as such, the filmmaker and choreographer give it the stature of a participant in the dance.[12]
Through movement, or compression and expansion of the visual image, or editing, the filmmaker is able to anticipate and
embellish movement and, ultimately, control the message being communicated in the dance. Any dance can become a
failure the minute the filmmaker allows his camera to take
off on its own flights of fancy, or the minute he allows the
camera to "assert its own personality."[13] As in ballet, where
the male figure often is most important as the support for a
ballerina in a pas-de-deux, the filmmaker serves his most important function in supporting the total sweep and message of
the movement going on before him. Walter Terry, in discussing Gene Kelly, states: "Not content with simply photo-
graphing dances, he used the camera's inherent mobility and
almost magical perceptiveness to seek out dance details or,
through absolutely appropriate fantasy, make the dancer a part
of the wind, the rain, the sky, just as a dancer really is in
his own dreams."[14] The Film Musical has broken past the
proscenium arch in recording dance; the camera's flexibility
makes it an explorer: it can delineate character more sharply with a multiplicity of shots and movements, it can create
"real" alter egos, move from reality into fantasy with no
jarring of sensibilities, and it can translate the rhythms of a
person's imagination and feelings into the rhythms of life.

The third essential element of the Film Musical is the
libretto or, as it is oftentimes called, the "book." The book
in the total structure of a Film Musical is the basic subject
matter or idea for the plot--minus the song and dance numbers as totally conceived segments of the plot--which determines what direction the musical will take in terms of conflict and theme. In the case of filmed musicals the book
would be a basic scenario. The fusion of music, dance, and
book ideally evolve a unity so balanced and integrated that the
three elements appear as one.[15] There is a tendency when a
musical does not achieve this fusion to concentrate most of the

criticism on the book, forgetting in the process the formal
distinguishing factor implied by the genre: the communication of the story through the use of music.   Music and dance,
in the main, are implemented in the context of a Film Musical to explore and bring to the surface the intricacies of the
underlying structure of the book.   An effective Film Musical
will take statements of importance, i.e., pieces of the dramatic action where the conflicts, motivational patterns, and
ideas concerned with the theme of the film are of heightened
importance, and express them in musical and/or choreograph-
ic terms; this is a demand--a demand of convention--implied
in the genre of the Film Musical.   In Silk Stockings (1957),
for instance, the starchy Ninotchka's (Cyd Charisse) first
"flowering of feeling" is structurally important and is done
by means of the song "All of You," sung by Fred Astaire,
and a dance number between the two which beautifully illustrates her (up to this point) hidden potential for feeling and
expressiveness.   Nothing of the movement of the film as a
whole is destroyed by an obtrusive number here because fidelity, not only to the story but also to the conventions of the
genre, has been maintained.   This fidelity to convention is
essential to the formal qualities of the Film Musical, and convention also plays an important role in the popularity of the
genre.

        The Film Musical, like other popular art forms, is
highly formulaic; it has always relied upon a solid core of
conventions, especially in its books, to engage the audience's
interest, but it has also been an evolutionary art form in
terms of the artistic inventiveness executed within the formulaic structures.   Up to the mid-1950s most musicals could be
located within one of the following formulas:[16]   1) The revue,
one of the earliest forms, generally presents a variety of acts
ranging from dramatic scenes to musical production numbers;
sometimes, but often times not, there is a thematic idea
which unites the acts; Hollywood Revue of 1929 and Ziegfield
Follies are good examples of this formula.   2) The screen
operetta is most often a love story set in some exotic locale;[17] the music is highly melody-oriented and does not often
draw on typical American jazz rhythms so often implemented
in the "musical comedy," and, for the most part, the lyrics
for the songs aspire to quasi-poetry and do not draw on common speech idioms of the present culture; The Desert Song
(1929), Maytime (1937), and The Student Prince (1954) are
good examples.   3) The backstage musical is concerned with
getting the big show ready for its Broadway debut and all the
problems accompanying this process; 42nd Street and Busby

Berkeley's "Golddiggers" series fall into this category as well
as later films like Summer Stock (1950) and The Band Wagon.
A variant of the formula is Singin' in the Rain (1952), which
basically uses the same conventions but deals with the motion
picture industry.   4) The Cinderella or "rags-to-riches" formula generally chronicles the rise in the world of a star or
some semi-waif like Deanna Durbin or Shirley Temple.   5)
The love/hate, mistaken notion or mistaken identity formula
is often seen in the Astaire-Rogers musicals, and a whole
complex of mistaken notions keeps Easter Parade (1948) (with
Astaire and Judy Garland) predictable yet lively; essentially
in this formula, hate at some point turns into love, and then
to further complicate the plot, one principal or the other generally accepts some idea (false, of course) about the other
which must be overcome if love is to triumph.   6) The musical biography traces the life or career of some individual
whose life is intimately associated with music or the performance of music; The Jolson Story (1946) and Rhapsody in Blue
(1945) (a biopic of George Gershwin) are two of the most popular.   The majority of these formulas had their inception on
the early Broadway stage, where producers and artists became aware of their consistent popular appeal and continued
to implement them.   The Film Musical essentially adopted the
formulas but, like the stage musical, continued to refine them
through a process of evolving inventiveness in the use of music and dance.

        A common critical complaint directed against the mu-
sical is that the creators are relying on the same old conventions in their books.   There is a good reason for drawing
upon formula: a formulaic book or storyline can prove to be
a necessary adjunct to the aesthetic form of the Film Musical.
By providing the audience with a storyline that is basically
familiar, and, in fact, almost archetypal,[18] the artists involved in the musical are able to, first, present the audience
with "familiar shared images and meanings [which] assert an
ongoing continuity of values";[19] and, second, they are able to
exercise a greater degree of artistic freedom in those areas
which define and distinguish the art: music and dance.   By
the same token they are able, through their artistic inventiveness, to present and confront the audience with, as John
Cawelti states in his essay on "The Concept of Formula in the
Study of Popular Literature," "a new perception or meaning
which we have not realized before."[20]   In drawing upon some
fairly well-established formulas, the artists in Film Musicals
are able to infuse new life into characters and situations about
which the audience has a reasonable amount of prior knowledge.

We all know that Gene Kelly is out to woo and win Leslie
Caron in An American in Paris (1951), but when will the crucial first romantic encounter come?   How will Kelly's character go about winning her?   In keeping with the conventions
of the genre he sings "Love Is Here to Stay" and the ensuing
dance of give and take solidifies the love relationship, yet it
is very different from other scenes of its kind.   This is not
to say that the book for a musical must be idiotically simple
so that artists can be more artistic; on the contrary, a musical book may be totally imaginative, unlike anything written
before, but it still must be able to assimilate the more abstract art forms of music and dance and use them to their
full advantage in the whole of the film.   Formula enables the
audience to draw easily discernible relationships between the
"conventional" story set in the everyday world and the stylized representation and interpretation of the inner mode of
the reality of feelings, emotions, passion, etc. brought to the
surface by means of music and dance; what then becomes important to recognize is that the burden of not only the genre's
popularity but also its artistic content falls into the realm of
how effectively the Film Musical presents its subject matter.

    The Film Musical is a highly conventional film genre
as opposed to the strict "art" film where convention becomes
subordinate to inventive themes or ideas.   In the musical the
elements of music and dance woven into the libretto not only
serve the end of reinforcing a formulaic type of film but also
serve in creating and distinguishing a distinctive film genre.
Moreover, if a new idea (a novel and progressive artistic concept) is expressed, it is, most often, found in the song and
dance sequences.   It is not surprising, then, in light of this,
to understand the popularity of the Film Musical: on the one
hand we have a genre with a solid core of conventions which
can be counted on to strike a responsive chord in the viewer,
and on the other we have the audience's obvious appreciation
of the talents of artists like Fred Astaire and Gene Kelly, or
composers like the Gershwins, Jerome Kern, Cole Porter,
Irving Berlin, Harold Arlen, and Jule Styne. [21]   The Film
Musical presents us with a popular phenomenon in terms of
the directors, composers, and choreographers who have consistently taken the conventional fabric of the musical and pro-
gressively and imaginatively shaped it into a form which can
present us with freshness of perception and variety of experience hitherto unseen, emphasizing in the process how both
common and new ideas are presented rather than what the implications of these ideas are.   Instead of always searching immediately outside a film genre to find some reason for its

popularity, we should begin by accepting the art form within its own sphere--recognizing first the parameters and dimensions of that sphere. Hopefully, this introductory analysis of the Film Musical's form will help balance our perspective, at least in terms of this genre. [22]

Notes

1. The Impact of Film: How Ideas Are Communicated Through Cinema and Television (New York: MacMillan Publishing Company, Inc. , 1973), p. 308.

2. See Pauline Kael's review of Funny Girl in Going Steady (Boston: Little, Brown and Company, 1968, 1969, 1970), pp. 133-137; in the review she does not even mention the composer of the score, Jule Styne.

3. Understanding Movies (Englewood Cliffs, N. J. : Prentice-Hall Inc. , 1972), p. 115.

4. "Rouben Mamoulian: 'Style Is the Man,'" in Discussion (The American Film Institute), No. 2 (1971), p. 9.

5. Lehman Engel, in his The American Musical Theater: A Consideration (New York: The MacMillan Company; a CBS Legacy Collection book, 1967), lists a variety of song types most often used in stage musicals; I believe the same list is applicable to the Film Musical:

> 1. Song ... The verse is free in form, usually establishes or sets up a subject, and is melodically secondary to the chorus--which introduces and develops the main theme. In musical theater and popular song practice, the 32-bar chorus (or variants) [AABA is the usual melodic structure] is the commonest form.... 2. Ballad. Most often a love song, but it can also be a narrative, soliloquy, or character song.... 3. Rhythm song. One primarily carried along on, or propelled by, a musical beat which is most usually a regular one [oftentimes uptempo].... 4. Comedy song. Divided into two main and quite opposite forms--each of which has many variants ... might be generally classified as the 'short joke' and the 'long joke'.... 5. Charm song. One usually combining music and lyrics in equal importance. The subject matter ... is light,

> and ... no attempt to make a comedy point. The
> musical setting is generally delicate, optimistic and
> rhythmic, and may have, more than the music of
> comedy songs, a life independent of its lyrics....
> 6. Musical Scene. A theatrical sequence ... set
> to music, for one or any number of characters. It
> may include a song and may be held together for-
> mally by its literary structure, guided by ... musi-
> cal balance. It may include speech, recitative,
> song, and incidental music (underscoring). (pp.
> 118-120)

6. Alec Wilder. American Popular Song: The Great Inno-
   vators, 1900-1950 (New York: Oxford University
   Press, 1972), states in his discussion of George
   Gershwin, "The constant, and characteristic, repeated
   note found throughout Gershwin's songs is a basic at-
   testation of this aggressiveness." (p. 122)

7. The word "particularization" is taken from Lehman Engel's discussion of music in Words with Music (New
   York: The MacMillan Company, 1972), pp. 92-112.

8. Engel, Words with Music, p. 108.

9. "The Band Wagon," in The Velvet Light Trap, No. 11
   (Winter, 1974), p. 33.

10. John Kobal. Gotta Sing Gotta Dance: A Pictorial History
    of Film Musicals (London: The Hamlyn Publishing
    Group Limited, 1971), pp. 299-300; all the subsequent
    quotations are from these pages.

11. The Dance Through the Ages (New York: Grosset and
    Dunlap, 1967), p. 261.

12. Gene Kelly substantiates this concept of choreographing
    the camera and having it act as a participant in the
    dance when he states: "You learn to use the camera
    as part of the choreography." From Tony Thomas'
    The Films of Gene Kelly: Song and Dance Man (Se-
    caucus, N.J.: The Citadel Press, 1974), p. 27.

13. Sorell, Dance Through the Ages, p. 291.

14. The Dance in America (New York: Harper and Row Pub-
    lishers, 1971; revised edition), pp. 228-29.

15. A good example of this is in Lehman Engel's Words with
    Music, pp. 115-16, where he relates that when some-
    one asked him after seeing Fiddler on the Roof what
    he thought of the score, he "could only reply that [he]
    had been totally unaware of it" because he was "com-
    pletely absorbed in the total experience."

16. The following formulas are also mentioned and illustrated
    a little more fully in the following books: John Kobal,
    Gotta Sing Gotta Dance (Mr. Kobal mentions the for-
    mulas but does not often define them; he does provide
    many examples); John Russell Taylor and Arthur Jack-
    son, The Hollywood Musical (New York: McGraw-
    Hill Book Company, 1971) (the authors here only men-
    tion formula tangentially); Arlene Croce, The Fred
    Astaire and Ginger Rogers Book (New York: Outer-
    bridge and Lazard, Inc., 1972) (Ms. Croce discusses
    the formulas used in the Astaire-Rogers films quite
    extensively).

17. Leonard Bernstein, in his chapter on "American Musical
    Comedy" in The Joy of Music (New York: Simon and
    Schuster, Inc., 1959), p. 167, cites the outstanding
    characteristic of the operetta as its use of exotic lo-
    cale.

18. Because so many of the "books" in Film Musicals are
    comedies I believe Northrop Frye's comments about
    archetypal structure in comedy is particularly relevant
    at this point; I will parenthetically cite The Pirate by
    way of illustration:

> What normally happens [in a comedy] is that a young
> man wants a young woman [Serafin woos Manuela in
> The Pirate], that his desire is resisted by some op-
> position, usually paternal, and that near the end of
> the play some twist in the plot enables the hero to
> have his will ... the movement of comedy is usual-
> ly a movement from one kind of society to another.
> At the beginning of the play the obstructing charac-
> ters are in charge of the play's society [like Don
> Pedro], and the audience recognizes that they are
> the usurpers. At the end of the play the device in
> the plot that brings the hero and heroine together
> causes a new society to crystallize around the hero
> [in The Pirate, Serafin (Gene Kelly) puts on a small
> show and uses his hypnotist act to draw the truth

160   Film Genre

out about Don Pedro], and the moment when this
crystallization occurs is the point of resolution in
the action, the comic discovery, anagnorisis or
cognito.
    The appearance of this new society is frequently
signalized by some kind of party or festive ritual,
which either appears at the end of the play or is
assumed to take place immediately afterward [in
most musicals it is the promise of marriage often
symbolized in the reprise of a love ballad or another song; in The Pirate Kelly and Garland (Sera-
fin and Manuela) perform Cole Porter's 'Be a Clown,'
symbolic of their union to one another and to a life
on the stage].

The preceding is from Anatomy of Criticism: Four
Essays (New York: Atheneum, 1957), p. 163.

19. John G. Cawelti, "The Concept of Formula in the Study
    of Popular Literature," in Journal of Popular Culture,
    Volume 3, No. 3 (Winter, 1969), p. 385.

20. Ibid.

21. Once again I refer the reader to the books on dance cited
    above, where the names of Astaire and Kelly are most
    often mentioned in regards to achievement in filmed
    dance, and also to Alec Wilder's American Popular
    Song, cited above for discussion of American compos-
    ers and their compositions.

22. The author wishes to express his gratitude to Mr. Gary
    Don Luckert, whose interest in and knowledge of the
    musical spurred my own interest, and to Mr. Jack
    Nachbar for his helpful suggestions in focusing and
    framing my subject matter.

MONSTERS FROM THE ID

Margaret Tarratt

> Few things reveal so sharply as science
> fiction the wishes, hopes, fears, inner
> stresses and tensions of an era, or de-
> fine its limitations with such exactness. [1]

Most writers in English, on science fiction films,
view them as reflections of society's anxiety about its increasing technological prowess and its responsibility to control the gigantic forces of destruction it possesses.   Francis
Arnold, for instance, was typical in relating the upsurge of
science fiction films in the '50s and '60s to the existence of
the Bomb and the first Sputnik. [2] It has long been a critical
commonplace to deplore the introduction of the "love interest"
into science fiction films.   Richard Hodgens, in "A Brief
Tragical History of the Science Fiction Film," while praising
The War of the Worlds, complained that "one unnecessary
modern addition ... was an irrelevant boy and girl theme, because [George] Pal apologized 'Audiences want it. '"[3]   In
"Glimpses of the Moon," Penelope Houston refers cynically
to "the inevitable girl" in such films. [4]   The plot synopsis of
20 Million Miles to Earth in the Monthly Film Bulletin[5] omits
the hero's romance, and this is no isolated example.   Yet the
"love interest" in science fiction films, far from being extraneous to the central concern of the works, usually forms
an integral part of their structure, as certain French critics
have recognized.

F. Hoda, in "Epouvante et Science Fiction,"[6] dwells
with interest on the "camouflaged sensuality" of the genre,
pointing out that many of the situations in films of this kind
could be reduced to representations of aggressive sexuality,
disguised to a greater or lesser degree.   Jean Loth, in "Le
Fantastique Erotique ou l'orgasme qui fait peur,"[7] suggested

that film monsters should be regarded as embodiments of
women's virginal sexual fantasies--a cross between fear and
desire; Raymond Lefèvre, in "Le Décor de la Peur,"[8] noticed
the masking of sadism and eroticism by fantastic decor and
poetic effects; while Fereydoun Hoveyda suggested that the importance of the science fiction film lay in its tentative breakdown of certain limitations concerning the representation on
the screen of love and hate and of human relationships. [9]
None of these writers, however, gives any detailed illustration in support of their theses.   The fullest analysis along
these lines so far is in Tom Milne's study of Mamoulian's
Dr. Jekyll and Mr. Hyde, [10] but this film is not examined in
a science fiction context.

Although the majority of science fiction films appear
to express some kind of concern with the moral state of contemporary society, many are more directly involved with an
examination of man's inner nature.   Curt Siodmak maintained:

> In its day, Frankenstein, the forerunner of a gen-
> eration of admitted mumbo jumbo and lots of enter-
> tainment, was a true trail blazer, and in effect
> opened up Hollywood-produced motion pictures to
> both psychiatry and neuro-surgery. What now seems
> primitive in Metropolis or the Jekyll-Hydean cycle
> of werewolf pictures are simply variations on the
> theme which Siegfried Kracauer in From Caligari to
> Hitler, characterised as a 'deep and fearful concern
> with the foundations of the self.'[11]

This article will argue that these films are deeply involved
with the concepts of Freudian psychoanalysis and seem in
many cases to derive their structure from it.   They may deal
with society as a whole, but they arrive at social comment
through a dramatization of the individual's anxiety about his
own repressed sexual desires, which are incompatible with
the morals of civilized life.   Freud described this process in
"Anxiety and Instinctual Life":

> The commonest cause of anxiety neurosis is uncon-
> summated excitation.   Libidinal excitation is aroused
> but not satisfied, not employed; apprehensiveness
> then appears instead of this libido that has been di-
> rected from its employment.... What is responsi-
> ble for anxiety in hysteria and other neurosis is the
> process of repression. [12]

The battles with sinister monsters or extra-terrestrial forces
are an externalization of civilized man's conflict with his
primitive sub-conscious or id. Freud writes of the id in the
following manner:

> We approach the Id with analogies; we call it a
> chaos, a cauldron full of seething excitations....
> It is filled with energy reaching it from the in-
> stincts, but it has no organisation, produces no col-
> lective will, but only a striving to bring about the
> satisfaction of the instinctual needs subject to the
> observance of the pleasure principle.... Contrary
> impulses exist side by side, without cancelling each
> other out or diminishing each other.... No altera-
> tion in its mental processes is produced by the pas-
> sage of time. Wishful impulses which have never
> passed beyond the id, but impressions, too, which
> have been sunk into the id by repression are vir-
> tually immortal; after the passage of decades they
> behave as if they had just occurred. They can only
> be recognized as belonging to the past, can only lose
> their importance and be deprived of their cathexis
> of energy when they have been made conscious by
> the work of analysis.... The id, of course, knows
> no judgments of value; no good and evil; no morali-
> ty.... Instinctive cathexes seeking discharge--that,
> in our view, is all there is in the id. [13]

    Forbidden Planet (1956, dir. Fred McLeod Wilcox) pro-
vides an explicit, if somewhat crude, example of the id in
action. The events take place several centuries in the future,
when man has penetrated what is significantly termed "inner"
as opposed to "outer" space. A party is sent to discover
what has happened to a group who had attempted to colonize
the planet Altair--420 years before. As they try to land, they
are warned off by Captain Morbius (Walter Pidgeon), leader
of the original expedition, who claims he is the only survivor,
needs no help and cannot be held responsible for the consequences of their landing. They are entertained by Morbius
who lives in the height of automated luxury. Unexpectedly,
his daughter Altaira (Ann Francis), appears in the room, an
innocent, briefly-clad siren whom Morbius had been trying to
keep away from the men. She shows considerable admiration
for the clean-limbed heroic spacemen, who become rivals for
her affection until Commander Adams (Leslie Nielsen) wins.
When he kisses her, her pet tiger, which had hitherto been
harmless when in her presence, no longer recognizes her and

advances, snarling, until the Captain is forced to shoot it.
Meanwhile, in the spaceship at night a curiously sexual,
heavy panting noise is heard, the ship is smashed up and one
of the men is later found torn to bits. Eventually they see
and fight the monster, a leaping tigerish shape outlined in
electrical sparks. Morbius, talking to the Captain, explains
that the planet was originally the domain of the Krell, a humane and hyper-intelligent species, whose scientific discover-
ies he is able to make use of with the help of a patent brain
booster. They became extinct at a time when they were on
the threshold of dispensing with their physical bodies. The
Captain, finding the monster is immune to all weapons, decides to have a brain boost himself in order to work out a
strategy against it. Returning to Morbius' house with his
scientist colleague (whose I.Q. is considerably higher than
his own), he persuades the Doctor's daughter to marry him
and leave with him for Earth. Dr. Morbius opposes this plan
violently, declaring that he and his daughter are "joined, body
and soul." The Captain's companion meanwhile, who had
sneaked off to get a brain boost himself, returns to die, gasp-
ing with his last breath: "The monster is from the id."

"The id--What's that?" asks the Captain. "An obso-
lete term once used to describe the elementary structure of
the subconscious," replies Morbius. The Captain, with com-
mendable celerity, now grasps the root of the problem. The
Krell, in the passion for scientific advancement, had ignored
the "mindless beast" of their own subconscious, which had ultimately destroyed them. "That thing out there is you!" he
accuses the Doctor, indicating the monster which is once
more advancing; "We are all part monsters in our subcon-
scious--that's why we have laws and religion. You sent your
secret id out, a primitive, more enraged and inflamed with
each frustration. You still have the mind of a primitive."
The Doctor was destroying the spacemen who threaten his relationship with his daughter. In despair, Morbius recognizes
the truth, turns off the electric current which animates the
monster of his id and significantly addresses the Captain as
"Son." The word "incest" is never mentioned, but his suppressed incestuous desires are clearly implied to be at the
root of all the trouble.

Forbidden Planet has aspects in common with many
science fiction films. Space travel is commonly accompanied
by publicly recognized sexual frustration amongst the all-male
crew. The scientist with his total dedication to advanced
knowledge is an unbalanced figure, ruthless in defense of his

own researches. The hero is an ordinary man with healthy
physique, leadership qualities, a controlled sexual drive and
only average intellect--a good all-rounder.

As Kingsley Amis pointed out,[14] this film has strong
structural and thematic connections with Shakespeare's Tem-
pest--expecially in its distrust of advanced science and its influence on man. In Forbidden Planet, science has advanced
to a point at which it becomes the equivalent of Prospero's
occult study. Morbius has entered the realm of "forbidden
knowledge," both sexually and intellectually, a realm both en-
ticing and fearful to characters such as Baron Frankenstein
or Colonel Merritt in Conquest of Space (Byron Haskin, 1955),
who dies attempting to sabotage his sacrilegious mission.

Traditionally, the idea of forbidden knowledge has had
a sexual as well as an intellectual connotation stemming from
the myth of Adam and Eve. Science fiction films take up this
dual interpretation. With them, we return to the problems
and anxieties of the middle ages, when men feared to enquire
too closely into the elements--thought to be inhabited by evil
demons. Bacon's famous challenge to the fear of natural science, in his Advancement of Learning, is a challenge which
seems to confront the heroes of science fiction. Freud drew
a parallel between the anxieties of modern man and the "demonological neurosis" of the seventeenth century.

> The states of possession correspond to our neurosis,
> for the explanation of which we resort to psychical
> powers. In our eyes the demons are bad and repre-
> hensible wishes, derivatives of instinctual impulses
> that have been repudiated and repressed. We mere-
> ly eliminate the projection of these mental entities
> into the external world, which the middle ages car-
> ried out; instead we regard them as having arisen
> in the patient's internal life where they have their
> abode.[15]

One of the classics of the science fiction genre, The
Thing from Another World (1951, dir. Christian Nyby, much
influenced by the producer, Howard Hawks), provides an out-
standing example of the "demonological neurosis." A group
of American airmen in Alaska are called in by scientists working on secret research at the North Pole. Much emphasis is
laid on the freezing conditions as well as the lack of women.
A radioactive craft has landed embedding itself in the ice.

Captain Pat Hendry, in charge of rescuing the spacecraft, is subjected to a good deal of ragging about an alleged
romance with the chief scientist's secretary, Nikki (Margaret
Sheridan). We learn that they had spent a disastrous evening
on leave together, in which Hendry had got drunk and made a
heavy pass at her, only to wake up and find she had gone
back to base. This incident had become common knowledge
in the camp. Hendry, to some extent ignorant of his own
drunken behavior, complains about Nikki's action and is enlightened by the indignant girl: "You had moments like an
octopus--I never saw so many hands in all my life." Hendry
suggests that their relationship started off on the wrong footing and asks if they can begin again. Following this is the
film's best sequence, in which the men attempt to extricate
the spacecraft by means of explosives, but destroy it while
salvaging its occupant, who is frozen into a slab of ice. On
the return journey, "The Thing" is not shown, but a couple
of dogs in the plane whine. One of the men recalls an incident in the war when he was stranded with a bomber group:
"An army nurse came ashore and caused as much disturbance
as this man from Mars."

On their arrival back at base, Hendry resists the
pressure of Dr. Carrington, who wishes to be allowed to examine the creature immediately, believing it necessary to
keep it alive at all costs. The Captain insists on awaiting
instructions and organizes a 24-hour watch to be kept. In another interlude with Nikki, she declares: "You're much nicer
when you're not mad," and offers to buy him a drink. "That
sounds promising," he replies, "You can tie my hands if you
want." In a subsequent scene we see him "bound" to a chair,
discussing men and women's relationships. "If a man tries
to kiss you the first time, he is a wolf. But after 1,000
drinks and 1,000 dinners he isn't?" asks Hendry. She agrees.
"Can't I be untied now?" he asks. Later she kisses him and
remarks that she would not have been able to be so nice to
him were he untied. Finally, when her back is turned, he
loosens his bonds. Nikki: "How long have you been loose?"
Hendry: "Long enough!"

Later that night, the Captain is told how the man on
watch is terrified by the monster's hands and eyes, and the
speculation as to whether or not it is alive. The guard cov-
ers the ice with his electric blanket so he will not see it, and
the creature thaws out. Observing it free, the watchman attacks it in blind panic, and in a subsequent struggle with the
airmen, it escapes into the Arctic night, leaving part of its

arm and hand behind. It later grows a new one. Examining
the severed arm, Dr. Carrington observes that it is entirely
composed of vegetable matter and concludes that on Mars,
vegetables have evolved in the same way that animals evolved
on earth. He also discovers a pocket of seed pollen in the
palm of the hand and marvels at the Thing's method of repro-
duction--"No pain, pleasure, emotions or heart. How superior!" The Thing is later found to feed off blood, but in
spite of this, Carrington longs to communicate with the superior intelligence, at whatever cost to human life. Again the
Captain resists his pressures, stressing the need for the
creature to be locked up. Later, it becomes necessary to
destroy it. As it seems invulnerable to firearms they attempt to burn it with Kerosene, but it escapes, leaving Hendry slightly wounded in the hand, to be ministered to by Nikki. Plans are made to electrocute the Thing. Dr. Carrington steps out to save it, urging it to communicate with them
on a rational basis, but is sent flying by a violent blow from
the creature's arm. Once the creature has been destroyed,
the men joke: "Our worries are over, whilst our Captain...."
Taking the hint, Hendry proposes to Nikki and she accepts.
Meanwhile, the newspaper reporter radios the story he has
been burning to deliver: "One of the world's greatest battles
has just been fought by the human race...."

The plot of this film could not meaningfully be described in less detail. A parallel is drawn between Captain
Hendry and the monster, most clearly through the motif of
the hand. We do not need Freud to suggest the phallic significance of this limb in dream symbolism since, in this film,
the hand is explicitly established as a sexual organ. In the
conflicts between the Captain and Nikki, his hands are his
sexual weapon, and in his use of them he becomes octopus-
like or monstrous. When he is bound to his chair, the purpose is to put his hands out of action. While the Thing is
seen lying in its ice prison, the guards are particularly
frightened by his eyes and hands and by whether or not he is
alive. The scientists establish not only that his hand is his
sexual organ, but that it grows again when severed--a human
fantasy symbolically warding off castration. In the struggle
against this monster of his id, Hendry is slightly wounded in
the hand, which is tended by Nikki. He undergoes a kind of
emasculation which makes him acceptable to her. The struggle against the Thing draws them closer together; by conquering the Thing he wins Nikki in marriage. His facing up to
the Thing and the desires of unbridled virility which it represents is a dramatization of Freud's description of the instincts

of the id being overcome when brought up into the level of
consciousness through analysis. As with the demonological
neurosis of the seventeenth century, the instinctual impulses
are externalized and dramatized. The Thing clearly represents Hendry's repressed sexual desires, the impulses of the
id. We are reminded of the parallel drawn by an airman between the arrival of a single woman in the midst of an all-
male military group and the arrival of the Thing amongst the
airmen. Like the Thing, Hendry is initially "frozen." The
Arctic landscape provides an objective correlative for his emotional and sexual life, repressed in the all-male disciplined
environment of an isolated base. Hendry, too, has his own
accidental thaw, through drink, when on leave. His subsequent instinctual predatory behavior is as unacceptable to Nikki as that of the Thing to the airmen. His renewed courtship
of Nikki is subject to a joking but rigid control of the instincts symbolized by the binding of his hands. Only in this
"civilized" manner can he awaken desire in her--the repeated
rituals of drinks, dinner and restrained behavior cited by
Kinsey[16] as the acceptable norm. In his courtship he must
fight his surging primitive instincts--a conflict we see settled
in the destruction of the Thing. The manner in which he
handles the military situation created by the Thing's presence
is an image of the way in which he handles himself in relation to Nikki. Unlike the scientist whose greed for knowledge
leads him into questionable moral paths, Hendry fears the
dangers of examining the Thing. Once it is free, he hopes
to control it, to keep it alive, but contained. He takes up his
General's cry of "Close the door," voicing the necessity to
protect human beings from the extremes of nature, whether
human or climatic. The Thing is found to be incompatible
with human life and must consequently be destroyed, however
fascinating it may be. As in Freud's description of the id,
the Thing cannot respond to human reason. Hendry's wounded
hand suggests the forcible taming of his aggressive sexuality
which civilized society demands. The structure of this film
can only be understood in a Freudian context. A number of
films, some less artistically accomplished than The Thing,
are structured in a similar manner.

    One such example can be found in Nathan Juran's 20
Million Miles to Earth (1957), in which a U.S. rocketship returning from a flight to Venus crashes into the sea off Sicily,
with its one survivor, Col. Calder (William Hopper), who is
tended by the zoologist's niece Marisa (Joan Taylor). A child
finds a sealed cylindrical container and sells it to the zoologist, Dr. Leonardo, who finds a glutinous jelly inside. Out

of this appears to hatch a small prehistoric-type monster with
a long tail. It is extremely aggressive and found to grow at
an alarming rate, and eventually escapes. Recaptured and
paralyzed by electric shock, it is kept in a Rome zoo for the
scientists to examine, but breaks loose again during a power
failure. After a spectacular fight with an elephant it is finally killed in the Colosseum. A small circle of men stands
round the corpse regarding it with expressions of regret.

This film has a number of aspects in common with
The Thing. At the outset, Colonel Calder and Marisa have
an antagonistic relationship. Her concern is for his health,
while he is obsessed with the need to safeguard his cargo.
The first appearance of the creature, as it struggles to free
itself from its prison of jelly, follows the goodnight wish of
Dr. Leonardo to his niece: "Pleasant dreams." The monster is a clear phallic symbol with its thrashing tail, its absence of internal organs, its dramatic growth and its reawakening to activity after it has been overpowered. Significantly, the planet it comes from is Venus, also the name of
the goddess of love. We are told that the atmosphere on
Venus is such that humans cannot breathe and survive in it
for long. Eight of the Colonel's crew died from exposure to
it. The Colonel wishes it to be kept alive so that scientists
may examine it to see under what conditions life could survive
on Venus. We do not have to stretch the interpretation too
far to recognize this as concern as to how far the aggressive
male sexual urge can be liberated in a love relationship without causing injury to the civilized way of life. The threat to
civilization from man's destructive urge has been voiced at
the beginning of the film with the image of an exploding atomic bomb, and this idea is kept in mind at several points in
the film, especially in the Roman background with its ancient
crumbling ruins and the Colosseum setting for the battle with
the elephant, which remind us of the Fall of the Roman Empire, popularly reputed to have sprung from an era of sexual
decadence.

As in The Thing, battles with the monster are inter-
spersed with increasingly romantic interludes. The more
committed the Colonel becomes to controlling the creature,
the less antagonistic is his relationship to Marisa. She is
profoundly disturbed by its appearance and is at one point attacked by it when it stretches out an arm from within its
cage. Like Captain Hendry in The Thing, Colonel Calder is
wounded in the arm--again a symbolic semi-emasculation--
when he tries to master it, declaring airily: "It's just a

matter of controlling the beast. " Once he has been wounded,
his relationship with Marisa becomes milder and more romantic.   He apologizes for his aggression and looks forward to a
time when they can pursue their relationship in a darkened
cafe at a table with a candle burning and a bottle of wine.
This is a symbolic representation of intercourse, the flame
of the candle symbolizing desire rather than destruction.   This
is made clear in a later scene, when Marisa tells the Colonel
of her nightmare, in which the candle in the dark cafe is
burning lower and lower.   Soon it will be out.   "If we hurry,"
suggests the Colonel, "perhaps we'll be in time. "   The situation in which they can enjoy this dreamed of intercourse can
only arise when the monster from Venus is put down, as the
Colonel ultimately recognizes.   If it is not quickly destroyed,
their romance will have burned itself out.   The Colonel is
unusual in this kind of film in combining the role of scientist
and hero.   Like Dr. Carrington in The Thing, he wishes the
monster to be scientifically examined, but, like The Thing,
the monster's potentially destructive power renders this too
dangerous a course of action.   In The Thing, the refrain is
"Close the door. "   In 20 Million Miles to Earth it is "Shut
the gate. "   In order to maintain the mores of civilization,
some instincts must be quelled, the moment they become apparent.   Both films suggest the fear of the violent primitive
drives of the male id.   The women are almost asexual figures of Arthurian romance, offering themselves to the knight
once he has slain the beast.

     In The Day the Earth Stood Still (Robert Wise, 1951),
the imperfect human male, a mixture of outward politeness
and inner violence, is contrasted with the refined Martian
Klaatu (Michael Rennie), who comes on earth to warn men
against the violence of their lives.   Significantly, the heroine's
husband has been killed in a war.   A gentle asexual figure,
Klaatu is tended by a powerful robot named Gort, who seems
to represent man's violence and even his sexuality (in the
scene where he advances threateningly on the cringing heroine
and carries her off to the spaceship, as F. Hoda observed[17]).
Out of control, Gort's powers are dangerous.   Under Klaatu's
orders he is an invaluable weapon.   After the girl, Helen
Benson (Patricia Neal), has been in contact with Klaatu, she
is unable to go through with the marriage that her jealous and
selfish fiancé urges on her.   As Klaatu enters his spaceship
to return to Mars, she looks at him wistfully.   He is a man
whose "baser instincts" or id, in the figure of Gort, are held
firmly under control.   The film suggests a concept of an ideal
man separated from his most primitive instincts, using them
only as a source of energy to aid his "higher" civilized aims.

It Came from Outer Space (Jack Arnold, 1953) is another film in which a similar pattern develops with slight
variations. The hero, John Putnam (Richard Carlson), a
dreamer-scientist, who wishes to hasten his marriage to his
slightly reluctant fiancée, Ellen (Barbara Rush), is the only
man in his town to realize that earth has been invaded by
alien beings. The creatures begin to "take over" the bodies
of people in the town so that they seem simultaneously to be
themselves, yet not themselves; something is different. The
scientist, who quickly comes to terms with the fact that they
have been invaded, tries to convince the Sheriff (who, as a
friend of Ellen's family opposed his marriage), but is repeatedly ridiculed and ignored. Eventually, Ellen herself is held
as a hostage. When she is seen again, her light-colored
girlish summer dress has been exchanged for a black one,
and she has adopted something of the air of the femme fatale.
All the invaders wish to do is to mend their spaceship and
take off again. A pact, sensibly made between humans and
invaders by Putnam, is finally broken by the Sheriff, whose
overriding instinct is to attack once he has been forced to accept their existence. The creatures manage to escape, but
not before they have been compelled to "show" themselves as
they really are--indistinct phallic shapes with an enormous
eye (a symbol of the genitals) in the middle of their heads. [18]

In this film, society, as epitomized by the Sheriff, is
unwilling to probe beneath the surface and refuses to believe
anything which does not accord with its own "civilized" desires. Hence, the thoughtful Scientist, who recognizes the
strength of his own sexual desire and who sees in marriage
something more than a mere social alliance, is automatically
a suspect figure. The invaders assume human form because
they recognize the human weakness of being unable to confront the existence of sexuality. But the existence of the
genitals cannot be ignored. Even the "nice" girl Ellen is
forced to reveal her innate sexuality. Putnam's dealings with
the invaders suggest that some form of harmony can be established between civilized and sexual man (a more sophisticated and humane view than in the films previously discussed),
but society in the form of the Sheriff, made to confront its
own sexual nature, can only attempt to overcome what is, in
fact, a superior force.

This film, like many science fiction films, provides a
good illustration of the tensions, examined by Kinsey, [19] between man's publicly accepted social and sexual mores and
the actual sexual needs of the individual. Forbidden Planet,
The Thing, 20 Million Miles to Earth, The Day the Earth

Stood Still and It Came from Outer Space are all films which
are concerned with the clash between the public and private
man, unwilling to defy convention, but disturbed by secret
impulses and desires that are incompatible with the social
superego to which they aspire. The legal proscription, still
widespread in the United States, of all sexual relationships
outside marriage, reflected in the bourgeois consciousness
of right and wrong, becomes a nagging source of disquiet,
particularly in The Thing, It Came from Outer Space or
Mamoulian's Dr. Jekyll and Mr. Hyde.

The conquest of the "monster of the id" is the structural raison d'être of many science fiction films. There are
also some science fiction films which, while based on psycho-
analytical concepts, concern themselves with a variation on
this theme. A number of them deal with impotence and frigidity. This group includes such films as Spider Woman,
Wasp Woman and The Fly, which explore insect phobia--fear
of castration and dread of the phallic mother. One of the
earliest science fiction films to look at the sexual nature of
woman is James Whale's The Bride of Frankenstein (1935).
Frankenstein itself provides a fairly straightforward example
of the kind of film discussed earlier, which examines the
tension between man's subconscious sexual desires and the
mores of civilization. The Bride assumes a knowledge of the
earlier film in its continued exploration of such secret desires. The film opens with a conversation between Shelley,
Byron and Mary Shelley--author of the novel Frankenstein.
Byron professes some amazement that such a dark story
could have been created by Mary, who appears a graceful
feminine figure. She is undisturbed by his suggestion of the
monstrous fantasies that lurk in her inner nature. Considering Byron's claim to be the "world's greatest sinner" and
Shelley's to be the "world's greatest poet," Mary suggests
that a simple love story would never have done for such an
audience: "So why shouldn't I write of monsters?" She then
offers to continue the tale, and her narration is carried over
the opening shots of the fire in which the monster is thought
to have met his death.

As with Hendry and the Thing, there is a close parallel relationship between Frankenstein and his Monster in the
Frankenstein films. Just as, at the beginning of The Bride
of Frankenstein, the Monster, thought to be dead, shows himself very much alive, so Frankenstein (Colin Clive), brought
home as a corpse on his wedding night, is revived in the
presence of his wife, who, incidentally, had once been warned

to beware her wedding night.   As with the creature in 20 Million Miles to Earth, this reawakening process symbolizes what Freud describes as "the revival of libidinal desires after they have been quenched through being sated. "[20]

The wedding night proceeds with a scene in which Frankenstein, still weakened through illness, lies alone in bed and discusses with reawakening enthusiasm the tempta- tions of aspiring to be a creator, with his wife (Valerie Hob- son).   She responds with shocked arguments that what he de- sires is "blasphemous. "   "We are not meant to know such things.   It is the work of the Devil. "   They are clearly dis- cussing the act of procreation or some form of sexual inter- course.   The analogy between love and science is taken up a little later by the eminent scientist Dr. Pretorius (Ernest Thesiger)--a man "booted out" of the university for knowing too much: "The creation of life is enthralling," he declares, "Science, like love, has her little surprises. "   In his efforts to convince Frankenstein to continue his experiments in crea- tion, he points to the Bible, quoting the exhortation to "in- crease and multiply. "   As if to underline his point he reveals some homunculi he has created, imprisoned in glass jars--a King, Queen, Archbishop, Devil and Ballerina.   The King, watched primly by the Archbishop and gleefully by the Devil (who is said to resemble Pretorius), makes frenzied attempts to climb out of his jar and make love to the Queen.   The Queen remains still, chattering anxiously.   The Ballerina, un- aware of anything, dances to one tune.   As in the relationship between Frankenstein and his wife, the male is the active transgressor, attempting from sexual motives to overcome the limits set by his creator.   The female adheres to the con- ventions, an innocent insipid performer, seeking admiration like the Ballerina, issuing anxious warnings against the preda- tory actions of the male, like the Queen.

The wedding night is disturbed by Pretorius, whose temptations to create life once more Frankenstein is unable to resist.   He is symbolically separated from his wife, and in a subsequent scene she hears a noise and cries out, "Is that you Henry?"   She then turns to find that she is being menaced by the Monster (Boris Karloff), who kidnaps her. Thus the connection between Frankenstein and his Monster is emphasized.   Pretorius and the Monster insist that Franken- stein's wife will not be returned to him until he creates a mate for the Monster.

Clearly, Frankenstein's primitive sexual drives are an

estranging factor between himself and his wife.   She speaks
to her husband and is answered by a Monster.   His only
chance of survival is to discover the secrets of her sexual
nature in order to meet the needs of his own erotic impulses.
The female monster he creates is played by Elsa Lanchester,
significantly the same actress who plays Mary Shelley in the
film's prologue.   The slow, tense attempts to stimulate this
corpse-like figure to life eventually succeed.   She seems to
look to Frankenstein for reassurance, but when confronted
with the Monster lets out a blood-curdling scream of terror
and revulsion.   The dual role played by Elsa Lanchester indicates the identification that should be made between the
ultra-civilized Mary Shelley and the primitive world of her
subconscious from which she draws her monster fantasies.
Valerie Hobson, as the gracious, civilized Elizabeth, is another substitute for Mary Shelley in the film.   The suggestion
is that even when woman's sexuality is most strongly aroused,
she can only meet the sexual male with complete frigidity.
There appears to be no distinction between woman's conscious
and unconscious desires.   This is why Mary Shelley is undisturbed by Byron's innuendos.   It is, after all, man who is
the "great sinner."   The point is made; the baffled Monster
threatens violence and at that moment, Elizabeth, escaped
from the Monster's prison, knocks on the door, calling to
Frankenstein.   The Monster, about to pull the lever which
will destroy the whole building and its occupants, agrees to
Frankenstein's escape.   "Yes, you go; (to Pretorius) You
stay.   We belong dead."

The innate female frigidity suggested by the reaction
of the female Monster to the Monster shows Frankenstein the
impossibility of satisfying his sexual nature.   It can only destroy, and he escapes thankfully with his wife, tacitly agree-
ing that this part of himself should be obliterated.

Much of the dialogue has a familiar ring to those
acquainted with later science fiction films--the assertion of
an area of knowledge forbidden to man, Biblical quotation to
support argument as in Conquest of Space or Them, the optimistic but ill-judged comment on the monster: "it just wants
someone to handle it" (cf. The Thing or 20 Million Miles to
Earth).   Another film which looks at the nature of woman
from a man's point of view, in rather different terms is The
Incredible Shrinking Man (Jack Arnold, 1957).

In this, as in most science fiction films, the apparently casual details of the opening scene are crucially important

to the film's thematic development. A couple are seen sun-
bathing on a boat. The man, Scott (Grant Williams), says
he is thirsty and wants the woman, Louise (Randy Stuart), to
fetch him some beer. She refuses until he makes a bargain
with her that he will make the dinner if she does so. They
then act out a scene in mock sixteenth-century dialogue, in
which he calls her "wench" and orders her down to the galley
in imitation of a time when man was master and woman
served him--a complete contrast to their own relationship.
They reveal that they have been living together for six years
and decide to get married. While the woman fetches the
drinks a cloud of mist appears on the horizon and rolls towards the boat, finally enveloping the man and leaving him
freezing cold.

In the next scene they are shown to be married. He
comments on a loss of weight, suggesting jokingly, "Maybe
it's the cooking round here." A little later, when they kiss,
he observes with dawning fear, "You used to have to stretch
when you kissed me." As he grows rapidly smaller from
day to day, he finds out that his sickness has been caused by
the radioactive mist to which he had been exposed and to
which the doctors and scientists can find no antidote. "I want
you to start thinking about us," he says to his wife, "--about
our marriage. There's a limit to your obligation." A model
of patience and understanding, she stands by him, tolerating
his increasing bad temper. "Every day I become smaller.
Every day I become more tyrannical in my domination of
Louise. I don't know how she stood it. Burning inside was
my desperate need for her." He starts up a friendship with
a female midget his own size but abandons it when he finds
he cannot stop shrinking. We see him dwarfed by a low cof-
fee table, with Louise, enormous in the foreground. Eventually, he is to be found living for safety in a doll's house in the
living room, complaining at the noise of his wife's feet as she
appears to crash down the stairs. She answers him patiently
and goes out shopping, inadvertently letting the cat in as she
does so. A terrifying scene follows in which the gigantic
predatory animal peers through the doll's house window and
makes a grab for him with his paw. In the ensuing struggle,
he escapes and falls through the stairs to the cellar, from
which he is unable to escape. In his new universe, away
from Louise's cooking, his main object must be to find food.
He sees a piece of cheese, but it is contained in a lethal
mouse trap which could well destroy him; a piece of bread
lies as bait in a spider's web and his adversary, a monstrous
spider, prowls round the cellar. "I had an enemy, the most

terrifying beheld by human eyes," he comments. There is
an immediate cut to Louise, upstairs, preparing to leave the
house. He finds a weapon for himself in a nail which, in
proportion to him is the size of a sword, and he decides to
pit his wits against the spider. At one point, unarmed and
threatened by the creature, he retrieves his weapon: "With
these, I was a man again ... I no longer felt hatred for the
spider. My enemy was not a spider but every unknown terror in the world.... One of us had to die." He finally
kills the spider in a nauseating scene in which he impales
her on his nail while black drops ooze on to his shoulder.
After the spider's death, "there was no thought of hunger or
shrinking." Completely reconciled to his state, he turns to
philosophizing about his role: "What was I, still a human
being, or a man of the future?"

Fear of castration by the female is the overriding
theme of this film and we are aware of the popular myth of
the dominant American woman, served by an emasculated
spouse. The opening scene observes the aggressive sexual
equality of modern times and looks back to the male-dominated situation it replaces. Our first image of the couple's
married life is outside the house. Louise feeds the cat and
prepares breakfast. His laughing fear of what her cooking
may be doing to him is taken up more strongly in the cellar
scenes, where food is left as bait to lure mice and flies to
their destruction--an analogy of the married woman's social
and sexual relationship to her husband. In his doll's house
he is reduced to the status of a toy. The giant clawing cat
is a replacement for Louise. She lets it in unconsciously.
Freud wrote of animal phobias:

> the anxiety felt in animal phobias is ... an affec-
> tive reaction on the part of the ego in danger: and
> the danger which is being signalled in this way is
> the danger of castration. This anxiety differs in no
> respect from the realistic anxiety which the ego
> normally feels in situations of danger, except that
> its content remains unconscious and only becomes
> conscious in the form of a distortion. [21]

This film is a first-person narrative from the man's
point of view. Superficially, he and his wife at first have a
good relationship. Later Louise behaves "perfectly" while he
feels guilt at his resentment of her. The film is clearly concerned with his fear of her influence on him within the marriage relationship which turns him into a toy and gradually
engulfs him.

In the cellar sequences, which symbolize his subconscious, his adversary comes out into the open, a female trying to trap him with food, implicitly associated with his wife in the cut mentioned above. He specifies that his real enemy is "every unknown terror in the world." By this, he means what Freud describes as fear, not merely of the mother but of the "phallic mother, of whom we are afraid; so that the fear of spiders expresses dread of mother-incest and horror of the female genitals."[22] Feeling "a man again" with his weapons, he impales her with his sword/penis. By confronting her sexually he proves his ability to resist her attacks and to conquer. After the fight neither the bait of food nor the fear of "shrinking," or castration, holds any power over him. He has freed himself from the constricting area of female domination and senses a new freedom for himself in the world, comforting himself that perhaps he will not be the only one to undergo this liberating experience in the future.

Don Siegel's Invasion of the Body Snatchers (1951) is not concerned with fears of woman but looks at a society characterized by lack of passion in every aspect. In some ways it has something in common with It Came from Outer Space. This film shows a silent conspiracy by which people are "taken over" by some curious plant life and as a result no longer feel pain, fear or joy, merely a vegetable contentment. Miles (Kevin McCarthy) and Becky (Dana Wynter) both have broken marriages behind them. Years ago at college they had been boyfriend and girlfriend but did not have sufficient courage or passion to leave to get married, as one of their friends in similar circumstances had done. Miles's conversations reveal the extent to which his interior and sex-life has been dried up and destroyed by the humdrum processes of everyday life. He claims that the reason his marriage broke up was that as a doctor, "I never was there when the food was on the table"--a comment both on the empty ritualization of the institution of marriage but also, at another level, implying that his job never left him enough time to sustain the sexual relationship. Both he and Becky pay more than lip service to society's clichés about human relationships. He chaffs his pretty nurse, telling her if she were not married, hers would have been a lost cause long ago. To Becky, he suggests that a doctor's wife needs infinite patience and the understanding of an Einstein. "What about love?" she asks. "That's for the specialists," he replies. Despite their growing feeling for each other, Becky resists a sexual relationship with conventional excuses that it is madness and the whole thing is so sudden--a point that is factually untrue, as he observes. Around them, the number of zombie-like creatures

grows.   A child rejects his mother, saying she is not his
mother.   She is the same as she was before but all feeling
has vanished.   The sickness is contagious, as more and more
people conspire to place the giant pods in contact with other
victims.   The psychiatrists, themselves afflicted with the
common illness, suggest that worry about what is going on in
the world causes the alienation problems: "The trouble is inside you."   In an impassioned speech, the Doctor describes
how he has watched humanity draining away from his patients
--"People I've known all my life.   Only when we have to fight
to stay human do we realize how precious it is."   When he
argues that love cannot so easily be discounted, with those
who try to infect him, they reply cynically: "You've been in
love before.   It doesn't last."   Becky cries out that she wants
his children, but she finally succumbs from exhaustion, becoming "an inhuman enemy bent on my destruction."   Standing
on the motorway, he yells at people in cars to stop and help
him escape to tell the truth.   They assume he is drunk or insane and pass by regardless.   "You fools! You're next!" he
yells.   The film ends on a false note of optimism and he is
finally believed, but this is not the ending that Siegel wanted
and certainly not the logical ending to the film.

    All the films discussed so far have been firmly struc-
tured round coherent themes relating the tensions of sexual
drives and the obligations on behavior imposed by civilized
society.   They are saturated with an awareness of Freudian
concepts.   The symbols are established from within the narrative context.   There is also a large group of films in which
such tensions are latent but not fully explored.   The films do
not appear to create their own symbolism.   Them! (Gordon
Douglas, 1954) is a good example of this.   It incorporates a
skeleton romance between two people working to destroy a
plague of monstrous aggressive ants--mutants from radioactive
fall-out.   Those who see the creatures view them with horror
and revulsion and there is a long scene in which the ants are
pursued through the nest they have made for themselves in the
city's sewers and an attempt is made to locate and destroy
the central egg chamber.   This labyrinthine motif might be
seen as a fantasy of anal birth[23] but the interpretation does
not clarify the preoccupations of the film in any significant
way.   The hero of The Projected Man (Ian Curteis, 1966),
who has himself hurled through space to prove a scientific
point to the corrupt authorities, is clearly motivated to an
equal extent by jealousy of the romance between his assistants,
one of them his former girlfriend (Mary Peach).   Returning
from the experiment with his face hideously burnt and scarred,

his aggression knows no bounds and he indulges in what might appear to be a gratuitous form of sexual menace as he carries off the office secretary, who is conveniently stripped to her underwear. His horrible appearance is the visible sign of the transformation he has undergone through jealousy, yet once more, nothing is closely worked out.

The Day the Earth Caught Fire (Val Guest, 1961) interweaves the imagery of the climatic changes with the story of a developing sexual attraction--at times it is not clear whether the hero and heroine are talking about themselves or about the weather. In the face of the potential destruction of the earth by fire their intolerant antagonism is shown to be petty and irrelevant. The reporter is brought to shake hands with his ex-wife's husband and to wish him well.

There are other science fiction films which are firmly entrenched in exploring different areas. 2001 (Stanley Kubrick, 1968), for example, is concerned with moral and metaphysical speculation combined with a delight in technical virtuosity for its own sake. A quasi-documentary such as Destination Moon (Irving Pichel, 1950) was an attempt to give a realistic picture of what the first moon landing might involve. Marooned (John Sturges, 1969) takes up the question most people were asking at the time of the first moon landing. What happens to the spacemen if their apparatus fails them and they cannot get back to earth? Such films, with their masculine emphasis and concentration on the mechanics of space-flight, suggest an image of man marveling at his own genitals. They do not have the social orientation of the heterosexual films.

This article has attempted to describe and analyze only one large and probably central area within the amorphous science fiction genre, and to point out some of the major preoccupations in these films with the problem of reconciling the desires of man as both sexual animal and social being. Although the current emphasis in science fiction films seems to be towards some form of pseudo-scientific "documentary," this is just a more subtle disguise for the overriding concern of the genre with "inner space" and "monsters from the id."

Notes

1. H. L. Gold, editor of Galaxy Science Fiction, quoted by Kingsley Amis in New Maps of Hell (London: Gollancz, 1961), p. 64.

2. "Out of this World," Films and Filming (June 1963), pp. 14-18.

3. Film Quarterly (Winter 1959), p. 32.

4. Sight and Sound (April/June 1953), p. 187.

5. November 1957, p. 141.

6. Positif (November/December 1954), pp. 1-16.

7. Cinema '57 (July/August 1957), pp. 9-14.

8. Image et Son (May 1966), pp. 31-36.

9. "La Science-Fiction à l'ère des Spoutniks," Cahiers du Cinéma (February 1958), pp. 9-16.

10. Mamoulian (London: Thames and Hudson, 1969), pp. 39-50.

11. "Sci-Fi or Sci-Fact?", Films and Filming (November 1968), p. 64.

12. "Anxiety and Instinctual Life," New Introductory Lectures on Psycho-Analysis, The Standard Edition of the Complete Psychological Works of Sigmund Freud, trans. James Strachey in collaboration with Anna Freud, assisted by Alix Strachey and Alan Tyson (London: Hogarth Press and the Institute of Psycho-Analysis, 1953-1974), XXII, pp. 82-83. Subsequent references to Freud are from this edition.

13. Freud, "The Dissection of the Psychical Personality," op. cit., XXII, pp. 73-74.

14. Amis, op. cit., p. 30.

15. Freud, "Introduction: A Seventeenth Century Demonological Neurosis," op. cit., XIX, 72.

16. Alfred C. Kinsey, Wardell B. Pomeroy and Clyde E. Martin, Sexual Behaviour in the Human Male (Philadelphia and London: Saunders, 1949), p. 268.

17. "Epouvante et Science Fiction," op. cit., pp. 1-16.

18. Freud, "The Uncanny," op. cit., XVII, 231.

19. Sexual Behaviour in the Human Male, pp. 263-296.

20. Freud, "The Acquisition and Control of Fire," op. cit.,
    XXII, 191.

21. Freud, "Inhibitions, Symptoms and Anxiety," op. cit.,
    XX, 126.

22. Freud, "Revision of Dream Theory," op. cit., XXII, 24.

23. Ibid., p. 25.

WINNING THE WEEPSTAKES: THE PROBLEMS OF AMERICAN SPORTS MOVIES

Nora Sayre

Box office poison comes in all weights and flavors, though, of course, each brand admits to exceptions: from Gone with the Wind to M*A*S*H, allegedly toxic subjects--such as the Civil War and the Korean War--have yielded hits. But some Hollywood producers assert that American sports movies (along with films about writers) rarely do well: the radiant athlete has no more drawing power than the poet or the prose-hound at his desk. Of late, it's been deduced that sports fans don't flock to sports movies; they simply prefer the real thing in the flesh or on the tube. Hence far fewer sports films are made today than in the '40s and early '50s, when many showed a profit, and television wasn't such a formidable rival.

Most sports pictures are characterized by a stunning lack of excitement; after all, it's the director who decides who wins or loses. And since actors aren't athletes, their grunts or gasps of effort fail to generate suspense, while the camera, the doubles, and the film editors do most of the actual work. Also, many fictional sports sequences are reduced to montage. (For the tension that's missing from the majority of these movies, recall the desperate tennis match in Hitchcock's Strangers on a Train, where Farley Granger must win the match in three sets if he's to prevent the murderer from planting a clue that will incriminate him. It's no mere question of winning--but of winning quickly enough.) But usually, you know that a movie star can no more lose a game or a match early in the movie than Belmondo or Clint Eastwood can be iced in the first reel of a thriller. Even the music throughout the opening credits always informs us whether a sports film is going to be triumphant or bitter: the mood is defined long before the hero fondles his first ball.

Meanwhile, the script of almost any sports film seethes with prophetic lines, ranging from "You know, this kid looks like a winner" to "See that? He's a natural, a champion!" or "The champ looks badly out of condition" and "Just imagine, darling, now we can buy our own home!" And sports movies always root the cinema audience firmly in one person's corner. One day, it would be nice to see a film that divided our affinities between two equally appealing competitors. Moreover, some performers make dreadfully unconvincing athletes: no matter how often Charlton Heston may swat his toes in daily life, he makes a most unlikely quarterback, and his performance reminds you of those actors who play reporters but are obviously unable to type.

In short, sports have inspired some of our very worst movies; from 1940 to the present, Hollywood has made a chiché out of sports. Most of these pictures distill a very native brand of sentimentality and brutality, an essence of syrupy sadism. The athletes' private lives usually slide into the rich soup of melodrama--"It's not just the money. (Sob.) You won so much more than that"--and their fictionalized biographies have to be inspirational. Here, adversity often helps to pad the picture: the damaged legs of Ben Hogan or Monty Stratton justified interminable hospital sequences, racking decisions about surgery, protracted preparations for the big comeback, and such lines as "Courage never goes out of fashion." Actually, a hale or healthy man hardly qualifies for a sports biography.

Rondo themes concern the transitory nature of success, the tragedy of being 35, the depravity of the sports industry (despite the occasional vow that "This is one game that's going to stay clean"), and the athlete's piercing dilemma about whether money or glory matters most. Still, amid the cataracts of clichés, there are a few solid considerations about the athlete who's treated as an object--a slab of meat which has no thoughts or feelings. From The Harder They Fall, where it's observed that "Fighters ain't human," to even a comedy like Pat and Mike, where Katharine Hepburn rebels against her owner-trainer ("I think I'm just an animal to him!"), the plight of the person who's regarded only as a piece of merchandise does make a few of these movies more interesting than the rest.

Inevitably, as in any film genre, the better sports films are built on imaginative characterization. If our emotions are to be involved in winning or losing, we need to give

---

a hoot about the individual who's sweating glycerin and gnawing his lip and panting like the athlete he isn't. Moreover, one of the most crucial ingredients of all sports films is the direction of the crowd. At best, the crowd can be a central character: its concentration and excitement should wring the same feelings out of the movie audience. An adroit camera may return to particular faces that cheer or jeer the hero, love or loathe him--fairly or unfairly. And a savage or fickle or indifferent crowd can intensify our support of an athlete in jeopardy. Yells of "Kill him! Kill him!" or "You're through! File for Medicare!" may net our sympathies for the most boring boxer or pitcher.

Raoul Walsh was exceptionally gifted at directing crowds: many of his extras are passionate participants, who act out the strategies that their favorite ought to use: they identify with him and make us do the same. However, a feeble crowd--which emits listless "Oooos" or "'Rays!" or "Awwws"--can cripple an entire movie. And the mossy device of cramming the crowd with all the key characters from the athlete's life--the good wife, the bad woman who let him down, the mother, the old trainer who always believed in him, the hoods who did or didn't bribe him, the unscrupulous promoter--should be retired for at least a decade or two.

The settings of sports movies are wonderfully consistent: the locker room in which the athletes suspect that success or failure is contagious, where they cluster around a winner or recoil from a loser (silence in the locker room always means the worst), and the old neighborhood candy store to which the champion returns--and where he's often reminded that crime or graft or cheating doesn't pay. There's also the starlit city rooftop where the future winner and his girlfriend stare up at the constellations which reflect the glory that lies ahead.

Despite the essential disclaimer of "I ain't got no time for girls," most of the male athletes are quite frighteningly dependent on their women. Eventually, they have to say, "I wouldn't be any good without you." The nice women wear white blouses, are expert at massaging the backs of necks, deft at packing suitcases and pasting clippings in scrapbooks. They knead and knot damp handkerchiefs while listening to the big game on radio--though it usually remains a mystery as to why they aren't there in person. (Still, radio endows sports commentators with some of the choicest lines in these movies, such as "There's something funny going on out there.") The wives of athletes can't be too graceful: they always run very clumsily in high heels when some crisis prompts a dash to their husbands' sides. Bad women can be identified by an excess of lipstick. However, mothers are far more central to sports movies than wives or girlfriends, and good sons make a ceremony of giving them money. Even though mothers disapprove of pool rooms or the time wasted in batting practice, the relationship with the sporting sons is playful. Paul Newman as Rocky Graziano keeps chucking his (Eileen Heckart) under the chin, James Stewart as Monty Stratton repeatedly asks Agnes Moorehead, "How's my girl?", Gary Cooper as Lou Gehrig says again and again that his mother is his "best Girl," and encourages her to sit on his lap. But it's clear that mothers aren't easily amused, and a fur coat rarely buys off their mistrust of the arena.

On the whole, it appears that partial or ultimate failure makes a meatier movie than success: on screen, repetitive triumph is cloying. Hence, the boxing films--which focus on fixed fights or champions who refuse to throw the fight--are far more engrossing than most other sports pictures. (Also, the subject did attract some of Hollywood's best talents.) Most of these movies bend the knee to Odets's Golden Boy, especially Body and Soul--which then became the model for the subsequent fight films. Seen today, these melodramas of the '40s and '50s have weathered well. Although they're couched in extreme terms of good and evil, of cleanliness destroyed by raging corruption, we now tend to forgive the overstatements, and to ignore the palpitating romanticism and the rampant moralism.

Robert Rossen's Body and Soul (1947), distinguished for its script by Abraham Polonsky and the camerawork by James Wong Howe (who filmed the fight scenes on roller-skates), is set in the depression. The film has a stinging social conscience: line after line stresses poverty and unemployment, plus the rot engendered by craving more money than one needs. John Garfield is the dapper but rueful middleweight who exults in his earnings and disregards the facts of fight-fixing until he finally revolts against the system. For a while, it's hard for him to perceive the consequences of being manipulated by crooks, even though his friends repeat that "They're making a money machine out of him, cutting him up" and "People want money so bad they make it stink. And they make you stink."

In his last fight, Garfield personifies the dogged

defiance of a wounded animal who won't give in, while the
crowd's impatience with light punches and its appetite for pain
accelerates.   There's a taut, reflective performance by Can-
ada Lee as a doomed ex-champion and a good ironic part for
Anne Revere as the boxer's spirited mother.   There's also a
turgid love story, and--as in most melodramas--an improbable upbeat ending, but the sense of hopelessness about American venality comes through most powerfully.   The film also
has a distinct historical significance: the credits read like a
roll call of the American Left of the late '40s.   Rossen, Polonsky, Garfield, Lee, and Revere were all later questioned
by the House Committee on Un-American Activities.   In 1952,
Ed Sullivan wrote that "Body and Soul is of tremendous importance to Americans fighting communism because it illustrates the manner in which Commies and pinks ... gave em-
ployment to one another."

        Like John Garfield, the boxers in The Set-Up and
Champion (both 1949) also refuse to throw their fights, and
these movies are designed to make you hate the world of boxing.   Robert Wise's The Set-Up revolves around a 35-year-
old who's expected to lose to a young opponent.   But he's
literally punished for winning: he's so badly beaten by the
gangsters who tried to buy him that he'll never be able to
fight again.   Throughout, Robert Ryan excels at suppressed
emotions: the tightlipped smile when he's pleased, the brief
swallow or widening eyes that register fear, the dregs of
dignity shored up by a shabby figure.   He brings a sensitivity
to the part which is sometimes a characteristic of the better
sports films, which may project vulnerability in unexpected
places, such as the soul of an athlete.   (John Hancock's Bang
the Drum Slowly, which is really a sophisticated weeper rather than a baseball picture, was effective when the athletes
made us conscious of their personal feelings--which they also
tried to hide.)   The Set-Up also contains a few Hollywood
chestnuts, such as the use of trains to sound mournful--has
any American movie train ever sounded cheerful, apart from
the Atchison, Topeka, and the Santa Fe?   But the crowd's
cruelty and the anxieties of the locker room, with its camaraderie and boastful apprehensions and stray hostilities, give
this somber film its high quality.

        Mark Robson's Champion, written by Carl Foreman
and produced by Stanley Kramer, unwisely sweetens Ring
Lardner's story about a monster who never paid for his trans-
gressions.   The story starts with him knocking out his crip-
pled brother, laying out his mother and his pregnant bride,

throwing a fight early in his career. But the movie makes
him a decent fellow to begin with; once he's tainted by success, the picture reeks of come-uppance, and he even has to
die of brain damage. (The Lardner fighter remained a
champ.) As usual, the movie bogs down in the hero's love
life, and one of the funnier sequences has Kirk Douglas pos-
ing for sculptor Lola Albright; rather like Rodin's "Balzac,"
he wears half a bathrobe, and he wrenches the head off his
likeness before embracing its creator. The boxing scenes
are suspenseless--they function only as drama, not as sport.
But Douglas' bumptious vitality and the alert, canny nature
of his characterization remind you of how well he can act.
His manic energies, which were later misplaced in so many
hack movies, are just right here.

        Somebody Up There Likes Me (1956), based on the
autobiography of Rocky Graziano, directed by Robert Wise
and scripted by Ernest Lehman, is one of the few movies
that contains any kindly reflections about the fight business.
It states that sport (with some help from love) can pluck
young thugs away from crime. Although the local cops predict that "the little greaseballs" will wind up in the death
house, these movie delinquents of the '50s merely smashed
windows or stole tires or worked over gum machines in the
subway--in short, it's odd to see a street movie that's bereft
of dope. (Among the hoodlets, watch for Sal Mineo and the
young Steve McQueen.) Despite some soft-centered moments
--as when a son has to weep at his mother's reproaches--
this rapidly paced, well edited film doesn't sag, even though
it's a two-hour uplift biography. Even the preoccupation with
alienation isn't pedantic, as it is in Rebel Without a Cause
and many others of the period.

        The focal exhilaration springs from Paul Newman's
performance. Much of the time, he's compiling an anthology
of Brando traits. Wiping his nose with his knuckles, pouting
and wincing and sulking and slouching like the master, droop-
ing when disappointed, squinting when distressed, Newman
hardly permits us to forget a single scene from On the Waterfront. But in spite of the fidelity to Brando, Newman's own
talent streams through. Agile and rubbery, pursing his lips
and popping his eyes, he appears as an uncontrollable creature, truly capable of violence, and he's excellent at rages.
Compare him here to Burt Reynolds aping Brando in The
Longest Yard, where, chewing gum or smirking or wrinkling
his nose, Reynolds surpasses flattery with his lumbering imitation. If you muse on Reynolds and Newman as Brando's

descendants, you'll rarely see such a harsh contrast between
mimicry and talent.

Unquestionably, Mark Robson's The Harder They Fall
(also 1956), based on Budd Schulberg's novel and scripted by
Philip Yordan, is the best of the fight films.   A gigantic
Argentinian with no aptitude for boxing wins a series of fights
that he doesn't know are fixed--until he's reduced to rubble
in the first match of his heavyweight career.   The film dwells
on the helplessness of those who are packaged or destroyed
by crooked managers, especially those fighters who are stupid
(or thought to be) or punchdrunk.

Humphrey Bogart, in his last picture, is an ex-sports
writer who agrees to promote the mammoth freak.   Protest-
ing against the hoods with whom he collaborates, committed
to what appalls him, Bogart's face often stiffens with disgust
--once more, sensitivity enhances a gritty role.   He and Rod
Steiger as the fight manager play marvelously together.
Steiger's pudgy smile and sadistic nasal monotone, the edge
of threat in everything he says, the sneer that stays in his
face well after he's fired off an insult, congeal in a portrait
of a compulsive worth loathing.

Although the hulk of a fighter is a pathetic figure, the
movie eludes sentimentality.   Throughout, Bogart can handle
moments that could squeeze corn from other actors: when he
lowers his eyes because he can't bear to watch the final fight,
his withdrawal expresses the savagery in the ring more than
the closeups of flying fists and bleeding gums.   Bogart's suffering as a spectator makes us feel the boxer's suffering--
and that's the kind of acting which is very scarce in sports
movies.   The novel's grim ending is softened in the conclusion of the film, but that probably prevents the movie audience
from slitting its collective throat.

Students of boxing films should also inspect Raoul
Walsh's Gentleman Jim (1942): lighthearted, stylish, down-
right charming, it's a mutant in the field.   Set in Victorian
San Francisco, it flirts with the career of James J. Corbett,
culminating in his defeat of John L. Sullivan.   The uproar and
the pandemonium at the ringside, where the fans drive their
fists through the air, shout advice, and pummel imaginary op-
ponents, make the fights in posh sporting clubs or near wharfs
compelling.   The characters range from benign swells to dock-
side Irish toughs, and the movie is pensive about social class:
everyone's fiercely aware of the pecking orders, yet they're

given lines that deny the existence of a class system. Errol
Flynn is so clean-cut that at first you hardly recognize him:
as a glossy upstart, he's good at preening himself or at waking up with a hangover, and I'd forgotten (or perhaps I never
knew) what fetching armpits he had. They're perpetually on
display throughout this movie, whenever his arm is raised
by the referee.

Football has fared pitifully in the movies of each era,
and it's fair to say that Knute Rockne--All American (1940)
is a far more representative sports flick than any of the
fight films. Directed by Lloyd Bacon, who once acted in
Chaplin's two-reelers, the film's written credits gravely
thank Notre Dame for its "gratuitous cooperation." There's
a lot of prose on the screen throughout the picture, as when
it's recorded that "The Viking boy added a rich sense of humor to his lust for life"--a point we eagerly remember when
he later informs some freshmen that "Football is a place for
clear minds." Pat O'Brien is flaccid as the legendary coach,
and seems unaroused by the games that ignite the crowds.
"Nobody can stop my team," he declares without conviction,
"Nobody." He also explains that football is essential to the
health of the nation, because the "spirit of combat," which
results in wars and revolutions in foreign countries, is chan-
neled into sport by Americans. (Perhaps the makers of Rol-
lerball were inspired by this very speech.) His only character trait appears to be a fear of baldness. It's announced
that Rockne's "ingenious brain perfected the forward pass"--
a fan cries, "It'll revolutionize football!"--and he also invents
a new kind of backfield shift. His hairline recedes to denote
the passage of time.

Ronald Reagan, bedecked with a small, shiny pompa-
dour, plays George Gipp, the "new sensation" of Rockne's
team. Coughing faintly, he soon succumbs to what's known
in the trade as "the movie disease"--a nameless affliction
that never dispatches villains. If you watch this film on TV,
you'll miss the famous scene of Reagan on his deathbed; it
was scissored due to "legal complications" with Gipp's family.
But you can revel in this passage by seeing Emile de An-
tonio's Millhouse (1971), which meticulously illustrates how
Richard Nixon ripped off the rhetoric of others, including
Martin Luther King. Just after Nixon accepted the 1968 nom-
ination in Miami Beach, he referred to Eisenhower in the
hospital, and hollered, "Let's win this one for Ike!" Millhouse then cuts to Knute Rockne, where the aging O'Brien in

a wheelchair reminisces to his losing team about Gipp.
There's a flashback to the dying Reagan, while his fever
chart goes crazy, when he whispered to Rockne, "Sometime,
when the team is up against it ... tell 'em to go out there
and give it all they've got--and win this one for the Gipper."
Inflamed by the story, Rockne's team leaps to its feet and
hurtles on to victory.

Number One (1969), directed by Tom Gries, converts
Charlton Heston into an aging quarterback who's told, "You
can't beat the clock. The party's over. The king is dead."
As a member of the New Orleans Saints, he fouls up consistently on the field, gritting his teeth in grief when the crowd
boos. Apparently, we're supposed to empathize with the character. But the director has merely given Heston a titanic
case of the sulks: his mood ranges from petulant to peevish,
between flighty spurts of violence, and sometimes the actor
forgets to limp when he's supposed to. To prove his man-
hood, he beats up a homosexual and rapes his wife in the
same scene. Rigid with misery, he seems to be wearing his
eyebrows lower than usual, but he's simply too large to look
rejected.

Evidently, football still can't escape the whiskery traditions of mawkishness (Brian's Song, made for TV in 1971
and later released to movie theatres) and brutality (Robert
Aldrich's The Longest Yard, 1974). Brian's Song, adapted
from a memoir of the late Brian Piccolo of the Chicago Bears
by the Bears' black star Gayle Sayers, is a male Love Story.
James Caan as Piccolo--all snowy grins and unflagging folk-
siness--and Billy Dee Williams as Sayers giggle and frisk together like amorous toddlers. They run side by side in leafy
slow-motion shots, and the film is an essay in winsomeness
until Piccolo gets terminal cancer. Then his admirers com-
pete to win the weepstakes. Like Ali MacGraw, Caan looks
outrageously healthy until just before he croaks. The thing
was a fervent success, and in 1972, Nixon told some TV
newscasters, "Believe me, it was one of the great motion
pictures I have seen." But whereas Love Story was forgiva-
ble because it made one remember Oscar Wilde's remark that
only a heart of stone could fail to laugh at the death of little
Nell, Brian's Song is repellent because it cheapens the life
and death of a real person.

"Are you sure we came to the right ballpark?" Lou
Gehrig's mother anxiously asks her husband in Pride of the

Yankees (1942).   Her doubts about reality may be shared by
some baseball buffs, since Gary Cooper is distinctly adrift as
a great hitter--particularly when his nostrils flare with determination while he flourishes the bat.   Indeed, there's very
little baseball in this home-spun picture, directed by Sam
Wood and co-scripted by Herman Mankiewicz.   Throughout,
Cooper is at his most diffident and obtuse.   When approached
by the renowned team, he asks warily, "You mean--the New
... York ... Yankees?", as though he fears that he might be
drafted to fight the Civil War.   Smitten with Teresa Wright,
he asks a teammate, "What does it mean when a girl says
that you remind her of a Newfoundland puppy?"   Although
sport is neglected, there are lengthy scenes devoted to deco-
rating his new home, and the choice of wallpaper seems more
important than any amount of home runs.   But there are some
beguiling appearances by Babe Ruth--at bat, catching Cooper
taking bites out of his new straw hat--and some touching sequences as Gehrig struggles against the muscular disease that
was to kill him.

        While Pride of the Yankees was fashioned with a light-
ness that's uncommon in sports films, The Stratton Story
(1949), also directed by Sam Wood, is the kind of movie that
makes you grateful for a watch with a luminous dial--so that
you'll know when you can be released.   James Stewart, as
Monty Stratton of the Chicago White Sox, appears (as so often)
to be chewing on an invisible potato.   With June Allyson, he
trudges through one of the most tepid courtships in film history, and it's difficult to decide whether Cooper or Stewart
was the less erotic actor.   (We should pause to acknowledge
Allyson as one of our more offensive actresses: the relent-
less perkiness, the monstrous maternal chuckles, must have
scared generations of men away from anything in puffed
sleeves.)   The movie's so undramatic that the sports colum-
nists are given special lines to spice matters up: "Ohhh,
those Yankees are murder" and "He's got to lose one sometime."   Like many of the sports films, this one includes
some real footage, but even that doesn't help.   A hunting accident that results in an amputation hardly gets a rise out of
Stewart: he tells his mother, "It looks like I kinda gummed
things up."   She replies, "We've always been able to handle
our share of troubles."   Still, the music throbs as he puts
on his false leg, and the voice-over narration, concerning
"the courage to refuse to admit defeat" sounds like a eulogy
to the cold war mentality.

Unless you linger over Esther Williams as Channel
swimmer Annette Kellerman in Million Dollar Mermaid, wom-
en athletes have been infrequent in Hollywood films. But
Hard, Fast, and Beautiful (1951), directed by Ida Lupino and
written by Martha Wilkerson, is a trashy but diverting fable
with some intriguing role reversals, even though it skirts the
issues of feminism. Claire Trevor is a ruthless mother who
propels her daughter to a world tennis championship. The
first shot of Trevor--driving her needle into some defenseless embroidery--tells you that she's a villain: anyone who
sews that way just can't be a good person. Meanwhile, her
lurid social ambitions reflect the '50s concept of tennis as
an upper-class exertion.

Fathers usually get short shrift in sports pictures, but
here the prodigy's begetter plays the wifely role. "Baby,"
he tells his daughter, "Remember it's just a game. Just a
game." She's delighted by winning, but apologizes to her boyfriend for her success; he forlornly answers, "Stay the way
you are, champ." As the father begins to waste away (he
too has the movie disease), it's demonstrated that a daughter
who prospers is murdering her father. Finally, the tennis
star learns to loathe her mother: on winning the great match,
she shoves the cup at Trevor and collapses into her fiancé's
arms. The mother is left alone, clutching the trophy in an
empty stadium while old newspapers blow across the vacant
tennis court. This is definitely a training film for mothers;
unlike coaches, who function as lovable Fascists, mothers
ought to girdle the letch for victory. Hard, Fast, and Beautiful is also a conspicuously cheap movie: the location shots
at Forest Hills confirm that no money was spent on extras,
and I'm very grateful to Eugene Stavis of the Cinemathèque
for pointing out that the announcer is wearing last year's suit.

Today, when the ethics of winning and losing are discussed, there are hordes out there who proclaim that Clarence Brown's National Velvet (1944) is their favorite sports
picture. It is certainly Elizabeth Taylor's sexiest role, in
contrast to her more mature lethargies. The passion and intensity that she brings to seducing a bad-mannered horse--
despite the warnings that "he'll toss you right off," which is
surely a reference to masturbation--were never equalled in
Butterfield 8 or Cleopatra, let alone The Sandpiper or The
VIP's. At 12, she possesses the same rich thick tremolo
that gurgles from her adult larynx; the voice slurs and ripens
further when she tearfully declaims, "I'd sooner have that
horse happy than go to heaven!" But the long steeplechase is

almost ridiculously exciting.   The movie concludes with the
statement that one big win is all that anyone needs in a life-
time--an eccentric philosophy for any film that deals with
sports.

     Apart from George Cukor's Pat and Mike (1951), where
Hepburn and Tracy clown close to the edge of sober issues--
such as an athlete's loss of independence or confidence--
sports comedies tend to wheeze and clank like cut-rate vehi-
cles.   Ever since Joe E. Brown blinked his way through a
ponderous travesty of Ring Lardner's great Alibi Ike in 1935,
the jokes have mainly relied on the linkage of sports to stu-
pidity.   However, Harold Lloyd's The Freshman (1925) explores the themes of rejection and humiliation more sharply
than some of the more earnest sports films do.   Lloyd frantically yearns for popularity, which can be achieved only by
making the football team.   Ridiculed by a ferocious coach
who despises the material he has to work with--"You dubs
are dead from the dandruff down!"--Lloyd becomes a dummy
for the team's tackle practice.   One bruiser after another
flings him to the ground.   Later, he reels and collapses all
over the field, people walk on his face, and he's always at
the bottom of the fleshpack.   Some real pathos lurches
through the slapstick, and The Freshman measures up to
Graham Greene's observation that, "As Chaplin learned long
ago, the man who falls downstairs must suffer if we are to
laugh; the waiter who breaks a plate must be in danger of
dismissal.   Human nature demands humiliation, the ignoble
pain and the grotesque tear: the madhouse for Malvolio. "

     If golf seems like an undramatic axis for a movie,
imagine Glenn Ford as Ben Hogan.   And if the imagination
shrivels, examine Follow the Sun (1951).   Eisenhower wasn't
even nominated, but the culture was preparing itself for him.
The script, developed from a Reader's Digest article, is full
of astonishments: "He played for the glory of winning,"
"People are pretty darn nice," and "Say, I know what your
trouble is.   That left elbow. "   Early losses, plus Hogan's
lack of rapport with the spectators, and a car crash that
wrecks a leg, create a crescendo of adversity--which is balanced by a sublime marriage and an adoring wife.   But every
obstacle is vanquished, and after Hogan receives a standing
ovation, he confesses that his fans have thawed him: "I used
to think that when I teed off in a tournament, I was all alone
out there. "

Some might excuse the dismal quality of the sports movies of the '40s and '50s because they were designed as popular entertainment. However, those decades also unleashed many splendid American pictures which were also produced for a mass audience. Yet sports movies still seem to have a fine potential: so many blunders have been made that the field seems as fresh for future filmmakers as newly fallen snow. For example, almost none of the models of the past have explored the athlete's relationship to the public--or given a public figure a private life that wasn't ludicrous. (Or hilarious. Or grotesque.) And, since the camera grows cleverer each year, mightn't we soon be allowed to believe that we're watching a real game? Also, no script has to hang on utterances like "Well, my gravy train is makin' no stops" or "It's hard to be a good loser, but it's even harder to be a good winner" or "This is a damn good racket." Moreover, a movie doesn't have to spell out everything that will happen in its first few minutes. There could even be surprises.

GENRE AND MOVIES [THE WESTERN]

Douglas Pye

... The generic and individual identities of narrative
works are created by a large number of elements in combination, many (all?) of which are necessary to those identities
without any one or small group being sufficient to define
them. In the American cinema, characteristics of the narrative tradition that run across generic boundaries contribute to
our sense of what "the Western" is as greatly as those features most obviously characteristic of the genre.

In an essay called "The Use of Art for the Study of
Symbols," E. H. Gombrich describes a parlor game he remembers from his childhood to illuminate the process of symbol formation in the visual arts. It is also evocative in relation to genre.

> We would agree, for instance, that the person to
> be guessed would be a film star.... The task
> would be to guess his identity through a series of
> appropriate emblems or comparisons. The guesser
> would ask the group in the know such questions as:
> If he were a flower what would he be? Or what
> would be his emblem among animals, his style
> among painters?... You might compare each of
> the answers to the indices of letters and numbers
> on the sides of an irregular map which combine to
> plot a position. The psychological category of bear-
> like creatures sweeps along a wide zone of the meta-
> phorical field, and so does the category of thistly
> characters, but the two categories are sufficiently
> distinct to determine an area that can be further re-
> stricted by further plottings. [1]

Later, Gombrich remarks of the categories that might be employed:

None of these, of course, can be said to have an
intrinsic meaning, but they can interest through
their very multiplicity and generate meaning within suitably narrow contexts.

The recognition of works as belonging to a specific
genre may be seen as the result of a similar process--the
intersection of a range of categories, the interplay of which
generates meaning within a context narrow enough for recognition of the genre to take place but wide enough to allow
enormous individual variation. If the categories are thought
of as involving conventions of various kinds, it is easy to
see why exhaustive classification of generic elements is impossible. Given the number and possible combinations of elements within a field, the range of meanings and associations
that can be generated through the constant movement of narrative and mise-en-scène will be infinite.

Within the American cinema in general, narrative traditions can be characterized in a number of ways: in terms
of linearity, psychological involvement, dramatic and tempo-
ral-spatial unity, illusionism, and so on. [2] In approaching
the Western I want to concentrate on a limited number of
conventions: some which relate to broad tendencies of narrative (inside and outside the cinema) and others which seem
more obviously determined by the historical moment, national
tradition and local circumstances.

Certain broad tendencies of narrative can be approached
through a theory of fictional modes of the kind Northrop Frye
constructs in The Anatomy of Criticism. [3] He distinguishes
five modes, defined in terms of the range and power of action of the protagonist.

1) Myth, in which the protagonist is superior in kind to
other men and his environment. The hero is in fact a
god.
2) Romance, in which the hero is superior in degree to
other men and his environment. Here the hero is mortal,
but his actions are marvelous and the laws of nature tend
to be to some extent suspended.
3) The high mimetic mode, in which the protagonist is
superior in degree to other men but not to his environment.
The hero in this mode is a leader whose authority, pas-
sions and power of expression are greater than ours but
who is subject to social control and to the order of nature.

This is the mode of tragedy and most epic.
4) The low mimetic mode, in which the protagonist is
superior neither to other men nor to the natural world.
He is one of us; we respond to his common humanity and
demand the same canons of probability we find in our own
lives. This is the mode of most realistic fiction.
5) The ironic mode, in which the protagonist is inferior
in power or intelligence to ourselves, so that we have a
sense of looking down on a scene of frustration or absurdity.

        Frye's framework is a useful one if we bear in mind
that the modes are not mutually exclusive but form points on
a sliding scale, so that they can occur in various combinations in individual works. Frye also adds a further distinction that is relevant here, between tragedy and comedy.
Again, these are tendencies, not exclusive categories, and
can be found together with any one or more of the five modes.
In tragedy the hero is isolated from his society in his fall
and death, and in comedy the theme is the reverse, the integration of the hero with his society. From the five modes
and the tragedy/comedy axis, several sources of conflict within the narrative emerge as characteristic--the nature of those
conflicts and their outcome contributing to the structure,
theme and mood of the work. The major sources of conflict
will be between man and man, man and nature, and man and
society--personal/heroic, elemental, and social.

        Whatever validity Frye's poetics have, such distinc-
tions are helpful in pointing to issues which must be significant in any discussion of narrative genres. [4] Although Frye's
modes are unsatisfactory as final categories, for the purposes
of this article, the notion of modes remains useful. Tendencies of this kind may well have a lot to do with genre recognition. At this level, literary and filmic narrative can be
seen as continuous, and we may find common tendencies
across a number of genres we commonly think of as distinct.
Generic differences emerge from the combination of these
basic tendencies and the more local conventions.

        A further general, and perhaps rather obvious, point.
In classical aesthetics, as mentioned earlier, "levels of style"
were prescribed for each major kind of literary work: a
particular manner accompanied the subject matter. So, in
tragedy, the fall and death of a hero would be handled in a
serious and elevated style. These levels of style never completely dominated Western literature[5] but they remained

important for each succeeding classicizing movement. Since
the early nineteenth century, however, and the achievement
of the realist novel, levels of style have effectively broken
down, with important consequences. There is no longer any
necessary correlation between subject matter and the manner
in which it is treated. In the terms I have already used, a
fictional mode does not determine a level of style. For instance, a work may contain strong elements of Romance and
yet be realized (in its setting, characterization, treatment of
action) in a manner that might be called low mimetic, or
realistic. This fluid relationship between mode and manner
of realization, and especially between a low mimetic manner
and high mimetic or romantic mode, is important for the
Western, the genre I intend to concentrate on.

Apart from the conventions which relate to broad tendencies of narrative are others more obviously determined
by local conditions of various kinds. They might include:

a) Plot. It might be possible to identify within a genre
recurring plots that carry with them associations and expectations.
b) Other structural features which might relate both to
mode and to plot: recurring "block" constructions, day
and night, journey and rest, action and repose.
c) Character. Individual incarnations of both central and
peripheral figures. In the Western, both the distribution
of identification figures and the expected hero, heroine,
villain configuration. A large list of conventional types
can easily be drawn up for the Western, together with
their most common roles in the action.
d) Time and space. Not just the expected temporal-
spatial continuity, but recurring historical and geographi-
cal settings.
e) Iconography, which might be extended to include the
soundtrack. In the Western, it would include landscape,
architecture, modes of transport, weapons and clothes;
but also music, recurring sounds, voices and kinds of
speech.
f) Themes. Particular concerns associated with or arising from a complex of elements.

Each of these contains a wide range of possibilities--
in combination, the possibilities are enormously multiplied
and, with the conventions of mode and so on, the permutations
are endless. The variable combination of elements within the
Western will therefore make each individual work unique in

some respects even if it appears highly stereotyped, but it
will be unique within a field plotted by the intersection of
these various matrices.   In terms of Gombrich's game, the
field would therefore be narrow enough to register as familiar to an audience and to invoke a wide spectrum of expectations which are aroused, defined, confirmed or surprised by
the moment-to-moment conjunction of elements within each
film.   The number of more or less familiar elements within
the total work is very large and the movement, both "on the
screen" and in the narrative, creates a dynamic which produces new combinations at each moment of the film.

      Seen in this way, a genre will be capable of taking an
enormously wide range of emphasis, depending on the interests and intentions of the individual artist.   Any one or more
than one element can be brought to the foreground while
others may all but disappear.   Plot, character, theme, can
each become central--the relationship of character to the natural world may be a major issue in some Westerns while in
others landscape may be simply a background to the action;
characters can be fully individualized, given complex or conflicting motivation, or may be presented schematically as
morality play figures, embodiments of abstract good or evil.
Part of the Western's richness must be due to this potential
range of emphasis and situation, but underlying this is the
peculiar impurity of its inheritance, the convergence of various currents which achieve a special resonance in America.

      One current that seems of particular importance is
Romantic narrative, in Frye's sense.   In this mode, the
hero is superior in degree to other men and to his environment but he is mortal--a hero but not a god.   His actions in
the story tend to be marvelous--he performs wonders--and he
often lives in close harmony with the natural world.   When
such a hero dies, it creates the sense of a spirit passing out
of nature, coupled with a melancholy sense of the passing of
time, the old order changing and giving way to the new.   The
mood that is evoked when the hero dies Frye calls "elegiac."
At the other end of the scale of Romance for Frye is romantic comedy, and he describes the mood corresponding to the
elegiac in romantic comedy as "idyllic."   In this form, the
simple life of the country or frontier is idealized, and the
close association with the natural world recurs in the sheep
and pleasant meadows of pastoral.   Interestingly, Frye identifies the Western as the pastoral of modern popular literature, with cattle and ranches instead of sheep and pleasant
pastures.   But it is clear that the Western as we know it is

more complex than such a definition will allow--it seems
more rewarding to think of its debt from Romance as dual,
with elements of the elegiac and idyllic modes.

This duality is present in Fenimore Cooper's Leatherstocking Tales, the first significant fiction of the West and a
formative influence on the tradition of Western fiction through
the nineteenth century. The five Leatherstocking Tales present an ambivalent vision of the process of Westward expan-
sion--the encroachment of civilization on the wilderness--
centering on the scout and hunter, Natty Bumppo. The setting of the tales moves gradually west from New York State
to the Great Plains of The Prairie, in which Natty, now a
very old man, dies facing the setting sun. Natty is in some
ways very much the hero of Romance (although his social
status gave Cooper difficulties): he has talents which set him
apart from all other characters and, more importantly, he is
endowed with an infallible moral sense--he has the ability to
know good from evil. Natty lives outside the settlements,
which he regards with deep suspicion as corrupt and ungodly,
wasteful of the goods God has provided for Man's use. And
yet, although his values are presented as ideal, the Westward
expansion of society encroaches more and more on the wilderness, pushing Natty further and further west. His death, and
in fact the tone of more than one of the tales, can be described as elegiac in Frye's sense. At the same time, Natty
lives in harmony with the natural world, reading the wilderness as the book of God, so that images of perfected natural
life recur in the tales, images in which the natural and moral
worlds are united, as they are in Frye's idyllic mode. Characteristically, the tales end with the genteel heroes and her-
oines, the army officers and their ladies, the kidnapped aristocratic girls, being reintegrated into society--the movement
Frye describes as characteristic of comedy--while Natty remains estranged from it, a movement into isolation that
evokes the elegiac mood, the inevitable passing of an ideal
order.

In Cooper, this current of Romantic narrative, capable
of inflection in more than one direction, meets other currents
of thought associated particularly with the idea of the West
and its significance for America, and this conjunction of romantic mode and complex thematic gave a basic shape to the
Western. It isn't necessary to do more than refer to the
complex of ideas about the West that dominated so much of
nineteenth-century American thought, since many of the ideas
have become commonplaces in the discussion of American

literature and film. But it is important to stress the variable associations of the terms "West" and "Frontier." From
the earliest times, these concepts could mean several things,
some of them apparently contradictory. If the West was seen
as a potential Eden, the garden of the world, it was also
seen as the wilderness, the great American desert. The life
of the frontier was both ennobling because it was close to nature, and primitive, at the farthest remove from civilization.
The Indian could be both a child of nature, primitive but innocent, and the naked savage. In Cooper, this dual vision
of the Indian is a feature of most of the tales--the virtuous
tribe of the Mohicans set against the unredeemable evil of
the Mingoes. These very familiar oppositions of garden/
desert, civilization/savagery, which are at the heart of ideas
about the West, were bound up with the Western from the
earliest times. They were not always overt, or as important to meaning as they are in Cooper, but they are always
at least latent within the material of the genre, providing the
Western with a unique potential for reflecting on American
themes. It is also worth emphasizing the continuity of the
developing images of the West in America with much older
ideas and myths. So the images of the garden connect with
much earlier images--the Garden of the Hesperides and other
earthly paradises to be found in the direction of the sunset--
and the opposition of garden and desert can easily take up
the Biblical images of the Promised Land and the Wilderness.
Similarly, views of the Indian are at least partially formed
from earlier images of the noble savage.

     The Western is founded, then, on a tremendously rich
confluence of romantic narrative and archetypal imagery modified and localized by recent American experience--the potential source of a number of conflicting but interrelated streams
of thought and imagery.

     After Cooper, the thematic concern with ideas of the
West is not maintained at the same level of fiction.[6] Stories
of pioneers feed into existing molds of ideas and into existing
romantic structures to create the story of Western adventure,
less concerned with American identity than with action and
excitement. In dime novels, the Western tale became increasingly extravagant and fantastic, although it was fed by
actual events--the Indian wars, the adventures of outlaws and
lawmen, the cattle drives. Actual people became the basis
of heroes of dime novel sagas in a constant process of roman-
ticizing actuality in the service of sentimental fiction and the
adventure story. The Western was also taken up on the stage,

becoming one form of melodrama, sometimes with famous
Western characters playing themselves, and in the Wild West
Show.

As well as these developments, the representations of
the West in American painting may well have influenced attitudes and helped to create a specifically visual repertoire of
Western imagery. It is difficult to locate with any precision
the film Western's debt to these sources, but there are several potentially interesting areas. It is plausible to suggest
that landscape painters, themselves probably influenced by
contemporary attitudes, should in turn have contributed to
ways in which the American landscape was thought of, both
in terms of its sublimity and wildness and in terms of the
American mission of domesticating the wilderness. [7] Also,
through most of the nineteenth century, there were painters
whose major interest was in recording the appearance and
customs of the Indians and frontiersmen, a documentary impulse that retains an important grip on the tradition. Thus
the fantastic invention of the dime novelists and their cover
designers co-existed with the much more sober accuracy of
painters (and photographers) interested in recording what they
saw; in between these extremes were various shades of invention, distortion and interpretation.

Frederic Remington, whose work was disseminated by
Harper's and Collier's Weeklies in the years between 1886
and 1909, contains in himself various impulses which indicate
the range of visual responses to the West during the period. [8]
Many of his drawings of Indians, hunters and cowboy life are
straightforwardly factual, but even here Remington presents a
range of incidents which define life on the range for his audience. A second category is more overtly dramatic--narrative
pictures with strong romantic or melodramatic feeling ("Fight
over a water hole," "A misdeal"). There are others that are
moralistic or thematic, the equivalent of much Victorian anec-
dotal painting: "Solitude" (a solitary buffalo in an open, hilly
landscape and near it, a single buffalo skull); "The Twilight
of the Indian" (an Indian behind a plough with a fence behind
him and in the background both wooden shack and tepee). It
is very difficult to separate different impulses in Remington--
the categories I have indicated are by no means clearly de-
fined--and this is a crucial point about the Western tradition
in general: by the end of the nineteenth century, there is no
possibility of disentangling the confused and conflicting impulses within the tradition.

I mentioned earlier the importance for the Western of the breakdown of levels of style, the split between the mode of fiction and its manner. With the development of the film Western, manner--the nature of the presented world--becomes particularly important. From early on, the Western film gravitated towards exteriors and a comparative solidity and fullness in the presentation of the fictive world (something we see already in Remington and other painters). However fabulous the story, there tends to be a kind of verisimilitude of surface. We can see this if we compare the minimal setting and costumes that will convey the idea of "Western Town" in a musical or in a number in a TV spectacular--flats seen in silhouette only, a pair of saloon doors, and a cast wearing jeans and wide brimmed hats--with almost any town scene in a film or TV Western. Clearly, the film setting is stylized, but it has a solidity of appearance that creates a sense of reality--an inhabitable world. The "realism" reveals itself in the large level of repetition and redundancy in such a scene --many details duplicate or double each other, providing much more than the bare minimum that would signify a western town, enough detail to convince us of the solidity of the presented world.

Obviously enough, this kind of realism is not peculiar to the Western--it is a feature of most narrative genres in the American cinema. But a tension between a realism of presentation and a much greater degree of abstraction at other levels does seem characteristic of many Westerns--the low mimetic realization "anchors" and gives credence to other, more abstract elements: romantic narrative structures, plots inherited from melodrama, the simple moral framework of sentimental fiction. In the last section of this essay I want to illustrate this kind of tension as one way in which the conflicting elements of the tradition contribute to the richness of the Western.

In some films, this tension produces a resonance we tend to associate with symbol. The simultaneous presence of the solid surface and a high degree of abstraction elsewhere causes an oscillation of response from one level to another, an awareness that the narrative flow is not the sole source of meaning, but that it is accompanied by another dimension, intimately tied to it, but supplying another kind of meaning. Neither the realism of the surface nor the underlying abstraction dominates in such a context, but a balance is achieved between the two, a relationship analogous to that between denotation and connotation in Roland Barthes. 9

The famous dance sequence in John Ford's My Darling
Clementine seems to me to work like this.   The whole passage is something of an interlude in the main development of
the narrative, contributing nothing to the revenge plot and
little to the Doc Holliday interest; in fact the episode tends
to unbalance the film structurally by being so markedly different from what has gone before.   Yet it is partly the re-
duction of narrative interest that gives the passage its particular force--the interruption of the main channel of communication has the effect of throwing others into relief, while the
specific detail is maintained at a level high enough to retain
the solidity of the presented world--in the acting, for instance, there is a splendid fullness and individuality.

The abstraction is present in the particularly bold conjunction of elements Ford brings together to form the central
complex of the sequence: the landscape of Monument Valley,
which is barren and inhospitable but beautiful, with the desert
coming right to the edge of the town; the partly built church;
the stars and stripes; the dance itself.   All these things have
associations of their own, but together they form an enormously rich associative cluster.   At the simplest level we
see the dedication of Tombstone's first church, one milestone
in the town's growth.   But the church is also a tangible sign
of community identity and solidarity and of the faith of the
settlers (less in religion perhaps, than in their own abilities
and their social future); and the flag is the emblem of their
sense of national identity.   These ideas are fused with the
more personal human values of family and community in the
dance, while the bold juxtaposition of desert and town suggests broader ideas of the conquering of the wilderness, the
growth of American civilization.   The abstractions invoked
are given particular force and the whole scene great emotional weight by the presentation of the dance itself--the inexpert
musicians, the naive enthusiasm and lack of pretension, and
the homeliness of dances and dancers--the density, at this
level, of circumstantial detail, which "grounds" the symbolized aspiration, giving it concrete form.

The sequence achieves formal completeness with the
integration of Wyatt Earp (Henry Fonda) and Clementine
(Cathy Downs) into the dance, and they too have both individual and representative significance, as characters within the
narrative and also as representatives of East and West--
Clementine the embodiment of Eastern refinement, Earp of
the "natural," untutored virtues of the frontier.   Their walk
away from the town towards the dance is given, through their

bearing and the visual presentation, a formality and dignity
that inevitably suggests a couple walking down the aisle, but
a couple that unites the traditional East/West opposition.
The interruption of the dance as Earp and Clementine reach
the floor has none of the tension or disruptive force interrupted dances take on in other Ford Westerns; it is a prelude
to a greater harmony, the community joining the dance
around the Marshal "and his lady fair"--an image which points
towards the possibility of a perfected society in the West
which will reconcile opposing forces in an ideal harmony.

      The ideas invoked in the sequence are commonplaces
of the tradition and Ford asserts them with extraordinary
economy in a kind of visual shorthand, so that both the basic
image structure of the sequence and its conceptual foundation
are highly abstract. But it is impossible to respond only at
this denuded level of meaning. If the conceptual, symbolized
meaning in a sense robs the scene of its individual life to
confer a wider, representative significance on it, the concrete realization constantly reasserts its specific and detailed
life in which the objects, people, movement and music are of
this moment only and refuse to be contained by any schematic
framework. Response oscillates between the levels of meaning, unable to choose definitely one or the other, rather in
the way Barthes describes as characteristic of "Myth."

      Different forms of this tension, in which other ele-
ments are in the foreground, can be found in many Westerns.
The famous "silent" opening of Rio Bravo, for instance, is
in its way equally abstract, without invoking themes to do
with Westward expansion at all. The abstraction here is in
the characters and action. The main characters are readily
identifiable genre types characterized in largely conventional
ways: the drunk, the smiling killer, the unbending sheriff.
Their presentation is so unambiguous and familiar, and the
intense and violent action so compressed in time that the sequence is almost melodramatic in effect and quite bewildering
in the opening moments of the film. Because it is the opening, we rely not on a context for action established by the
director during the film, but almost exclusively on genre recognition and expectation, and Howard Hawks plays directly on
our experience in his use of Dean Martin, John Wayne and
Claude Akins. His use of conventions of character and action
is more than economical, although it is certainly that--it involves a kind of balancing act in which the emblematic presentation of character and the extreme compression of intense
action borders on the unacceptably schematic. But abstraction

is in fact necessary to the sequence's functions in establishing the basic situation of the film and stating its central
theme. It is precisely the abstraction which signals the scene
so clearly as thematic statement. The rest of the film can
be seen as developing and exploring in various forms the issue of self-respect, between the moral poles presented so
boldly in the opening action. In fact, the abstraction remains
within dramatically acceptable limits partly because Hawks
makes his statements not in dialogue but through action which
has a specific life of its own in addition to its thematic role,
and partly (a related point) because the whole scene is sufficiently grounded in the detail we conventionally expect of a
saloon: decor, other characters, actions, costume and so on.
But even so, there is a remarkably low level of redundancy
in the sequence, as in fact throughout the film: Hawks ex-
cludes a great many familiar Western elements and narrows
his focus to a small group of characters in, for a Western,
a very restricted setting.   More than any other conventions,
he invokes those of character and action, excluding virtually
all thematic material related to history, and never activating
the symbolic potential of the form as Ford does so frequently.
This is interesting in relation to Hawks's earlier Westerns,
Red River and The Big Sky, which involve wider "epic" and
historical dimensions in which Hawks seems only marginally
interested.   In both films, the central concern is a very
small group of characters and their relationships, but the
presence of the epic material has the effect of dissipating to
some extent the effectiveness of that focus.   The compression
of Rio Bravo is the result of a self-discipline based on understanding the possibilities inherent in the generic material.

        Concentration on positively valued films like My Dar-
ling Clementine and Rio Bravo inevitably tends to suggest that
one can ignore the vast mass of Western movies and TV series that constitute the bulk of the genre. In practice, this
huge number of more or less undistinguished films is ignored
by criticism, and it is difficult to conceive of a situation in
which they will ever receive detailed study. But it is important to bear in mind that these films have made possible the
achievements of the recognized directors, keeping alive the
conventions; the elements of the tradition are found in all
Westerns, of whatever quality.

        For example, The Lone Ranger, which had a long run
in the cinema and on TV as a children's series, exists at the
pulp end of the Western spectrum, while The Searchers is by
one of the acknowledged masters of the American cinema and

is arguably one of the greatest Westerns ever made. It is
not a juxtaposition that can be held very long but long enough
to point to common elements. The Lone Ranger represents
the inheritance of Romantic narrative in one of its simplest
forms; it centers on the anonymous masked hero who possesses extraordinary powers which set him apart from ordinary men. He is virtually invulnerable--the nearest thing to
a god without being immortal. He rides a horse of incredible beauty which, like its master, has extraordinary gifts.
And he is accompanied by a faithful Indian companion--a fact
which draws attention to the direct line of descent from Fenimore Cooper. In fact, The Lone Ranger can be seen as a
debased and simplified version of Cooper's tales, with the
hero riding off from the settlements after each adventure,
away from all human company except that of his Indian friend,
retaining his emotional isolation and his celibacy. There is
none of Cooper's complexity, of course, but instead a simple
moral scale of polarized good and evil, with the basic terms
and the hero's status never questioned.

     The Searchers incorporates elements of Romance that
are very similar, and again the line of descent from Cooper
can be fairly easily traced. One thread within the film is
the idea of the solitary, invulnerable, wandering hero, Ethan
Edwards (John Wayne), for whom life within the settlements
is impossible. He appears from the wilderness as the story
opens, and when his job is finished he returns to the desert
again. In common with the hero of Frye's Romantic mode,
Ethan's power of action is greater than that of other men.
At the same time the film is structured around a version of
the romantic quest, which brings to mind the grail quest
(Ethan's grail being Debbie), and is largely set in desert terrain which evokes the imagery of the Waste Land familiar
from versions of the grail legend but also, through the repeated Biblical allusions, the journey of the Israelites to the
Promised Land and their years wandering in the Wilderness.
The settlers are in a sense both attempting to find a Promised Land and are still wandering in the Wilderness, living
in the barren landscape of Monument Valley. They are also
led by an Old Testament soldier-priest in the figure of the
Reverend Samuel Johnson Clayton, captain of the Texas Rang-
ers. These elements are very powerful in The Searchers,
but they are combined with others in such a way that they are
never dominant. In particular, Ford gives great complexity
to the Romance structure by combining it with features more
characteristic of lower modes. So, unlike the Lone Ranger,
Ethan is humanized, his mortality and human needs

emphasized. The aspiration to achieve autonomy and emotional isolation is held in tension with the love for his sister-
in law that binds him to the settlements, and this tension con-
tributes to the psychic split which brings him close to madness. Again, Ethan does not possess the perfect moral sense
of Cooper's Leatherstocking; in this respect, he is more like
the characteristic heroes of realist fiction, only too fallible
morally.

I think it is reasonable to claim that The Searchers
consistently achieves the resonance of symbolic drama that
My Darling Clementine achieves only in one passage, and that
it does so partly as a result of the fusion of modes and impulses which are held in productive tension: romantic narrative and a version of the hero of Romance with a low mimetic
insistence on human needs and moral fallibility; a high level
of abstraction (or unreality) in the setting--the farm set in
the middle of barren desert--with a fullness of naturalistic detail in the presentation of the settlers' lives. Part of any
claim for the greatness of The Searchers needs to be based
on these tensions, which make what could have been simply a
story of Indian savagery and revenge into a work that it makes
sense to discuss as a film about America--a symbolic representation of the American psyche--as one might discuss The
Leatherstocking Tales or Moby Dick. Ford's achievement is
based on a profound understanding of his tradition--even the
comic domestic scenes, the grotesquery of sexual relationships
in the film, which are often ignored or apologized for, belong
to a tradition stretching back to "Rip van Winkle," in which
marriage and settlement are presented as crippling or at least
inhibiting, a tradition which Leslie Fiedler has discussed at
some length. 10

Less complex than The Searchers, but interesting in
this context, is Delmer Daves's 3. 10 to Yuma. What is most
frequently commented on in the film is its "realism," its evo-
cation of an unusually barren and unromanticized West in
which environment dominates man, and its refusal of "romantic" (in both senses) characterization. From the outset, the
barren landscape suggests the bleakness of life in this West.
The hold-up which follows the extended shot of the stage approaching across the desert is undramatic, unclear, shrouded
in dust. The iconographical profile of the hero, Evans (Van
Heflin), when he appears, conflicts with expectation--he is
with his two sons, dressed in functional, worn working clothes,
without a gun, and he is almost immediately deprived of his
horse and forced to chase his cattle on foot. The insistence

on the harshness of the environment is reinforced by discussion of the drought which dominates the lives of the ranchers in the area. The hero is also, unusually, motivated exclusively by money--his need to raise cash to buy water for his parched ranch; and this need is played on throughout, the captured outlaw, Wade (Glenn Ford), tempting him with offers of more and more money if he will release him. Both towns in the film are unprepossessing, dominated by harsh sunlight and hard shadows; the inhabitants are reluctant to risk anything over the outlaw, as if the heat and drought have sapped physical and moral resolve. These elements of the film are firmly low mimetic, in terms of the relationship of man and the natural world and the stature of the hero (he is one of us). Daves goes even further in this direction by handcuffing Glenn Ford when he is first captured, and so effectively preventing the possibility of conventional confrontations between hero and villain.

But it is partly, perhaps, the consistency with which the low mimetic manner is maintained that begins to suggest, paradoxically, through its absence for most of the film, the existence of another dimension. Daves consistently refuses possible developments through action, in favor of a concentration on the tension between Evans's desperate need for money (his motive for taking in Wade), with its accompanying sapping of moral energy, and the moral obligation to complete his undertaking in the face of Wade's bribes. The film moves towards Evans's final decision to take Wade from the hotel to the train, not as a moral obligation or a way of making the necessary money (it is going to be paid anyway) but as a completely free act. It is at this point that the suppressed dimension of the film emerges clearly with the thunder which accompanies the build up to Evans's decision but which his wife somehow fails to hear. He takes the thunder as promising the long needed rain but also, it seems clear, as confirmation of the rightness of his resolve. The simultaneity of moral climax and thunder signals dramatically an other than contingent relationship between man and the natural world, the drought as expression of and punishment for the spiritual state of the people. Their atrophy of will and resigned selfishness stand in a necessary relationship to the blight on the land in a way that clearly evokes the Waste Land of Grail legends. Evans's action ends the drought as the quester's can in legend--it is free of the considerations of money and family that have dominated him earlier--"The awful daring of a moment's surrender/Which an age of prudence can never retract." What is interesting in 3.10 to Yuma is not the

presence of this Romantic dimension but its sudden revelation.
Not only does the selective hearing of the characters (we hear
the thunder, why can't the wife?) break with the established
naturalism of the film's manner, but the climactic thunder,
which is acceptable in other conventions, has such obvious
dramatic and symbolic significance in this resolutely low
mimetic context that the context cannot contain it. The thunder and the rain at the end assert with melodramatic force
the existence of, on the whole, unprepared dimensions (the
solemn sympathy of men and nature characteristic of Romance)
in a way that seems to threaten the film's unity. In other
words, there seems in 3.10 to Yuma a collision of mode and
manner rather than a productive tension between them, a ca-
pitulation of sense to meaning, which makes the end of the
film unfortunately glib.

These attempts to approach particular films in terms
of genre are necessarily tentative. The description of tendencies within generic traditions needs finally to be based on
more detailed study of the available materials. In this respect, the Western is likely to remain central to genre criticism. It is unique in the accessibility of its pre-history and
the continuity of its traditions, which make an accurate description of the evolution of conventions adopted by the cinema
both possible and necessary. Comparative work is needed on
the antecedents of other genres, the tendencies which seem to
contribute to their recognition, and most especially on the
ways in which modes intersect other, often more obvious, conventions. Inevitably this kind of emphasis will contribute to
the modification of notions of authorship in the American cinema. It may also provide materials for other approaches--
accounts, for instance, of the sociological and psychological
contexts of genre--which should tell us more about the social
significance of popular forms and the ways in which conventions are sustained.

Notes

1. E. H. Gombrich, "The Use of Art for the Study of Symbols," in Psychology and the Visual Arts, ed. James
Hogg (Baltimore: Penguin, 1969).

2. See, for instance, Thomas Elsaesser in Monogram I.

3. Northrop Frye, Anatomy of Criticism (Princeton University Press, 1957). Especially the Theory of Fictional
Modes.

4. For a critique of Frye's theory of modes see Tzvetan
    Todorov, The Fantastic: A Structural Approach to
    Literary Genre, trans. Richard Howard (University
    of Cleveland Press, 1973).

5. Erich Auerbach, Mimesis (New York: Doubleday, 1957).

6. Henry Nash Smith traces the development of Western fic-
    tion after Cooper in Chapters 7-10 of Virgin Land
    (Harvard University Press, 1950).

7. American Frontier: Images and Myths, Catalogue of the
    1974 London Exhibition of paintings of the West, U.S.
    Information Service, contains a useful introduction on
    this topic. Roderick Nash's Wilderness and the Amer-
    ican Mind deals in greater detail with developing
    American attitudes to wilderness.

8. Frederic Remington: 173 Drawings and Illustrations
    (New York: Dover Books, 1972).

9. Roland Barthes, "Myth Today," in Mythologies, trans.
    Annette Lavers (London: Jonathan Cape, 1972).

10. Leslie Fiedler, Return of the Vanishing American (Lon-
    don: Jonathan Cape, 1968).

SELECTED BIBLIOGRAPHY

The Bibliography is divided by genres, with an opening section on "Theory" and a final section for "Miscellaneous"
criticism. Included in the Bibliography are books and articles concerned with any genre or genres. Omitted are those
works which are primarily discussions of a particular director within a genre, on the grounds that these are more properly considered works of auteur criticism, and that they
would make the Bibliography too unwieldy.

THEORY

Alloway, Lawrence. "The Iconography of the Movies,"
 Movie, No. 7 (February-March 1963). Reprinted in
 Movie Reader, ed. Ian Cameron. New York and Wash-
 ington: Praeger, 1972.

Amelio, Ralph J. The Filmic Moment: An Approach to
 Teaching American Genre Film Through Extracts.
 Dayton, Ohio: Pflaum, 1974.

Bourget, Jean-Loup. "Social Implications in the Hollywood
 Genres," Journal of Modern Literature, 3 (April 1973),
 191-200.

Buscombe, Edward. "The Idea of Genre in the American
 Cinema," Screen, 11, No. 2 (March-April 1970), 33-
 45.

Cavell, Stanley. The World Viewed: Reflections on the On-
 tology of Film. New York: Viking, 1971, Chap. 5.

Cawelti, John G. "The Concept of Formula in the Study of
 Popular Culture," Journal of Popular Culture, Vol. 3,
 No. 3 (Winter 1969), 381-390.

_____. The Six-Gun Mystique. Part IV. Bowling Green,

Ohio: Bowling Green University Popular Press, 1971.

Collins, Richard. "Genre: A Reply to Ed Buscombe,"
    Screen, 11, Nos. 4-5 (August-September 1970), 66-75.

Dienstfrey, Harris. "Hitch Your Genre to a Star," Film Cul-
    ture, 34 (Fall 1964), 35-37.

Durgnat, Raymond. "Genre: Populism and Social Realism,"
    Film Comment, 11, No. 4 (July-August 1975), 20-29,
    63.

Frye, Northrup. Anatomy of Criticism: Four Essays. New
    York: Atheneum, 1970.

Genre. Department of English, SUC at Plattsburgh, Platts-
    burgh, New York 12901.

Grant, Barry K. "From Film Genre to Film Experience,"
    Paunch, Nos. 42-43 (December 1975), pp. 123-137.

Hess, Judith W. "Genre Films and the Status Quo," Jump
    Cut, No. 1 (May-June 1974), pp. 1, 16, 18.

Kaminsky, Stuart M. American Film Genres: Approaches to
    a Critical Theory of Popular Film. Dayton, Ohio:
    Pflaum, 1974.

McCarthy, Todd and Charles Flynn, eds. Kings of the Bs:
    Working Within the Hollywood System. New York:
    Dutton, 1975.

McConnell, Frank D. The Spoken Seen: Film and the Ro-
    mantic Imagination. Baltimore and London: Johns
    Hopkins University Press, 1975, Chap. 5.

Manchell, Frank. Film Study: A Resource Guide. Ruther-
    ford, N. J.: Fairleigh Dickinson University Press,
    1973, Chap. 2.

Pye, Douglas. "Genre and Movies," Movie, No. 20 (Spring
    1975), pp. 29-43.

Ryall, Tom. "The Notion of Genre," Screen, 11, No. 2
    (March-April 1970), 22-32.

Sacks, Sheldon. "The Psychological Implications of Genre

Distinctions," Genre, 7 (April 1968), 106-115.

Sobchack, Thomas. "Genre Film: A Classical Experience,"
    Literature/Film Quarterly, 3 (Summer 1975), 196-204.

Tudor, Andrew. "Genre: Theory and Mispractice in Film
    Criticism," Screen, 11, No. 6 (1970), 33-43.

————————. Theories of Film. New York: Viking, 1974,
    Chap. 5.

Yacowar, Maurice. "Recent Popular Genre Movies: Awash
    and Aware," Journal of Popular Film IV, 4 (1975),
    297-305.

                        COMEDY FILMS

Agee, James. "Comedy's Greatest Era," in Agee on Film.
    New York: Grosset and Dunlap, 1967, Vol. 1, 1-20.

Bergman, Andrew. We're in the Money. New York: Harper
    and Row, 1972.

Bergson, Henri. "Laughter," in Comedy, ed. Wylie Sypher.
    New York: Doubleday, 1956, pp. 61-190.

Callenbach, Ernest. "The Comic Ecstasy," Films in Review,
    5, No. 1 (January 1954), 24-26.

Durgnat, Raymond. The Crazy Mirror: Hollywood Comedy
    and the American Image. New York: Delta, 1972.

Dyer, Peter John. "They Liked to Break the Rules," Films
    and Filming, 6, No. 1 (October 1959), 12-14, 38-39.

Geduld, Carolyn and Harry. "From Kops to Robbers: Trans-
    formation of Archetypal Figures in the American Cine-
    ma of the 20's and 30's," Journal of Popular Culture,
    I, No. 2 (1967-68), 389-394.

Higham, Charles, and Joel Greenberg. Hollywood in the
    Forties. London: Zwemmer, and New York: Barnes,
    1968.

Kaminsky, Stuart M. American Film Genres: Approaches to
    a Critical Theory of Popular Film. Dayton, Ohio:

Pflaum, 1974, Chap. 9.

Kracauer, Siegfried. "Silent Film Comedy," Sight and Sound,
    21 (August-September 1951), 31-32.

McCaffrey, Donald W. "The Evolution of the Chase in the
    Silent Screen Comedy," Cinema Journal, 4 (1964), 1-8.

Maltin, Leonard. Movie Comedy Teams. New York: New
    American Library, 1970.

Mast, Gerald. The Comic Mind: Comedy and the Movies.
    Indianapolis and New York: Bobbs-Merrill, 1973.

Montgomery, John. Comedy Films 1894-1954. London:
    George Allen & Unwin, Ltd. , 1968.

Olson, Elder. The Theory of Comedy. Bloomington, Indiana
    and London: Indiana University Press, 1968.

Robinson, David. The Great Funnies: A History of Film
    Comedy. New York: Dutton, 1969.

Sufrin, Mark. "The Silent World of Slapstick (1912-1916),"
    Film Culture, 2, No. 4 (1956), 21-22.

CRIME FILMS*

Alloway, Lawrence. Violent America: The Movies 1946-
    1964. New York: Museum of Modern Art, 1971.

Baxter, John. "Something More than Night," The Film Jour-
    nal, 2, No. 4 (1975), 4-9.

---

*In the genre of Crime Films I have included detective films,
police films, mystery films (since the mystery to be solved
is almost always a crime), spy films--in short, all films
dealing with the perpetration or prevention of crime (with the
exception of the Gangster film, since that group of films is
clearly defined to the extent that it can be understood as com-
prising a distinct and separate genre). This classification
allows one to avoid the intentional fallacy inherent in the dubiously labeled genre of "The Thriller," a term which is
more appropriately used to describe tone, and which, unlike the horror film, is much too vague as a generic category.

Cameron, Ian.   A Pictorial History of Crime Films.   London:
    Hamlyn, 1975.

Connor, Edward.   "The Mystery Film," Films in Review, 5,
    No. 3 (March 1954), 120-123.

Cutts, John.   "Oriental Eye," Films and Filming, 3, No. 11
    (August 1957), 16.

Davis, Brian.   The Thriller.   London: Studio Vista, and
    New York: Dutton, 1973.

Deming, Barbara.   Running Away from Myself.   New York:
    Grossman, 1969.

Durgnat, Raymond.   "Spies and Ideologies," Cinema, No. 2
    (March 1969), pp. 5-13.

Everson, William K.   The Detective in Film.   Secaucus,
    N. J. : Citadel Press, 1972.

Godfrey, Lionel.   "Martinis without Olives," Films and Film-
    ing, 14, No. 7 (April 1968), 10-14.

Gow, Gordon.   Suspense in the Cinema.   Cranbury, N. J. :
    A. S. Barnes, 1968.

Grace, Harry A.   "A Taxonomy of American Crime Film
    Themes," Journal of Social Psychology, 42 (August
    1955), 129-136.

Gregory, Charles.   "Knight Without Meaning?: Marlowe on
    the Screen," Sight and Sound, 42, No. 3 (Summer
    1973), 155-159.

Hammond, Laurence.   Thriller Movies.   Secaucus, N. J. :
    Derbibooks, 1975.

McConnell, Frank D.   The Spoken Seen: Film & the Roman-
    tic Imagination.   Baltimore and London: Johns Hopkins
    University Press, 1975, Chap. 5.

Miller, Don.   "Private Eyes: From Sam Spade to J. J.
    Gittes," Focus on Film, No. 22 (Autumn 1975), pp.
    15-35.

Oliver, Bill.   "The Long Goodbye and Chinatown: Debunking

the Private Eye Tradition," Literature/Film Quarterly, 3, No. 3 (Summer 1975), 240-248.

Parish, James Robert, and Michael R. Pitts. The Great Spy Pictures. Metuchen, N.J.: Scarecrow Press, 1974.

Reck, Tom S. "Come Out of the Shower and Come Out Clean," Commonweal, 26 September 1969, pp. 588-591.

Sarris, Andrew. "Films in Focus," Village Voice, 22 July 1971, p. 55.

Thomson, H. Douglas. "Detective Films," Sight and Sound, 4, No. 13 (Spring 1935), 10-11.

Wolfe, Tom. "Pause, Now, and Consider Some Tentative Conclusions About the Meaning of the Mass Perversion Called Porno-Violence...." Esquire, LXVIII, 1 (July 1967), 59, 110-111.

DISASTER FILMS

Annan, David. Catastrophe: The End of the Cinema? U.S.A.: Bounty Books, 1975.

Kaplan, Fred. "Riches from Ruins," Jump Cut, No. 6 (March-April 1975), pp. 3-4.

Rosen, David N. "Drugged Popcorn," Jump Cut, No. 8 (August-September 1975), pp. 19-20.

EPIC FILMS

Baxter, John. Hollywood in the Sixties. London: Tantivy, and New York: Barnes, 1972.

Durgnat, Raymond. "Epic, Epic, Epic, Epic, Epic," Films and Filming, 10, No. 3 (December 1963), 9-12.

Dyer, John Peter. "Some Mighty Spectacles," Films and Filming, 4, No. 5 (February 1958), 13-15, 34.

Everson, William K. "Film Spectacles," Films in Review, 5 (November 1954), 459-471.

Robinson, David. "Spectacle," Sight and Sound, 25, No. 1
    (Summer 1955), 22-27, 55-56.

Zinsser, William K. Seen Any Good Movies Lately? New
    York: Doubleday, 1958, Chap. 3.

                            EROTIC FILMS

Atkins, Thomas, ed. Movies and Sexuality. Hollins College,
    Va.: The Film Journal, 1973.

Bazin, Andre. "Marginal Notes on Eroticism in the Cinema,"
    in What is Cinema? Berkeley: University of Califor-
    nia Press, 1971, Vol. II, 169-175.

Blake, Roger. The Porno Movies. Cleveland: Original Cen-
    tury Books, 1970.

Buckley, Peter. "A Dirty Movie Is a Dirty Movie Is a Dirty
    Movie," Films and Filming, 18, No. 11 (August 1972),
    24-29.

Chappell, Fred. "Twenty-Six Propositions about Skin-Flicks,"
    in Man and the Movies, ed. W. R. Robinson. Balti-
    more: Penguin, 1967, pp. 53-59.

Corliss, Richard. "Cinema Sex: From The Kiss to Deep
    Throat," Film Comment, 9, No. I (January-February
    1973), 4-5.

Dowdy, Andrew. The Films of the Fifties: The American
    State of Mind. New York: Morrow, 1975.

Durgnat, Raymond. Eros in the Cinema. London: Calder
    and Boyars, 1966.

_____. "Eroticism in Cinema," 8 pts. Films and Filming,
    8, No. 1 (October 1961)-8, No. 8 (May 1962).

Georgakas, Dan. "Porno Power," Cineaste, VI, 4 (1974),
    13-15.

Hanson, Gillian. Original Skin: Nudity and Sex in Cinema
    and Theatre. London: Tom Stacy, Ltd., 1970.

Heard, Colin. "Sexploitation," Films and Filming, 15, No.

11 (August 1969), 24-29.

Hoffman, Frank A. "Prolegomena to a Study of Traditional Elements in the Erotic Film," Journal of American Folklore, 78 (April-June 1965), 143-148.

Knight, Arthur, and Hollis Alpert. "The History of Sex in Cinema," 20 pts. Playboy 12, No. 4 (April 1965)- 16, No. 1 (January 1969).

Kyrou, Ado. Amour-Erotisme & Cinema. Paris: le Terrain Vague, 1966.

Lo Duca, Giuseppe. L'Erotisme au Cinema. 3 vols. Paris: Jean-Jacques Pauvert, 1957.

Morthland, John. "Porno Films: An In-Depth Report," Take One, 4, No. 4 (March-April 1973), 11-17.

Paul, William. "Emerging Paradoxes of the New Porn," Village Voice, 3 June 1971, pp. 63, 73.

Rhode, Eric. "Sensuality in the Cinema," Sight and Sound, 30, No. 2 (Spring 1961), 93-95.

Robinson, David. "When Is a Dirty Film...?" Sight and Sound, 41, No. 1 (Winter 1971-72), 28-30.

Sarris, Andrew. "Reflections on the New Porn," Village Voice, 1 Sept. 1975, pp. 71-72.

Sontag, Susan. "The Pornographic Imagination," in Styles of Radical Will. New York: Delta, 1969.

Turan, Kenneth, and Stephen F. Zito. Sinema: American Pornographic Films and the People Who Make Them. New York: New American Library, 1975.

Tyler, Parker. Screening the Sexes: Homosexuality in the Movies. New York: Doubleday, 1973.

Walker, Alexander. Sex in the Movies. Baltimore: Penguin, 1968.

Wortley, Richard. Erotic Movies. London: Roxby, 1975.

GANGSTER FILMS

Alloway, Lawrence. Violent America: The Movies: 1946-
    1964. New York: Museum of Modern Art, 1971.

Baxter, John. The Gangster Film. New York: A. S.
    Barnes, and London: A. Zwemmer, 1970.

Bergman, Andrew. We're in the Money. New York: Harper
    and Row, 1972.

Farber, Manny. "The Outlaws," Sight and Sound, 37, No. 4
    (Autumn 1968), 170-176.

Gabree, John. Gangsters: From Little Caesar to The God-
    father. New York: Galahad Books, 1973.

Kaminsky, Stuart M. American Film Genres: Approaches
    to a Critical Theory of Popular Film. Dayton, Ohio:
    Pflaum, 1974, Chaps. 2 and 6.

Karpf, Stephen. The Gangster Film: Emergence, Variation
    and Decay of a Genre, 1930-1940. New York: Arno
    Press, 1973.

Kinder, Marsha. "The Return of the Outlaw Couple," Film
    Quarterly, XXVII, 4 (Summer 1974), 2-10.

McArthur, Colin. Underworld USA. New York: Viking,
    1972.

Parish, James Robert, and Michael R. Pitts. The Great
    Gangster Pictures. Metuchen, N.J.: Scarecrow Press,
    1976.

Peary, Gerald. "Notes on Early Gangster Comedy," Velvet
    Light Trap, No. 3 (Winter 1971-72), pp. 16-18.

Sacks, Arthur. "An Analysis of the Gangster Movies of the
    Early Thirties," Velvet Light Trap, No. 1 (June 1971),
    5-11, 32.

Warshow, Robert. "The Gangster as Tragic Hero," in The
    Immediate Experience. New York: Atheneum, 1970.

Whitehall, Richard. "'Crime, Inc. ,' A Three-Part Dossier
    on the American Gangster Film," Films and Filming,

10, No. 4 (January 1964) - 10, No. 6 (March 1964).

_____ . "Some Thoughts on Fifties Gangster Films," Velvet Light Trap, No. 11 (Winter 1974), pp. 17-19.

HORROR FILMS

Brock, Brower. "The Vulgarization of American Demonology," Esquire, LXI (June 1964), 94-99.

Brustein, Robert. "Reflections on Horror Movies," Partisan Review, XXV, 2 (Spring 1958), 288-296.

Butler, Ivan. Horror in the Cinema. New York: A. S. Barnes, 1970.

Clarens, Carlos. An Illustrated History of the Horror Film. New York: Capricorn Books, 1968.

Dillard, R. H. W. "Even a Man Who Is Pure at Heart: Poetry and Danger in the Horror Film," in Man and the Movies, ed. W. R. Robinson. Baltimore: Penguin, 1967, pp. 60-96.

Douglas, Drake. Horror. New York: Macmillan, 1966.

Dyer, Peter John. "All Manner of Fantasies," Films and Filming, 4, No. 9 (June 1958), 13-15 ff.

_____ . "The Roots of Horror," International Film Annual No. 3, ed. William Whitebair. New York: Taplinger, 1959, pp. 69-75.

_____ . "Some Nights of Horror," Films and Filming, 4, No. 10 (July 1958), 13-15 ff.

Everson, William K. Classics of the Horror Film. Secaucus, N.J.: Citadel Press, 1974.

_____ . "A Family Tree of Monsters," Film Culture, 1, No. 1 (January 1955), 24-30.

_____ . "Horror Films," Films in Review, 5, No. 1 (January 1954), 12-23.

Eyles, Allen, et al. The House of Horror: The Story of

Horror Films. London: Lorrimer, 1973.

Fisher, David. "The Angel, the Devil and the Space Travel-
ler," Sight and Sound, 23, No. 3 (January-March 1954),
155-157.

Frank, Alan G. Horror Movies: Tales of Terror in the
Cinema. London: Octopus, 1974.

Gifford, Denis. Movie Monsters. New York: Dutton, 1969.

_____. A Pictorial History of Horror Movies. New York:
Hamlyn, 1973.

Halliwell, Leslie. "The Baron, the Count, and their Ghoul
Friends," 2 pts. Films and Filming, 15, Nos. 9 (June
1969), 13-16, and 10 (July 1969), 12-16.

Higham, Charles, and Joel Greenberg. Hollywood in the
Forties. London: Zwemmer, and New York: A. S.
Barnes, 1968.

Hill, Derek. "Horror," Sight and Sound, 28, No. 1 (Winter
1958-59), 6-11.

Huss, Roy, and T. J. Ross, eds. Focus on the Horror
Film. Englewood Cliffs, N.J.: Prentice-Hall, 1972.

Hutchinson, Tom. Horror & Fantasy in the Cinema. London:
Studio Vista, 1974.

Kaminsky, Stuart M. American Film Genres: Approaches to
a Critical Theory of Popular Film. Dayton, Ohio:
Pflaum, 1974, Chap. 7.

Kane, Joe. "Beauties, Beasts and Male Chauvinist Monsters,"
Take One, 4, No. 4 (March-April 1973), 8-10.

Laclos, Michel. Le Fantastique au Cinéma. Paris: Jean-
Jacques Pauvert, 1958.

Lee, Walt, ed. Reference Guide to Fantastic Films: Science
Fiction, Fantasy and Horror. 3 vols. Los Angeles:
Chelsea-Lee Books, 1972.

Lenne, Gérard. Le cinéma "fantastique" et ses mythologies.
Paris: Editions du Cerf, 1970.

Losano, Wayne A.   "The Vampire Rises Again in Films of
        the Seventies," The Film Journal, 2, No. 2 (1973), 60-
        62.

Naha, Ed.   Horrors From Screen to Scream.   New York:
        Avon, 1975.

Pirie, David.   A Heritage of Horror: The English Gothic
        Cinema, 1946-1972.   London: Gordon Fraser, 1973.

Steiger, Brad.   Monsters, Maidens and Mayhem: A Pictori-
        al History of Horror Film Monsters.   New York:
        Merit, 1965.

Tyler, Parker.   "Supernaturalism in the Movies," Theatre
        Arts, 29, No. 6 (June 1945), 362-366 ff.

Ursini, James, and Alain Silver.   The Vampire Film.   New
        York: A. S. Barnes, and London: Tantivy, 1975.

White, Dennis L.   "The Poetics of Horror: More than Meets
        the Eye," Cinema Journal, X, 2 (Spring 1971), 1-18.

Willis, Don.   A Checklist of Horror and Science Fiction
        Films.   Metuchen, N.J.: Scarecrow Press, 1972.

MUSICAL FILMS

Bach, Steven.   "The Hollywood Idiom: Give Me That Old
        Soft Shoe," Arts Magazine, No. 42 (December 1967-
        January 1968), pp. 15-16.

Bergman, Andrew.   We're in the Money.   New York: Harper
        and Row, 1972.

Cutts, John.   "Bye Bye Musicals," Films and Filming, 10,
        No. 2 (November 1963), 42-45.

Delamater, Jerome.   "The Musical," in Stuart Kaminsky,
        American Film Genres: Approaches to a Critical The-
        ory of Popular Film.   Dayton, Ohio: Pflaum, 1974.

Domarchi, Jean.   "Evolution du film musical," Cahiers du
        Cinema, No. 54 (1955), pp. 34-39.

Dowdy, Andrew.   The Films of the Fifties: The American

State of Mind. New York: Morrow, 1975.

Godfrey, Lionel. "A Heretic's Look at Musicals," Films and Filming, 13, No. 6 (March 1967), 5-10.

Higham, Charles, and Joel Greenberg. Hollywood in the Forties. London: Zwemmer, and New York: A. S. Barnes, 1968.

Jablonski, Edward. "Filmusicals," Films in Review, 6, No. 2 (February 1955), 56-69.

Kobol, John. Gotta Sing Gotta Dance: A Pictorial History of Film Musicals. London: Hamlyn, 1972.

Licata, Sal. "From Plymouth Rock to Hollywood in Song and Dance: Yankee Mythology in the Film Musical," Film & History, IV, 1 (February 1974), 1-3.

Lockhart, Freda Bruce. "The Seven Ages of the Musical," in International Film Annual, No. 1, ed. Campbell Dixon. London: John Calder, 1957, pp. 107-115.

McVay, Douglas. The Musical Film. New York: A. S. Barnes, 1967.

Newton, Douglas. "Poetry in Fast and Musical Motion," Sight and Sound, 22, No. 1 (July-September 1952), 35-37.

Pantasios, Anastasia J. "Rock Music and Film," Mise-en-Scène, No. 1 (n. d.), pp. 42-47.

Patrick, Robert, and William Haislip. "'Thank Heaven for Little Girls': An Examination of the Male Chauvinist Musical," Cineaste, VI, 1 (1973), 22-25.

Pechter, William S. "Movie Musicals," Commentary, 53, No. 5 (May 1972), 77-81.

Schuerer, Timothy E. "The Aesthetics of Form and Convention in the Movie Musical," Journal of Popular Film, III, 4 (Fall 1974), 307-324.

Sidney, George. "The Three Ages of the Musical," Films and Filming, 14, No. 9 (June 1968), 4-9.

Springer, John. All Talking! All Singing! All Dancing!: A
    Pictorial History of the Movie Musical. New York:
    Citadel Press, 1966.

Stern, Lee Edward. The Movie Musical. New York: Pyra-
    mid, 1974.

Taylor, John Russell, and Arthur Jackson. The Hollywood
    Musical. New York: McGraw-Hill, 1971.

Vaughan, David. "Dance in the Cinema," Sequence, No. 6
    (Winter 1948-49), pp. 6-13.

Wiener, Thomas. "The Rise and Fall of the Rock Film,"
    2 pts. American Film, 1, No. 2 (November 1975),
    25-29, and No. 3 (December 1975), 58-63.

                    SCIENCE FICTION FILMS

Amelio, Ralph J., ed. Hal in the Classroom: Science Fic-
    tion Films. Dayton, Ohio: Pflaum, 1974.

Arnold, Francis. "Out of this World," Films and Filming,
    9, No. 9 (June 1963), 14-18.

Atkins, Thomas, ed. Science Fiction Films. New York:
    Monarch Press, 1976.

Baxter, John. Science Fiction in the Cinema. New York:
    Paperback Library, 1970.

Bouyxou, J. P. La Science Fiction au Cinéma. Paris:
    Union Générale d'Editions, 1971.

Brustein, Robert. "Reflections on Horror Movies," Partisan
    Review, XXV, 2 (Spring 1958), 288-296.

Chappell, Fred. "The Science Fiction Film Image," The
    Film Journal, 2, No. 3 (1974), 8-13.

Denne, John D. "Society and the Monster," December, 9,
    Nos. 2-3 (1967), 180-183.

Dowdy, Andrew. The Films of the Fifties: The American
    State of Mind. New York: Morrow, 1975.

Edelson, Edward. Visions of Tomorrow: Great Science Fic-
    tion from the Movies. New York: Doubleday, 1975.

Evans, Walter. "Monster Movies: A Sexual Theory," Jour-
    nal of Popular Film, III, 1 (Winter 1974), 31-38.

Geduld, Harry M. "Return to Méliès: Reflections on the
    Science Fiction Film," The Humanist, XXVII, 6 (No-
    vember-December 1968), 23-24, 28.

Gifford, Denis. Movie Monsters. New York: Dutton, 1969.

_____. Science Fiction Films. New York: Dutton, 1971.

Gow, Gordon. "The Non Humans," Films and Filming, 20,
    No. 12 (September 1974), 59-62.

Grant, Barry K. "From Film Genre to Film Experience,"
    Paunch, Nos. 42-43 (December 1975), pp. 123-137.

Hodgens, Richard. "A Brief and Tragical History of the Sci-
    ence Fiction Film," Film Quarterly, XIII, 2 (Winter
    1959), 30-39.

Huss, Roy, and T. J. Ross, eds. Focus on the Horror Film.
    Englewood Cliffs, N.J.: Prentice-Hall, 1972.

Hutchinson, Tom. Horror and Fantasy in the Cinema. Lon-
    don: Studio Vista, 1974.

Johnson, William, ed. Focus on the Science Fiction Film.
    Englewood Cliffs, N.J.: Prentice-Hall, 1972.

Kaminsky, Stuart M. American Film Genres: Approaches to
    a Critical Theory of Popular Film. Dayton, Ohio:
    Pflaum, 1974, Chap. 7.

Kane, Joe. "Nuclear Films," Take One, Vol. 2, No. 6
    (1969), 9-11.

Landrum, Larry. "A Checklist of Materials about Science
    Fiction Films of the 1950s: A Bibliography," Journal
    of Popular Film, I, 1 (Winter 1972), 61-63.

Lee, Walt. Reference Guide to Fantastic Films: Science
    Fiction, Fantasy, and Horror. 3 vols. Los Angeles:
    Chelsea-Lee Books, 1972.

Lenne, Gérard. Le Cinéma "fantastique" et ses mythologies.
    Paris: Editions du Cerf, 1970.

Menville, Douglas. A Historical and Critical Survey of the
    Science Fiction Film. New York: Arno Press, 1975.

Murphy, Brian. "Monster Movies: They Came from Beneath
    the Fifties," Journal of Popular Film, I, 1 (Winter
    1972), 31-44.

Naha, Ed. Horror from Screen to Scream. New York:
    Avon, 1975.

Parish, James Robert, and Michael R. Pitts. The Great
    Science Fiction Pictures. Metuchen, N. J.: Scare-
    crow Press, 1977.

Rogers, Ivor A. "Extrapolative Cinema," Arts in Society,
    VI (Summer-Fall 1969), 287-291.

Siclier, Jacques, and André S. Labarthe. Images de la Sci-
    ence Fiction. Paris: Editions du Cerf, 1958.

Sobchack, Vivian. "The Alien Landscape of the Planet Earth,"
    The Film Journal, 2, No. 3 (1974), 16-21.

Sontag, Susan. "The Imagination of Disaster," in Against In-
    terpretation. New York: Delta, 1966.

Stanbury, C. M. "Monsters in the Movies: A Mythology of
    the Absurd," December, 10, No. 1 (1968), 74-76.

Steinbrunner, Chris, and Bart Goldblatt. Cinema of the Fan-
    tastic. New York: Saturday Review Press, 1972.

Tarratt, Margaret. "Monsters from the Id," 2 pts. Films
    and Filming, 17, Nos. 3 (December 1970), 38-42, and
    4 (January 1971), 40-42.

Wharton, Lewis. "Godzilla to Latitude Zero: The Cycle of
    the Technological Monster," Journal of Popular Film,
    III, 1 (Winter 1974), 31-38.

Willis, Don. A Checklist of Horror and Science Fiction Films.
    Metuchen, N. J.: Scarecrow Press, 1972.

SPORTS FILMS

Farber, Manny. "The Fight Films," in Movies. New York: Stonehill, 1976; or, Negative Space. London: Studio Vista, 1971.

Jahiel, Edwin. "The Ring and the Lens: Films on Boxing," Film Society Review (September 1966), pp. 26-28.

Sayre, Nora. "'Win This One for the Gipper!' And Other Reasons Why Sports Movies Miss the Point," Village Voice, 1 December 1975, pp. 30-32, 35, 37.

WAR FILMS

Belmans, Jacques. "Cinema and Man at War," Film Society Review, 7, No. 6 (February 1972), 22-37.

Deming, Barbara. Running Away from Myself. New York: Grossman, 1969.

Dworkin, Martin S. "Clean Germans and Dirty Politics," Film Comment, 3, No. 1 (Winter 1965), 36-41.

Gillett, John. "Westfront 1957," Sight and Sound, 27, No. 3 (Winter 1957-58), 122-127.

Grossman, Edward. "Bloody Popcorn," Harper's, 241 (December 1970), 32-40.

Guy, Rory. "Hollywood Goes to War," Cinema (Los Angeles), 3, No. 2 (March 1966), 22-29.

Higham, Charles, and Joel Greenberg. Hollywood in the Forties. London: Zwemmer, and New York: Barnes, 1968.

Hughes, Robert, ed. Film: Book 2: Films of Peace and War. New York: Grove Press, 1962.

Isaacs, Hermine Rich. "Shadows of War on the Silver Screen," Theatre Arts, XXVI, 11 (November 1942), 689-696.

Jacobs, Lewis. "World War II and the American Film," Cinema Journal, VII (Winter 1967-68), 1-21. Rpt. in

Film Culture, No. 47 (Summer 1969), pp. 28-42.

Jones, Dorothy B. "War Films Made in Hollywood, 1942-1944," Hollywood Quarterly, I, 1 (October 1945), 1-19.

Jones, Ken D., and Arthur F. McClure. Hollywood at War: The American Motion Picture and World War II. New York: A. S. Barnes, and London: Thomas Yoseloff, 1973.

Kagan, Norman. The War Film. New York: Pyramid, 1974.

King, Larry L. "The Battle of Popcorn Bay," Harper's, CCXXXIV (May 1967), 50-54.

Kozloff, Max, William Johnson and Richard Corliss. "Shooting at Wars: Three Views," Film Quarterly, XXI, 2 (Winter 1967-68), 27-36.

Kuiper, John B. "Civil War Films: A Quantitative Description of a Genre," Journal of the Society of Cinematologists, 5 (1965), 81-89.

Landrum, Larry N., and Christine Eynon. "World War II in the Movies: A Selected Bibliography of Sources," Journal of Popular Film, I, 2 (Spring 1972), 147-153.

Lewis, Leon, and William David Sherman. "War Movies," in The Landscape of Contemporary Cinema. Buffalo: Buffalo Spectrum Press, 1967.

Lingeman, Richard R. "Will This Picture Help Win the War?" in Don't You Know There's a War On?: The American Home Front, 1941-1945. New York: Putnam, 1970.

McClure, Arthur F. "Hollywood at War: The American Motion Picture and World War II, 1939-1945," Journal of Popular Film, I, 2 (Spring 1972), 123-135.

Manchel, Frank. Film Study: A Resource Guide. Rutherford, N.J.: Farleigh Dickinson University Press, 1973, Chap. 2.

Mann, Klaus. "What's Wrong with Anti-Nazi Films?" Decision, II, 2 (August 1941), 27-35.

Manville, Roger. Films and the Second World War. New
    York: Delta, 1976.

Morella, Joe, et al. The Films of World War II. Secaucus,
    N. J. : Citadel Press, 1975.

Soderbergh, Peter A. "Aux Armes! The Rise of the Holly-
    wood War Film, 1916-1930," South Atlantic Quarterly,
    LXV, 4 (Autumn 1966), 509-522.

Spears, Jack. "World War I on the Screen," 2 pts. Films
    in Review, XVII, Nos. 5 (May 1966), 274-292, and
    6 (June-July 1966), 347-365.

Tyler, Parker. "The Waxworks of War," in Magic and Myth
    in the Movies. New York: Simon and Schuster, 1947.

Whitehall, Richard. "One ... two ... three," Films and
    Filming, 10, No. 11 (August 1964), 7-12.

Zinsser, William. Seen Any Good Movies Lately? New
    York: Doubleday, 1958, Chap. 13.

WESTERN FILMS

Agel, Henri, ed. The Western. Etudes Cinématographiques
    12-13, Vol. II. Paris: Lettres Modernes, 1961.

Alloway, Lawrence. Violent America: The Movies 1946-1964.
    New York: Museum of Modern Art, 1971.

Amelio, Ralph J. "Bonanzaland Revisited: Reality and Myth
    in the Western Film," See, IV, 1 (1970), 24-28.

Armes, Roy. "The Western as a Film Genre," in Film and
    Reality. Baltimore: Penguin, 1975.

Austen, David. "Continental Westerns," Films and Filming,
    17, No. 10 (July 1971), 36-42.

Baker, Bob, et al. "ABC of the Western," Kinema, No. 3
    (August 1971), pp. 20-34.

Bazin, Andre. "The Western, or the American Film par ex-
    cellence," and "The Evolution of the Western," in
    What Is Cinema? Vol. II. Berkeley: University of
    California Press, 1971.

Beale, L. "The American Way West," Films and Filming,
    28, No. 7 (April 1972), 24-30.

Bellour, Raymond, and Patrick Brion, eds. Le Western:
    sources, thèmes, mythologies, auteurs, acteurs, film-
    ographies. Paris: Union Général d'Editions, 1966.

Blount, Trevor. "Violence in the Western," Kinema, No. 3
    (August 1971), pp. 14-19.

Bluestone, George. "The Changing Cowboy: From Dime
    Novel to Dollar Film," Western Humanities Review,
    XIV (Summer 1960), 331-337.

Boatright, Moody C. "The Formula in Cowboy Fiction and
    Drama," Western Folklore, XXVIII, 2 (April 1969),
    136-145.

Brauer, Ralph. "Who Are Those Guys? The Movie Western
    During the TV Era," Journal of Popular Film, II, 4
    (Fall 1973), 389-404.

Buscombe, Edward. "The Idea of Genre in the American
    Cinema," Screen, 11 No. 2 (March-April 1970), 33-45.

Cawelti, John G. "Cowboys, Indians, Outlaws: the West in
    Myth and Fantasy," American West, I (Spring 1964),
    28-35, 77-79.

_____. "The Gunfighter and Society: Good Guys, Bad
    Guys, Deviates, and Compulsives--A View of the Adult
    Western," American West, V, 2 (March 1968), 30-
    35 ff.

_____. "Prolegomena to the Western," Studies in Public
    Communication, No. 4 (Autumn 1962), pp. 57-70.

_____. "Reflections on the New Western Films," Univer-
    sity of Chicago Magazine (January-February 1973), pp.
    25-32.

_____. The Six-Gun Mystique. Bowling Green, Ohio:
    Bowling Green University Popular Press, n. d.

_____. "Zane Grey and W. S. Hart: The Romantic West-
    ern of the 1920s," Velvet Light Trap, No. 12 (Spring
    1974), pp. 6-10.

Collins, Richard. "Genre: A Reply to Ed Buscombe,"
    Screen, 11, Nos. 4-5 (August-September 1970), 66-75.

Cowie, Peter. "The Growth of the Western," in International
    Film Guide 1966. London: Tantivy, and New York:
    Barnes, 1966.

Elkin, Frederick. "The Psychological Appeal of the Holly-
    wood Western," Journal of Educational Sociology, 24,
    No. 2 (October 1950), 72-86.

Esselman, Kathryn C. "When the Cowboy Stopped Kissing
    His Horse," Journal of Popular Culture, VI, 2 (Fall
    1972), 337-349.

Etulain, Richard W., and Michael T. Marsden, eds. "The
    Popular Western," Journal of Popular Culture, VII, 3
    (Winter 1973), 645-751.

Everson, William K. A Pictorial History of the Western
    Film. New York: Citadel Press, 1967.

Eyles, Allen. The Western: An Illustrated Guide. New
    York: A. S. Barnes, 1967.

Fenin, George N. "The Western--Old and New," Film Cul-
    ture, 2, No. 2 (1956), 7-10.

_____, and William K. Everson. The Western, from
    Silents to Cinerama. New York: Orion Press, 1962.

_____. _____. The Western: From Silents to the Sev-
    enties. New York: Bonanza Books, 1973.

Folsom, James K. "'Western' Themes and Western Films,"
    Western American Literature, II, 3 (Fall 1967), 195-
    203.

Ford, Charles. Histoire du Western. Paris: Editions
    Pierre Horay, 1964.

Franklin, Eliza. "Westerns, First and Lasting," Quarterly
    of Film, Television and Radio, 7, No. 2 (Winter 1952),
    109-115.

French, Philip. Westerns. New York: Viking, 1974.

Friar, Ralph and Natasha. The Only Good Indian ... The Hollywood Gospel. New York: Drama Book Specialists, 1972.

Godfrey, Lionel. "A Heretic's View of Westerns," Films
and Filming, 13, No. 8 (May 1967), 14-20.

Homans, Peter. "Puritanism Revisited: An Analysis of the
Contemporary Screen-Image Western," Studies in Public Communication, No. 3 (Summer 1961), pp. 73-84.

Kaminsky, Stuart M. American Film Genres: Approaches
to a Critical Theory of Popular Film. Dayton, Ohio:
Pflaum, 1974, Chaps. 2 and 11.

Kitchen, Lawrence. "Decline of the Western," The Listener,
14 July 1966, pp. 54-57.

Kitses, Jim. Horizons West. Bloomington, Ind. , and London: Indiana University Press, 1970.

Larkins, Robert. "Hollywood and the Indian," Focus on Film,
No. 2 (March-April 1970), pp. 44-53.

Lovell, Alan. "The Western," Screen Education, No. 41
(September-October 1967), pp. 92-103.

MacArthur, Colin. "The Roots of the Western," Cinema,
No. 4 (October 1969), pp. 11-13.

McMurtry, Larry. "Cowboys, Movies, Myths, and Cadillacs:
Realism in the Western," in Man and the Movies, ed.
W. R. Robinson. Baltimore: Penguin, 1967.

Markfield, Wallace. "The Inauthentic Western," American
Mercury, LXXV (September 1952), 82-86.

Nachbar, Jack. "A Checklist of Published Materials on
Western Movies," Journal of Popular Film, II, 4 (Fall
1973), 411-428.

_____, ed. Focus on the Western. Englewood Cliffs,
N. J. : Prentice-Hall, 1974.

_____. "Seventy Years on the Trail: A Selected Chronol-
ogy of the Western Movie," Journal of Popular Film,
II, 1 (Winter 1973), 75-83.

Nussbaum, Martin. "Sociological Symbolism of the 'Adult

Western,'" Social Forces, 39, No. 1 (October 1960),
    25-28.

Park, William. "The Losing of the West," Velvet Light
    Trap, No. 12 (Spring 1974), pp. 2-5.

Parkinson, Michael, and Clyde Jeavons. A Pictorial History
    of Westerns. London: Hamlyn, 1972.

Pye, Douglas. "Genre and Movies," Movie, No. 20 (Spring
    1975), 29-43.

Rieupeyrout, Jean Louis. Le Western, ou, Le Cinéma amér-
    icain par excellence. Paris: Editions du Cerf, 1953.

_____. "The Western: A Historical Genre," Quarterly of
    Film, Radio and Television, 7, No. 2 (1952), 116-128.

Ross, T. J. "Fantasy and Form in the Western: From
    Hart to Peckinpah," December, XII, 1 (Fall 1970),
    158-169.

Ryall, Tom. "The Notion of Genre," Screen, 11, No. 2
    (March-April 1970), 22-32.

Schein, Harry. "The Olympian Cowboy," American Scholar,
    24 (Summer 1955), 309-320.

Smith, Henry Nash. Virgin Land: The American West as
    Symbol and Myth. New York: Vintage, 1950.

Spears, Jack. "The Indian on the Screen," Films in Review,
    X (January 1959), 18-35.

Vallance, Tom (also credited to Eric Warman). Westerns:
    A Preview Special. London: Golden Pleasure Books,
    1964.

Warshow, Robert. "Movie Chronicle: The Westerner," in
    The Immediate Experience. New York: Atheneum,
    1971.

Willett, Ralph. "The American Western: Myth and Anti-
    Myth," Journal of Popular Culture, IV, 2 (Fall 1970),
    455-463.

Williams, John. "The 'Western': Definition of the Myth,"

in The Popular Arts: A Critical Reader, ed. Irving
and Harriet A. Deer. New York: Scribner's, 1967,
pp. 98-111.

Wright, Will. Sixguns and Society: A Structural Study of the
    Western. Berkeley: University of California Press,
    1976.

                        MISCELLANEOUS

Anderson, J. L. "Japanese Swordfighters and American Gun-
    fighters," Cinema Journal, XII, 2 (Spring 1973), 1-21.

Bourget, Jean-Loup. "Romantic Drama of the Forties: An
    Analysis," Film Comment, 10, No. 1 (January-Febru-
    ary 1974), 46-51.

Crozier, Ralph C. "Beyond East and West: The American
    Western and the Rise of the Chinese Swordplay Movie,"
    Journal of Popular Film, 1, No. 3 (Summer 1972),
    229-243.

Davis, John. "Warner's Genres of the '30s and '40s," Velvet
    Light Trap, No. 15 (Fall 1975), pp. 56-60.

Durgnat, Raymond. "Genre: Populism and Social Realism,"
    Film Comment, 11, No. 4 (July-August 1975), 20-29,
    63.

Flanigan, b. p. "Kung Fu Krazy, or the Invasion of the 'Chop
    Suey Easterns,'" Cinéaste, VI, 3 (n. d.), 8-11.

Haskell, Molly. "The Women's Film," in From Reverence to
    Rape: The Treatment of Women in the Movies. Balti-
    more: Penguin, 1974.

Querry, Ronald B. "Prison Movies: An Annotated Filmogra-
    phy, 1921-Present," Journal of Popular Film, II, 2
    (Spring 1973), 181-197.

Ransom, James. "Beach Blanket Babies," Esquire, LXIV,
    No. 1 (July 1965), 90-94, 108.

Richie, Donald. Japanese Cinema: Film Style and National
    Character. New York: Doubleday, 1971.

Staehling, Richard. "From Rock Around the Clock to The
     Trip: The Truth About Teen Movies," in Kings of
     the Bs, ed. Todd McCarthy and Charles Flynn. New
     York: Dutton, 1975, pp. 220-251.

Addendum

THEORY

Solomon, Stanley J. Beyond Formula: American Film Gen-
     res. New York: Harcourt Brace Jovanovich, 1976.

Wood, Robin. "Ideology, Genre, Auteur," Film Comment,
     13, No. 1 (January-February 1977), 46-51.

CRIME FILMS

Cauliez, Armand Jean. Le Film criminel et le film policier.
     Paris: Editions du Cerf, 1956.

Solomon, Stanley J. Beyond Formula: American Film Gen-
     res. New York: Harcourt Brace Jovanovich, 1976.

GANGSTER FILMS

Mitchell, Edward. "Apes and Essences: Some Sources of
     Significance in the American Gangster Film," Wide
     Angle, I, No. 1 (Spring 1976), 22-29.

Solomon, Stanley J. Beyond Formula: American Film Gen-
     res. New York: Harcourt Brace Jovanovich, 1976.

Tudor, Andrew. Image and Influence: Studies in the Soci-
     ology of Film. London: George Allen & Unwin Ltd.,
     1974.

HORROR FILMS

Greenberg, Harvey R., M.D. The Movies on Your Mind.
     New York: Saturday Review Press and Dutton, 1975.

Solomon, Stanley J. Beyond Formula: American Film Genres. New York: Harcourt Brace Jovanovich, 1976.

Tudor, Andrew. Image and Influence: Studies in the Sociology of Film. London: George Allen & Unwin Ltd., 1974.

MUSICAL FILMS

Solomon, Stanley J. Beyond Formula: American Film Genres. New York: Harcourt Brace Jovanovich, 1976.

SCIENCE FICTION FILMS

Greenberg, Harvey R., M.D. The Movies on Your Mind. New York: Saturday Review Press and Dutton, 1975.

Solomon, Stanley J. Beyond Formula: American Film Genres. New York: Harcourt Brace Jovanovich, 1976.

WAR FILMS

Isenberg, Michael. "An Ambiguous Pacifism: A Retrospective on World War I Films, 1930-38," Journal of Popular Film, 4 (1975), 98-115.

Jeavons, Clyde. A Pictorial History of War Films. Secaucus, N.J.: The Citadel Press, 1974.

Solomon, Stanley J. Beyond Formula: American Film Genres. New York: Harcourt Brace Jovanovich, 1976.

WESTERN FILMS

Blumenberg, Richard. "The Evolution and Shape of the American Western," Wide Angle, I, No. 1 (Spring 1976), 39-49.

Solomon, Stanley J. Beyond Formula: American Film Genres. New York: Harcourt Brace Jovanovich, 1976.

Tudor, Andrew. Image and Influence: Studies in the Sociology of Film. London: George Allen & Unwin Ltd., 1974.

---

*Film titles are shown in capital letters: book titles are under-scored.